A Sor Juana Anthology

A Sor Juana Anthology

Translated by Alan S. Trueblood

With a foreword by Octavio Paz

Harvard University Press

Cambridge, Massachusetts, and London, England

Copyright © 1988 by the President and Fellows of Harvard College

Printed in the United States of America

This book has been digitally reprinted. The content remains
identical to that of previous printings.

Library of Congress Cataloging-in-Publication Data

Juana Inés de la Cruz, Sister, 1651–1695.
    [Selections. English & Spanish. 1988]
    A Sor Juana anthology / translated by Alan S. Trueblood: with a
foreword by Octavio Paz.
        p.   cm.
    English and Spanish.
    Includes index.
    ISBN 0-674-82120-3 (alk. paper) (cloth)
    ISBN 0-674-82121-1 (paper)
    I. Trueblood, Alan S. II. Title.
  PQ7296.J6A28 1988
861—dc19   87–27693
                    CIP

In memory of my father

Foreword

Octavio Paz

OF ALL THE MAJOR POETS of the Americas, Sor Juana Inés de la Cruz has until recently been the most neglected. I have long felt that she should be better known in English-speaking countries, and it was at my urging that Alan Trueblood agreed to translate, and Harvard University Press to publish, a generous sampling of her work. The selection and arrangement of the writings were made jointly by Alan Trueblood and me. We have endeavored to provide a choice of the best of her poetry and to exemplify as well her skill as a writer of prose and of poetic drama.

Among her few compositions in prose, to mention these first, we have naturally chosen to translate the famous *Reply* to the Bishop of Puebla, the autobiographical letter in which she defends the right of women to education and intellectual pursuits. The boldness of this work was anticipated by her one known foray into theology, the missive mentioned by Alan Trueblood in his Introduction, in which she took the position that the greatest benefactions of God are negative: "to reward is a benefaction, to punish is a benefaction, to suspend benefactions is the greatest benefaction, and to grant no favors is the greatest favor." This idea risked being considered more than theological subtlety. If the greatest divine favor was indifference, was not freedom of the will being allowed too much scope?

In an open letter, signed "Sor Philothea de la Cruz," introducing Sor Juana's *Missive,* her friend the Bishop, even as he published it, made no secret of his disagreement. Nor did he stop at expressing his objections to her theology; he also reproved her intellectual and literary inclinations. As a defense of the right of women to education and culture, Sor Juana's *Reply* to the Bishop's letter won her as well the hostility and criticism of other superiors. Her lot as a woman writer punished by haughty opinionated clerics reminds us of the fate that has befallen independent intellectuals of our own century in societies ruled by intolerant bureaucracies.

Sor Juana's dramatic production is represented here by excerpts from her sacramental play *The Divine Narcissus,* a work both fascinating and complex. Excluded, of necessity, are her secular plays for the public theater and the briefer dramatic pieces she wrote for performance at the viceregal court, reminiscent of the masques of the Elizabethans and the ballets produced at Versailles. These witty, remarkably crafted works tremble like towers of refracted light built to be admired one moment and fade the next.

In our selection of Sor Juana's lyric poetry we have sought to convey some idea of the range of kinds she cultivated: poetry of circumstance centering on her connections with the viceregal court, love poetry, poetry markedly personal in tone rooted in her individual situation, light verse, religious lyrics. Of the latter, the most memorable are the *villancicos* which reflect the outlook of the common people. In many we find the soft phrases of the Mexican Indian tongue, along with the language of Congolese blacks, Latin, and the coarse Basque speech. Such receptivity of Spanish baroque aesthetics to New World exoticism must not be confused with a concern for nationality. The predilection for native languages and dialects reveals not so much a presentiment of future nationality as a keen awareness of the universality of the Spanish tongue. Indians, colonials of European extraction, mulattoes, and Spaniards are all one. Sor Juana's interest in pre-Columbian religions may be understood in the same way. The function of the Church is no different from that of the Empire: reconciling antagonisms, overcoming differences through a higher truth.

Before referring to Sor Juana's longest and most important poem, *First Dream,* I must say some words about the meaning of her quest for knowledge and the significance of her bowing to ecclesiastical pressure, renouncing this quest, and lapsing into silence during the last two years of her life. The knowledge she sought was not contained in sacred books; she aspired to the integration of particular truths and insisted on the unity of all knowledge. To her the world was a problem. The universe is a vast laboratory in which the soul is lost. Such a view could not have been further removed from the image of the world found in the Spanish classics, in which knowledge and action are one; to know is to act and all action, like all knowledge, is directed toward the Beyond. Within this tradition, disinterested knowledge appears as blasphemy or madness. For Sor Juana, consequently, to deny this world and affirm the next could not have the same meaning it had for the great spirits of the Counter-Reformation and for the evangelists of New Spain. For Saint Teresa or for Ignacio de Loyola, giving up the world meant not abandonment or silence but a change of course: history, and with it human action, opens itself up to the Beyond and so becomes freshly fertile. Mysticism itself is not so much a matter of leaving this world as of inserting one's personal life into sacred history. Catholicism, whether militarist, evangelical, or reformist, endows history with meaning; in the end, renunciation of the world becomes a form of historic action. In Sor Juana's case, on the other hand, the truly personal portion of her work was oriented not toward action or contemplation but toward knowledge; to know means to question the world without judging it. There was no room for this new form of knowledge within the postulates of her historical universe. For more than twenty years Sor Juana held out. She gave in only when the doors closed definitively upon her. The conflict had penetrated deep within: knowing is a dream. When at the end of her life, history—the ecclesiastical hierarchy—woke Sor Juana from her dream, she fell silent. Her awakening put an end to the golden dream of the viceroyalty.

First Dream (translated here in its entirety) is a poem of knowledge. A perceptive contemporary thus summarized its action: "It being night-time, I fell asleep; I dreamt that I wished once for all to understand all things which make up the universe. Even on breaking them down into categories, I failed to grasp a single one. In the midst of my disillusionment day broke and I awoke."

The universe of *First Dream*—poor in color, abounding in shadows, chasms, and sudden illuminations—is a labyrinth of symbols, a rational delirium. In this it stands apart from the poetry of Góngora and indeed from all other major baroque poetry. Its intellectual bearings are to be found in hermetic and Neoplatonic philosophy. Sor Juana creates an abstract and hallucinatory world, composed of cones, obelisks, pyramids, geometric precipices, and aggressive mountain peaks, a world governed by mechanics and myth. This is scientific poetry—and also poetry of nocturnal terror. The final victory of the sun is cyclic and partial; its light triumphs over half of the world but is defeated in the other half. Rebellious night, "though rushing [off], regaining her composure," rebuilds her empire in the territories left unprotected by the sun. There other spirits dream Sor Juana's dream.

Sor Juana's night is not the carnal night of lovers. Nor is it the night of the mystics. It is an intellectual night, with the loftiness and the fixity of an immense eye; a night precariously erected upon emptiness; sheer geometry; an obelisk of silence, tensed toward the heavens through and through. Only in this verticality does it recall the nights of Spanish mysticism. But the mystics are swept up by celestial forces, as can be seen in certain paintings by El Greco. In *First Dream* the impulse toward heaven comes from below, from the human soul; heaven is closed off, its heights inimical to soaring. Humanity is faced with silence; the urge to know is illicit; the soul that dreams of knowledge is rebellious. Consciousness, alone in the night, is all drought, vertigo, gasping breath. And yet not everything is hostile. In the midst of humanity's very solitude, its headlong rout, it experiences an inward steadying. Knowledge is a dream, but that dream is all we know of ourselves and in it lies our greatness. As in a game of mirrors in which the soul becomes lost every time it comes within reach of itself and is won back whenever it loses itself, the poem's emotion arises from awareness of this ambiguity. The dizzying, cyclic night of Sor Juana all at once discloses its still center. *First Dream* is the poem not of knowledge but of the act of knowing. Thus does Sor Juana transmute her personal and historical destinies, draw victory from defeat and song from silence. Once again poetry is fed by history and biography. Once more it transcends them.

Ever since reading Alan S. Trueblood's translations of the poetry of Antonio Machado, I have admired his talent as a translator. No less difficult than the apparent simplicity of Machado are the verbal and conceptual labyrinths of Juana Inés de la Cruz. Indeed the difficulties may in fact be greater in her case. Not only are we far removed from baroque rhetoric; most of the religious, moral, and metaphysical concerns of the seventeenth century are foreign to us. To translate a text of another age requires splitting the sensibility and the intellect in two, becoming a person of another age without ceasing to be one of our own. Nevertheless, with the same understanding of the original and the same sensitivity he showed in translating Machado, Trueblood has now managed, in the case of Sor Juana's poems, without being unfaithful to them, to create texts in English which have a poetic value of their own. He has thus achieved what for Valéry was the ideal of verse translation: to produce similar effects by different means.

Contents

Preface

LIKE EVERY INTIMACY, the closeness that develops between the translator and the poet being translated carries with it certain demands and tolerates certain licenses. These vary with each instance of interlingual re-creation and sometimes lead the translator in unexpected directions that entail departures from accustomed practice. Quite early in my experience of Sor Juana's verse it became clear that I could not ignore in English the decisive role played in it by rhyme. This despite a conviction that primacy given to rhyme is probably the commonest error of judgment a translator can make when the receiving language is English. For rhyme in English, being much harder to come by, stands out more forcefully and in sharper relief than in Spanish, where it flows readily from the pen. (One need only compare Sor Juana's verse with that of her older contemporary Andrew Marvell for confirmation of this truth.) Perhaps to counteract this facility Spanish often resorts to assonant or vowel rhyme. Though English vowels lack the rich sonorities of the Spanish, they are much more varied and subtly shaded. Although full rhymes are less frequent, there is considerable scope for vowel rhymes, which together with slant- and near-rhymes can cushion the strong impact of rhyme in English.

Sor Juana's incisive verse uses rhyme to reinforce its clarity of line and sharpness of contour, to support its verbal dexterity and rhetorical expansiveness. Except for an occasional calculated comic effect, however, rhyme is handled with an ease and naturalness that both obviate triteness and blend effortlessly with the colloquial tone she often adopts. I have retained rhyme where it could be managed without awkwardness, though I have often changed its patterns and usually been content to suggest its presence without attempting to match the full network Sor Juana deploys. In some instances rhyme proved impossible to achieve in any acceptable scheme, while in at least one other, the long philosophical poem *First Dream,* I found it could be dispensed with altogether without serious loss.

Certain selections in this anthology are presented through excerpts rather than in full. This is a license which Sor Juana's verse is able to tolerate in translation, a by-product of its very rhetorical expansiveness. Though normally one would refrain from breaking into the intactness of poetic form, there are instances in Sor Juana in which expansiveness, for a contemporary ear, turns into repetitiveness. The ability to ring endless changes on a given motif, much prized by Sor Juana and her contemporaries, risks generating monotony for today's reader. Accordingly, where judicious pruning seemed desirable, or at least not harmful, I have not hesitated to practice it.

In selecting the contents of this anthology, I have greatly benefited from the suggestions of Octavio Paz, from which I have departed only when poems proved recalcitrant to translation or when I have added compositions particularly appealing or challenging to me. The order in which the selections appear follows as closely as possible the order in which they are presented and discussed in Octavio Paz's book on Sor Juana.

The Spanish texts are from Sor Juana Inés de la Cruz, *Obras selectas,* ed. Georgina Sabat de Rivers and Elias L. Rivers (Barcelona: Noguer, 1976). I am grateful to the editors and publisher for permission to reproduce these texts. For works that do not appear in this edition—certain *villancicos* and a *loa*—I have relied on volumes II and III of Sor Juana Inés de la Cruz, *Obras completas,* ed. Alfonso Méndez Plancarte (Mexico City: Fondo de Cultura Económica, 1952 and 1955). I have profited from the useful annotation in both editions.

For the English versions I have sometimes abbreviated or reworked the headings of the poems. These were supplied by Sor Juana's unknown first editor, not by herself, and are occasionally confusing or misleading. In translating biblical references and citations, I have in most cases followed the Vulgate used by Sor Juana, as presented in modern English editions of the Douay and Rheims versions.

The numbering of the poems in the English is sequential as found in this volume. The poems are referred to by this numbering in my Introduction and notes. For the Spanish versions I have retained the numbering found in the Méndez Plancarte *Obras completas,* which is standard today. The original Spanish headings of the poems are preserved as well. A concordance at the back of the book supplies equivalences between the two types of numbering.

I am indebted to Octavio Paz not only for proposing this anthology but for his careful perusal of the manuscript and his valuable suggestions. To Nina M. Scott I owe thanks for the care with which she read the manuscript and for her many helpful comments. I am grateful to Stephanie Merrim for critical assistance, to Jane Bragdon for various kinds of help, and to Stuart Blazer for comments on the translations. I am happy to acknowledge once again my gratitude to Ann Louise McLaughlin of Harvard University Press for editorial advice and suggestions from which this book has greatly benefited. It is a pleasure, finally, to thank Maud Wilcox, Editor-in-Chief of the Press, for her extensive assistance with this volume.

Little Compton, Rhode Island   A.S.T.

Introduction

FROM THE CITY OF MEXICO, heart of the autocratic and theocratic viceroyalty of New Spain, the voice of Sor (Sister) Juana Inés de la Cruz reaches us across a gap of three centuries, still fresh, still ringing true, at times sounding almost familiar. Can that voice bridge the further distance between the English- and the Spanish-speaking worlds? Such is my hope in offering this selection of her poetry and prose in English. For of all the memorable Hispanic voices of the latter half of the seventeenth century—and they were not lacking in those dominions on which the sun never set—Sor Juana's most clearly pierces constraints to proclaim the will and the right of the individual—and particularly of the individual woman—to realize herself intellectually, artistically, and emotionally. For us, as for a select few of her contemporaries, Sor Juana's own achievement offers the best proof of the validity of her claim.*

This is all the more remarkable when one considers that woman's subordination was absolute in colonial Spanish America. In the secular sphere she was to be a homemaker, assuring males at all social levels a dependable domesticity that would free them for the careers or labors to which tradition or chance assigned them. If instead of marrying she became a nun, as bride of Christ she had a duty to be completely submissive to His living body, the Church—that is, after her mother superior, to the male clerical hierarchy from

<hr>

* I am much indebted to the masterly study of Octavio Paz, *Sor Juana Inés de la Cruz, o Las Trampas de la Fe* (Barcelona: Seix Barral, and Mexico City: Fondo de Cultura Económica, 1982; 3rd ed., 1985), for the orientation and many of the particulars of this overview of Sor Juana and her writings. Paz's book has been published in English as *Sor Juana, or, The Traps of Faith,* trans. Margaret Sayers Peden (Cambridge, Mass.: Harvard University Press, 1988.)

confessor and canon upward, which exercised His authority and interpreted His Scripture on earth.

Genius is no respecter of circumstance. Still, the milieu from which Sor Juana sprang would appear especially unpropitious to the nurturing of an exceptionally gifted child. She was born into a family of modest means, small landholders on a large hacienda called San Miguel de Nepantla located between the volcanoes of Popocatépetl and Ixtacihuatl, southeast of the city of Mexico. Recent criticism, on the basis of persuasive, though not conclusive, new evidence, has tended to push her birthdate back three years, from 1651 to 1648. Like her two sisters, she was illegitimate. The father, Pedro Manuel de Asbaje, a Spanish captain, is nowhere in evidence in the accounts of her early life. He is noticeably absent from the autobiographical pages of her epistolary *Reply to Sor Philothea*. The disinclination of her mother, Isabel Ramírez, to marriage is not only a likely factor in that of Juana Inés later on; it also suggests a self-reliant and enterprising nature, for it meant that Isabel took over the direction of the farm leased to her father. Juana's determination to follow her own intellectual and creative bent and the skill she later displayed in doing so in the face of strong odds must have owed something to the mother's independent spirit.

By Sor Juana's own account, her talent showed up at an extremely early age. She mentions exhausting to such good effect the contents of her grandfather's small library that when she was sent to the city of Mexico—she would then have been around ten years old—people were amazed at her store of knowledge and her well-stocked memory. It is impossible to know for sure what motivated her mother in sending so young a child to the capital to live in the family of a sister whom marriage had placed in easier circumstances. Isabel Ramírez had by this time entered into a second nonsanctified union and borne the first of three more children. Her motives were probably both economic—straitened finances—and self-sacrificing: recognition of the child's unusual talents and determination not to stand in the way of their development. In any case, the separation and move to the capital set Juana on the solitary course to which the superiority of her mind predestined her, a course followed henceforth with the avidity and tenacity of the inspired autodidact.

Sor Juana's compulsion not only to amass knowledge but to exercise and extend the keen powers of her mind was strong enough to overcome the handicap, of which she was fully aware, of having neither the guidance of a teacher nor the stimulus of whetting her mind against those of fellow students. For, as a woman, she had no chance at the classically oriented education which the cultural establishment of her day, however religiously conformist and tradition-bound, had to offer. She does mention receiving twenty Latin lessons—all she needed for eventual access to the ecclesiastical and secular riches of that language and indeed for composing her own Latin verse. She also mentions in a recently discovered document her gratitude to a confessor for finding her a tutor, probably in theology and probably after she became a nun.

When a new viceregal couple, Antonio Sebastián de Toledo, Marquis de Mancera, and his wife, Leonor Carreto, arrived in 1664, the brilliance of the child prodigy was on everyone's lips. The Viceroy and Vicereine proved to be protectors of the arts, and soon Juana was not only presented at the viceregal court but taken under the wing of the Vicereine to live there as a maid-in-waiting. Participation in the active ceremonial and social round of life at court did not inhibit Juana's scholarly inclinations. If anything, these would have been favored by the relatively enlightened outlook of the viceregal couple. Juana's outgoing manner, her charm and beauty, heightened the impact of her learning and evidently of her wit as well. Some idea of the progress of her mind may be gained from an episode recalled much later by the Marquis de Mancera. He relates that, wishing to test once and for all the authenticity of Juana's learning, he summoned into confrontation and disputation with her some forty theologians, biblical scholars, philosophers, mathematicians, historians, poets, humane scholars, and intelligent nonspecialists, only to witness the astonishing ease with which she answered all their questions and replied to all the arguments they posed. However embroidered in the telling, the account (which probably echoes the feat of the twelve-year-old Jesus with the doctors in the temple) provides a glimpse of the range and power of Juana's intellectual drive, even if it does not touch on the marked scientific bent of her mind or her interest, both theoretical and practical, in music and the fine arts.

Some five years of residence at court brought Juana an experience of worldly social success that at times she must have regarded with disbelief. Nothing could have led her to anticipate the popularity and the renown she soon enjoyed and the close bond that developed between her and the Vicereine. Though favored originally as something of a phenomenon in a milieu avid for entertainment, she cannot have been long in developing the social and diplomatic skills needed to maintain her position. With neither family nor fortune to fall back upon, she was dependent in the last analysis upon her own charm and wits for survival. This factor may account for passages of flattery which strike today's reader as embarrassingly overdone but must at that time have been taken as their objects' due.

That her brilliance aroused envy from the beginning is clear from her verse. An almost complete lack of chronological guideposts makes it impossible to date with any certainty her poems from these years, since after taking the veil she continued in effect to participate at a distance in the life of the court. Nor are we able to postulate early composition on stylistic grounds, for her poems show dexterity and polish from the start, as two sonnets that *are* datable (from 1666 and 1667) attest. Significantly, these are what might be called poetry of etiquette (one is funerary, the other complimentary), occasional verse like so much more written over the years, some of it clearly at the behest of others. Such verse includes greetings on birthdays and saints' days; lines accompanying gifts or expressing appreciation for them; panegyrics; verse figuring in poetry contests, some of it on sacred themes; verse to accompany both courtly and popular dance music; now and then a wittily barbed satire, the target of which must have been evident to contemporaries; a petition or two (one surprisingly to a vicereine for an English prisoner); glosses on set lines or sonnets with set rhymes, both no doubt reflective of parlor games at court or in the convent locutory.

In all these verses Sor Juana is following established conventions; a personal sensibility scarcely speaks in them. Nevertheless, in three sonnets written on the death of "Laura" (Leonor Carreto, the former vicereine), which occurred in April 1674 as she traveled to Vera Cruz with her husband on their way back to Spain, we do catch between the lines a glimpse of the emotional bond between the two women. There is perhaps also in one of the three, which I have included (poem 35), a hint of the role of the Vicereine in encouraging her to write.

Another category of courtly verse embraces what, broadly speaking, may be called the casuistry of love. Here again Sor Juana is cultivating a tradition of long standing stemming from Petrarchan and Neoplatonic idealization of the beloved and including what Lope de Vega had called "definitions" of emotional states and analyses of their interactions: love, jealousy, separation ("absence"), reciprocation and nonreciprocation, rejection, deprivation. Sor Juana surely enjoyed her share of male attention and special pleading during her years at court. One senses at times a certain coquettishness in her tone which would quite naturally have become flirtatious in the atmosphere of the balls, entertainments, and pastimes, the gallantries and repartee of social intercourse. The expertise with which she expounds the processes of the emotions is by no means purely perfunctory. Behind the personas of her verse one divines a sensibility developed through emotional experience at the very least observed and shared at close hand.

Though Juana's turning from the worldliness of the court to the seclusion of the cloister may seem abrupt and startling today, it would have appeared less so to her contemporaries. The city of Mexico was full of convents which housed women of the upper classes for whom marriage, for whatever reason, was ruled out. Juana had neither a dowry nor a pedigree. Since all education was the prerogative of the Church, the path of an exceptional woman who had the temerity to value cultivation of her mind above all else, including marriage, inevitably led to the convent. A woman as clear-sighted as Juana could not have failed to see the fundamental incongruence between her brilliant but superficial situation at court and her profound *amor intellectualis.* In entering a convent, she must have accounted the obligations of communal life (which she clearly took into consideration) less distracting and less in conflict with her deepest values than the worldliness of the court.

A tentative first step in the direction of the convent came in 1667, when she entered the Discalced Carmelite order as a novice. The reformed rule of this order proved too strict, and after three months she retreated. The definitive step came in early 1669 when she entered the more permissive Convent of Santa Paula of the Hieronymite order, where she was to remain cloistered the rest of her life.

Life in the convent of Santa Paula was in no sense austere. Juana's religious duties consisted mostly of attendance at divine offices and observance of the canonical hours. In addition, she soon assumed responsibility for keeping the convent's accounts. The rule specifying that meals should be taken in common was not enforced. The nuns had private living quarters, usually occupying two floors, with their own kitchens, baths, sleeping quarters, and parlors. They brought servants with them—in Sor Juana's case a mulatto slave-girl given to her by her mother. Juana's parlor became her study, where she amassed her own library and spent hours reading, studying, reflecting, and writing. Her correspondence with persons of learning, both secular and clerical, in Spain and the Spanish New World became extensive as her fame spread.

Though now lost, it helped her create the sort of contact with intellectual peers for which opportunities were limited locally. An annex to the convent housed a girls' school; Juana's teaching duties included directing the musical and dramatic activities for which Santa Paula, founded some hundred years previously, had become known.

Juana's move to the Hieronymite convent did not interrupt her association with the viceregal couple and their circle. The move simply placed it on a more independent footing, allowing her to give priority to her intellectual vocation. The Marquis de Mancera and his wife became frequent visitors. After attending vespers, they would repair with Sor Juana to the locutory, together with acquaintances from court circles and persons of literary inclinations. Sor Juana thus became the center of a *tertulia*, a conversational gathering; a contemporary participant recalls her adroitness in intricate scholastic disputation, her comments on sermons, her skill at improvising verse. Presents went back and forth between court and convent, though this was in fact against the rule.

At this time and subsequently there was prudence as well as pleasure behind Juana's care to maintain her connection with the Viceroy and Vicereine. Their protection and that of their successors would serve to hold at bay critical voices motivated by religious zeal and voices of the invidious carping against her worldliness. In her *Reply to Sor Philothea* she mentions a mother superior who for a time forbade her to read. It is also evident that her confessor, the stern Jesuit Antonio Núñez de Miranda, though initially sympathetic, had been pressing her more and more insistently to give up her intellectual pursuits and worldly connections when she defied and broke with him in 1681 or 1682.

The viceregal term of the Marquis and Marquise de Mancera came to an end in 1673. They were succeeded by the Archbishop of the city of Mexico, Friar Payo Enríquez de Ribera, with whom Sor Juana was on good terms. But the period of her closest relations with the viceregal court and of her plenitude as writer and scholar began in 1680 when Friar Payo was succeded by Tomás Antonio de la Cerda, Marquis de la Laguna, and his wife, María Luisa, who was Countess de Paredes in her own right. She was almost the same age as Sor Juana, and the two women became close friends. María Luisa is the Phyllis and the Lysis who figure frequently in Sor Juana's verse of the 1680s. She and her husband were even more enthusiastic devotees of the arts than the Manceras, and she encouraged Sor Juana's poetic vocation. It was María Luisa who, on her return to Spain in 1688, would supervise the first publication a year later of Sor Juana's poetry, a volume grandly called *Inundación castálida* (*The Overflowing of the Castalian Spring, by the Tenth Muse of Mexico*). It was at María Luisa's request that Sor Juana composed her finest sacred work, the sacramental play *The Divine Narcissus*, which also appeared in print in 1689.

With the departure of the Marquis and Marquise de la Laguna in 1688, storm clouds began to gather for Sor Juana. Her relations with the new viceregal couple, the Count and Countess de Galve, while cordial, were more ceremonial, less close, to judge by the formal nature of the few compositions in which the two figure. The austere prelate, Francisco Aguiar y Seijas, Archbishop of Mexico, her most authoritative superior, was not only fiercely misogynous but also strongly opposed to secular drama. (Sor Juana had written two plays for public performance: *The Trials of a Household* and *The Greater Labyrinth Is Love*.) Yet the tertulias at the convent were evidently still flourishing. An occasional participant was the Bishop of Puebla, Manuel Fernández de Santa Cruz, Sor Juana's friend of long standing. On one occasion Sor Juana made bold to take issue with a Maundy Thursday sermon centering on Christ's injunction to the disciples to love one another as he had loved them. It had been delivered some forty years earlier by the eminent Portuguese preacher Antonio de Vieira, a Jesuit. The fine points of her argument need not concern us; it is difficult enough to imagine at this distance the ambience in which they could raise such a storm. Impressed by Sor Juana's disputational brilliance, the Bishop of Puebla asked her to put her demonstration in writing. When she sent it to him, Santa Cruz had it published under the glowing title *Carta atenagórica* (Missive Worthy of Athena). But he also included with it an admonishing letter addressed to her, signed Sor Philothea de la Cruz, an evident pseudonym for the Bishop himself.

There are two principal hypotheses with regard to the Bishop's motivation. Clearly there was rivalry between him and Aguiar y Seijas, whom documents prove to have been made Archbishop of Mexico in preference to Santa Cruz. In publishing a confutation of an eminent Jesuit, Santa Cruz was indirectly attacking the Jesuit archbishop, covering his traces, perhaps with intentional transparency, in the prefatory letter. (The fact that Sor Juana had reached back forty years for this battle of wits shows how avid was the search for theological niceties in this closed clerical society and reveals as well something of the pent-up taste for mental gymnastics which her self-education had left unsatisfied.) On this view, Sor

Juana, to her detriment, is a missile in an undeclared war, and Santa Cruz appears willing to violate her confidence (for she obviously had no expectation of publication) for his own purposes.

A second hypothesis holds that the Bishop saw a storm brewing between the unbending misogynist cleric and the proud cloistered nun who dared to point her words and her interests toward the world beyond the convent walls. On this reading, the Bishop's covering letter is a lightning rod intended to deflect the thunderbolt he saw coming from the archbishopric of the capital city now that Sor Juana no longer could count on strong viceregal protection.

In any case, it is thanks to Sor Juana's unfortunate overreaching (which would hardly have appeared such in other late-seventeenth-century societies) that we possess the *Reply to Sor Philothea*, the most remarkable document in the whole corpus of her writings. It is dated March 1, 1691. As she rises spiritedly to her own defense in reply to Sor Philothea, her voice breaks out of the hothouse atmosphere that would stifle it and comes through to us as ringingly as it does in her finest verse. Once we have found our way through the clustering formulas of self-abasement with which she tries to shield herself at the outset, and have adjusted to her excessive indulgence in Latin citations and in expostulations based on Scripture and the Church Fathers, we find ourselves listening to the remarkable story of an intellectual and artistic vocation that refused to be denied. Not that all her statements can be taken at face value; they are sometimes at variance with one another. The affirmation that she has never written anything for her personal satisfaction, only under compulsion or at the request of others, is countered by the confession that both intellectual inquiry and verse-writing were spontaneous with her, and took place "without my having any say in the matter."

Present-day scholarship has shown that Sor Juana is not above tailoring quotations or taking them out of context in self-defense and in defense of the right of women to pursue lives of learning, to cultivate artistic gifts, even to embrace public careers. Although there is no doubt of Sor Juana's interest in theology and in the techniques of scholastic argumentation on which it still rested in the Mexico of her day, there is as much astuteness as doctrine in her justifying the study of logic, rhetoric, physics, music, history, and a host of other subjects as means of enhancing her understanding of Holy Scripture.

The *Reply* offers fascinating glimpses into the workings of her mind. On the one hand, she reveals the characteristic tendency of the self-taught to be led far and wide by intellectual curiosity without necessarily pausing to delve deeply along the way. In fact it is evident that some of her knowledge stands at one remove from its sources—that is, is assimilated from manuals, compendiums, digests, anthologies, and the like. It could hardly be otherwise in view of her dependence on the books which chance brought into her possession. On the other hand, if a key to intelligence is the ability to establish connections and see relationships, Sor Juana convincingly demonstrates her own when she remarks on the interrelatedness of all branches of learning and on her technique of making one branch shore up her deficiencies in another or shed light on its obscurities. Perhaps the most vivid picture of the unceasing activity of her mind—her need to question and understand the smallest phenomena of her everyday surroundings—comes in her account of the three months when, forbidden to open a book, she "studied in everything God had created." These pages of the *Reply* exemplify a bent of her mind that in other circumstances might have asserted itself in productive scientific inquiry.

The longest section of the *Reply*, a vigorous justification of learning and literary activity in women, eloquently marshals a vast number of precedents and exemplars from biblical and patristic sources and saints' lives, as well as from classical antiquity and the contemporary world. This speaks for itself, and readers may be left to explore on their own its emphases and subtleties. Two final revelations deserve mention, however. First, there is confirmation that the convent setting was no unmixed blessing, since obligations toward the community of sisters and their demands upon her made Sor Juana's conventual life something of a *pis aller*—certainly no ivory tower. Second, the *Reply* shows graphically how keenly she suffered not only from the rancorous envy of her detractors but from a failure of understanding on the part of those most friendly to her.

The belief in herself and in the legitimacy of her stance which pervades the *Reply* marks the apogee of Sor Juana's quest for what we—not she—would call intellectual independence. The distinction of her mind had from childhood set her apart, forcing her at an early age to recognize that she had only herself to rely on. She became adept in handling human relationships; she learned to maneuver diplomatically between court and convent. Undoubtedly she used the favors her viceregal connections brought to her community to stave off criticisms of her privileged position within its walls, just as she neutralized the hostility of her confessor, Núñez de Miranda, and others in the ecclesiastical establishment on the strength of these same connections.

Circumstances had changed, however. The Count and Countess de la Laguna, her warmest and most enthusiastic patrons, were thousands of miles away in Madrid. The publication of her poetry there by María Luisa in 1689, while it consolidated her fame outside of New Spain, seems to have increased resentment of her preeminence and her womanhood in the literary and clerical establishment at home in Mexico. The episode of the *Missive Worthy of Athena* in the end distanced her from Santa Cruz, who seems to have withdrawn his support when, instead of heeding his advice and turning to heavenly muses, she firmly defended her cultivation of earthly ones. The hostility of Aguiar y Seijas was evidently exacerbated by her unwitting role as pawn in the feud between him and Santa Cruz. Rather than an organized cabal against her there was simply a recrudescence of the ecclesiastic pressures that had been there from the start. Sor Juana must have felt increasingly isolated and increasingly vulnerable. Remarkably enough, she still managed to hold out against such pressures well into 1692, with what her sympathizers must have seen as reckless defiance. In that year civil disorders caused by poor harvests that led to hunger riots seriously weakened the position of the viceroy, the Count de Galve, and strengthened the hand of Archbishop Aguiar y Seijas as he organized a penitential orgy of mea culpas. Whatever viceregal backing Sor Juana still enjoyed was seriously compromised. Everything was conspiring to sap her self-confidence and destroy her self-esteem. It was this moral collapse, strengthened perhaps by earlier spiritual misgivings, that led to her capitulation. This began on her initiative with a reconciliation with her former spiritual director, Núñez de Miranda. A document of 1693 survives in which she repents of having "lived so many years without religion in a religious community." Other documents suggest, perhaps with some exaggeration, extremes of self-castigation. More significantly, the last two years of her life are marked by complete silence, preceded by what appears to be her last poem (36), unfinished and probably dating from late 1692, when the second volume of her works would have reached her from Spain. Perhaps all is not rhetorical convention in the self-deprecation with which she meets the eulogies of the "pens of Europe." A little more than two years later, in April 1695, Sor Juana died of the plague while ministering to her sick sisters.

SOR JUANA'S POETRY marks a final upsurge of the Spanish baroque, a style brilliantly inaugurated at the beginning of the century by Góngora, who not surprisingly is the major influence on Sor Juana's literary manner and expression. It is a style steeped in the by now very familiar cultural idiom inherited from antiquity and enlarged upon by the Renaissance, whose points of reference are Greco-Roman myth, history, legend, and law, variously updated; commonplaces of philosophy and Ptolemaic cosmology; rarities of natural history and varied spoils of other branches of learning, all often applied more decoratively than organically. Glitter is added by imagery in which values placed on persons, objects, and feelings are underscored by the munificence or refinement of their metaphorical equivalents: precious metals and stones, splendid fabrics and materials, rare fragrances, the ever-present rose and rarer blooms, peacocks, phoenixes, and nightingales, often with inherent symbolic significance. Precisely because of the familiarity of this idiom, a premium is placed on novelty and ingenuity in its handling. Wit expressed in conceit, wordplay which startles and diverts by unexpected couplings of terms usually far apart or belonging to different orders of phenomena, is the fundamental figure of thought. Paradox, antithesis, hyperbole, and periphrasis are constant props. Patterns of scholastic logic, parallelisms, inversions, plain or incremental repetitions, are favorite ways of disposing concepts syntactically. Governing all is a rhetorical tendency that highly prizes ingenuity in unraveling variant expressions of an unvarying conceit. Sor Juana's dexterity in manipulating this poetic idiom was the amazement of her contemporaries. Her verse achieves at times almost mathematical effects of symmetry and congruity, reinforcing the impression of an *esprit de géométrie* which one gains, inter alia, from the references to mathematics in the *Reply to Sor Philothea*. Much as one may admire the high polish or the ductility of her verse, however, the modern reader is more likely to be struck by breakthroughs of stylistic originality and moments of plain earnestness, simplicity, colloquiality.

Beyond the conventional aspects of Sor Juana's treatment of love, certain markedly idiosyncratic features of her court and love poetry call for comment. The first relates to personas and addressees. One notes the insubstantiality of the male addressees, who often go by conventional names such as Silvio or Fabio. When the addressee is feminine, however, she emerges with greater concreteness and familiarity. On the other hand, the perspective of the personas in certain poems seems more masculine than feminine. Noticeable also is a dwelling on obstacles to fulfillment—nonreciprocation, separation, widowhood—or on substitutes such as dialogues with portraits or with the speaker's image of the loved one, remembered and elaborated inwardly. There is finally, as already noted, a more than conventional understanding of profane love, of the intensity of erotic feeling. (See, for example, poem 16 or the seventh quatrain of poem 25.)

To address the last point first. Most obviously Sor Juana was no ordinary nun. Besides the exceptional worldly experience she brought into the convent, she was familiar with the secular writings of poets like Lope de Vega and Quevedo and was sensitive to their revitalizing of amatory convention by the sheer force of personal feeling. Everything we know about her suggests that, as an artist, she was (like Jane Austen) endowed with an unusual degree of imaginative empathy. There are no reliable grounds for supposing that a disappointment in love lay behind her taking the veil.

The first two points mentioned are really one, for the emphasis on the female goes hand in hand with an obstructing of the relations between female and male. The situation has inevitably led in some critical quarters to an assumption of lesbianism or bisexuality. At this distance one can only say that no such assumption is necessary to account for the shadowiness of masculine figures and the warmth of emotion in the poems addressed to other women, most especially to Lysis or Phyllis. The important male figures in Sor Juana's early life had been missing (her own father), possibly hostile (her mother's second lover), or, so to speak, sexless (her grandfather). Moreover, the poetic tradition to which she was heir was exclusively masculine in outlook. In the Mexico of her day it would have been unthinkable for a woman openly to celebrate love for a man or make him the object of an amatory cult.

Most important of all, Sor Juana's ruling passion was intellectual. It is evident that what most engaged her was the impassioned pursuit of "beauties with which to stock the mind," to paraphrase poem 28. One need not read between the lines of the *Reply to Sor Philothea* to see that her choice of conventual life over marriage was one of mind over heart and body—over motherhood and domesticity. Amid the jocularity of her reply to the gentleman from Peru (poem 1), the same point is made: her body is "foreclosed to the other sex . . . neuter or abstract."

What then of the very human warmth of certain poems to Phyllis and Lysis? There lies behind it what Octavio Paz has characterized as "amistad amorosa," a mixture of love and friendship in which affection, devotion, gratitude, respect, and a Neoplatonically accented idealization all have a part. There is more than a touch of flattery at times and, most of all perhaps, a need for closeness to another person which neither the convent nor her library could satisfy.

But let us take a closer look at various poems in this anthology. Poem 3 is addressed to María Luisa, the Vicereine, apparently after her return to Spain. Though it is not translated in full, the excerpts given exemplify the Petrarchan and Neoplatonic character of the speaker's sentiments. Phyllis is idealized as a divinity possessed of every perfection, who holds the speaker in thrall with bonds of love, the binding force of the universe. Incapable of attaining perfection herself, the speaker suffers in bondage but eventually succeeds in locating her love in the "sexless" soul (ll. 111–112) and thus communing at a distance with the beloved.

Other poems offer variations on the thematic nexus of separation–distance–absence. In poem 17, an impending separation precipitates floods of tears, carrying conventional Petrarchan lachrymosity to baroque extremes. (One is reminded of Henry Vaughan's "Magdalen.") Poem 19, addressed to memory, focuses on its equivocal role for the absent lover. Separation becomes banishment in poem 6. In poem 20, death is the implacable agent of separation: the persona is a widow. In poem 18, finally, an absent Fabio is implored to return. Occasionally the obstacle to fulfillment is not physical but psychological: ambivalence and misgivings in poem 21. Elsewhere the speaker gladly embraces solitude in order to commune at will with a surrogate for the beloved: a failure to communicate directly with the lady addressed in poem 5 receives the simple explanation, "I could see you in my soul / and talk to you all day long." In poem 23 the elusive surrogate is itself addressed and by the end of the sonnet has been triumphantly told, "in vain shall you elude my fruitless clasp, / for fantasy holds you captive in its grasp."

The most frequent surrogate, however, is a portrait. Sor Juana writes deft variations on the thematic interplay between portrait and subject, stimulated by the concept of pictorial framing into ingenious effects of framing within stanzas of verse. Sufficient for the miniature of the Countess de Paredes described in poems 9 and 10 is, in each case, a single *décima*— ten octosyllables using four rhymes in the original. In poem 11, on the other hand, the speaker takes twenty-six quatrains as sharply delimited as cloisonné work to move from addressing Lysis to addressing her portrait. She then in a two-quatrain coda first returns to Lysis, then blurs the line between the two, addressing them simultaneously. Still another variation (poem 13) presents a (self-?) portrait of the poet, itself speaking to a "certain person," doubtless Lysis. The portrait slips in and out of identity with its subject, Sor Juana again skillfully setting off this intricate yet clearly delineated interplay in another *sfumato* ending which deprives portrait and subject alike of materiality.

Portraiture takes a graver, more disquieting turn—one congenial to the baroque sensibility—when the illusion of life which it creates is seen as emblematic of the deceitful hollowness of the actual world. From the pulpit and in the confessional Sor Juana must have been frequently exposed to reminders of the *Dies irae,* and for all her fascination with the phenomena of the human and material world there were surely moments when such admonitions touched a sensitive spot. So, at least, one may account for the chilling power of poem 27, in which she passes the lesson on to the beholder of a portrait of herself. The sonnet strikes one today as providing a grim hint of the vulnerability that will lead to her ultimate capitulation. The very cleverness of poem 26, on the other hand, with its deprecation of learning and extolling of pious ignorance, strikes one as the dutiful recitation of a lesson memorized. This poem opened the 1689 edition; one wonders if it was not placed first disingenuously, for purposes of edification.

More characteristic of Sor Juana are those instances in which, by way of reaction, she resorts to the evidence of the contact senses as touchstones of reality, a procedure in keeping with the empirical, prescientific turn of mind so amusingly evident in the *Reply to Sor Philothea:* "What could I not tell you, my Lady, of the secrets of nature which I have discovered in cooking . . . If Aristotle had been a cook, he would have written much more." Saint Teresa had noted that "the Lord moves among the saucepans." Perhaps it was Sor Juana's own experience of sampling food in preparation that enabled her to cap the love lore of poem 15 with a grain of salt: "Love's delicacy consists in being loved; / one pinch too much or little spoils love's taste." Elsewhere, treating hope not as a Christian virtue but as a purveyor of deception, she tells us at the end of a sonnet (33):

Myself, I'll act more wisely toward the world:
I'll place my eyes right at my fingertips
and only see what my two hands can feel.

In the arresting imagery of another sonnet (22), the conventional "rhetoric of tears" is superseded as an earnest of sincerity, "since, in that flood of tears, you saw and touched / my broken heart within your very hands." If the worn Petrarchan image of the moth and the flame is rather perfunctorily reiterated in poem 3, the succeeding evocation of a child running a finger along a knife blade is uncomfortably sensory. As a teacher, Sor Juana must have had ample occasion to observe human nature in children. With perhaps some reinforcement from *Lazarillo de Tormes*, she shows us in poem 37 a boy irrationally bursting into tears in the presence of a bogeyman he himself has fashioned.

Despite Sor Juana's fondness for portraiture and her strong interest in music, her imagination is essentially verbal. Even when she appears to be giving in to an inexhaustible propensity for spinning conceits, we find her applying to language the same questioning scrutiny she brings to phenomena of nature, speculating on the capacity of words to signify or bending them in new directions as signifiers. This frequently results in self-reflexive language and in effective new twists to old conceits. She has hardly begun poem 4, for example, when she pauses to ask herself how the small word "mine" (*mía*) in the first line is able to carry the weight of meaning she is giving it. The poem is more than half over before she resumes what was presumably her intended line of thought. One may assume that the last word of poem 12, once again "mine" (*mío*) is used advisedly. Similar semantic speculation but from a different angle underlies the subtlety of the ending of poem 7: "I will own my very soul / as if it were not mine."

Repeatedly Sor Juana's pen talks about itself as it writes. In my selection this twice leads to novel conceits in which the pen's strokes express its share in the grief it is articulating: in the elegiac sonnet on the Marquise de Mancera (poem 35) and in the second quatrain of poem 17. The frequent plays on the boldness of the pen's flights, in which *pluma* is both pen and feather as a synecdoche for wing, are perhaps inevitable. More original conceits are grounded in the writing process. The riot of sumptuary imagery which constitutes the portrait of the Countess de Paredes in poem 8 begins with an injunction to the Sun and Stars: "may the sun turn its beams into quills, / may all the stars compose their syllables." (There is esoteric significance behind the imagery here, as Octavio Paz has shown.) Subsequently we are told of the mouth: "its rubric is written in carmine, / its clause penned in coral and pearl." Is there perhaps an autodidact's longing behind the momentary suspension of decorative lavishness that gives us the far-fetched, essentially cerebral, yet delightful figure: "Your cheeks are April's lecture halls, / with classic lessons to impart to May"?

A lighter ingenuity prevails in the portrait of Little Liz (poem 39):

On her smooth forehead
Love loves to write.
The eyebrows alone
take up the whole page.

The keen receptiveness of the senses evident in conceits examined earlier furnishes expressive vehicles for similes and metaphors. The throes of a widow's grief Sor Juana likens to the sap of the burning log which flares up as if with life when the log is actually being consumed by flames (poem 20). In the unfinished verse epistle to the wits of Europe (poem 36), their encomiums are likened (ll. 81–92) to the sun's rays striking an opaque body and showing up the roughnesses of its surface. Sor Juana lingers over the details of the phenomenon with the same prescientific urge to observe and explain so evident in the *First Dream*. The same tendency is visible when she invokes effects of distance upon sound, of "left-handed perspective" on the sight, conveying almost technically her sense of the Europeans' generous distortions of her modest merits. Even when manipulating the venerable imagery of the four elements of Aristotelian physics, Sor Juana enlivens it dynamically:

I, like air filling a vacuum,
like fire feeding on matter,
like rocks plummeting earthward . . .

so, she tells María Luisa (poem 3) does she gravitate to her. The frequently invoked conflict of fire and water is carried beyond its age-old symbolism—love's passions and sorrows— to point implicitly or explicitly toward the figures of Phaethon and Icarus, the former especially dear to Sor Juana as an emblem of unrepentant boldness, one to be developed at length in the *First Dream*.

Sor Juana occasionally brings unprecedented touches of indigenous exoticism into the literary canon: the (Indian) "herb-doctors of my country" figure instead of Medea as casters of spells in poem 36. The baroque opulence of the portrait of poem 8 is put aside refreshingly when she tells María Luisa: "Your slender form, like the banana plant, / light as a streamer, flutters in the breeze."

The poems which bring Sor Juana closest to the modern reader may well be the sonnets in which, with scarcely any mediation of a persona, she apostrophizes extrapersonal forces or symbols and makes painfully clear the price she has had to pay for her intellectual and artistic distinction: poem 28, "World, in hounding me, what do you gain?"; poem 29, in which "She ponders the choice of a way of life binding until death"; poem 30, in which, addressing Fate, "She shows her distress at being abused for the applause her talent brings"; poem 32, one more sonnet addressed to Hope, in which "She suspects that the relief Hope gives is only cruelty in disguise." In such poems she puts aside the ornate idiom of the late baroque and clearsightedly, in sober tones, addresses herself to her personal situation. Even when the address is oblique and mediated by a literary topos, as when she addresses the rose (poem 31), one senses just beneath the surface an access of genuine world-weariness. If in the sonnet on Pyramus and Thisbe (34) one at first catches an undertone of irony, carried over perhaps from the original Ovidian version of the story (*Metamorphoses* 4), it is put aside in the outburst *ad feminam* of the concluding tercet.

Certain poems already mentioned have provided glimpses of Sor Juana in a lighter mood. In poems 1 and 2, for example, she banters gaily with her admirer from Peru, toying with tools of her trade such as the Muses and the Olympian pantheon. One senses here an irrepressible spirit of fun which, to judge by the testimony of contemporaries, must often have been on display in the tertulias of the locutory of Santa Paula. To enjoyment of the ridiculous is added in her most famous poem (37)—the quatrains on the inconsistencies of the "double standard"—a steady bombardment of more calculated witticisms driven home by inversions of phrasing and neatly turned antitheses which streamline them stylistically. The poem is a lighter pendant to the almost programmatic feminism that speaks out in the *Reply to Sor Philothea*.

When Sor Juana states in the *Reply*, "I am not aware that anyone has seen an unseemly ditty by me," she is conveniently—or genuinely—forgetting five bawdy sonnets—one (poem 38) is included here—surely penned well before 1691, the date of her protestation. Since these sonnets are written to rhymes set in advance, they were presumably intended for private consumption as part of a poetic competition among friends. They demonstrate to perfection her technical skill, her lack of prudery, her ready wit.

In three other poems in a lighter vein (41, 39, and 40), written to dance tunes, Sor Juana's humor is more purely verbal, manifesting itself in the wordplay of ingeniously spun conceits. Poem 41, evidently a courtly lyric celebrating, under the name of Narcisa, some beautiful singer heard in the palace, has the airy levity of the nascent rococo. The verbal portraits of the more rustic figures who go by the nicknames of Liz and Gila in the other two poems, written to popular dance tunes, "The Wool Carder" and "Saint John of Lima," have the grace and charm of Goya's soon-to-be-painted tapestry cartoons. As if to underscore their greater earthiness, the imagery of the two gives a large place to the senses of smell and taste. The portrait of Gila is an exercise in astringency, taking its cue from the name of the city (Lima) where the dance supposedly originated; the word in Spanish also means lime.

Sor Juana's rural origins and her experience directing dramatic and musical activities in the patio of Santa Paula help account for her skill in stylizing the popular lyricism of song and dance. Her capacity for empathy with the spirit of the common people put her much in demand as a composer of *villancicos*, lyrics for interludes of song and dance during religious festivities. If one excepts the more structured and concentrated religious emotion of her play *The Divine Narcissus*, it is in this popular vein that Sor Juana achieves her most memorable religious expression. Her devotional verse proper is meager in quantity and not particularly distinguished in quality. In the single sample included in this book (poem 25) she is content to follow current practice in employing the language of profane love for the expression of the sacred kind.

Sor Juana's villancicos were written over a period of fifteen years (1676–1691). The sampling here includes lyrics prepared for the feasts of the Nativity, the Assumption, and the Immaculate Conception, and for the saint's day of Catherine of Alexandria. They were commissioned by cathedrals in Puebla, Oaxaca, and the capital for use during the celebration of matins. Matins were comprised of three nocturnes, each consisting of three Psalms and three Lessons with polyphonic responses; within each nocturne three villancicos could be inserted. Although the number of villancicos varied, nine were most often included. Their most frequent pattern was one of variations on known lines, which then recurred as a refrain. Occasionally there are introductory sections, and sometimes the villancicos are varied enough to be called medleys. The practice of allowing for such intervals of popular devotion amid the solemnities of matins on religious holidays had developed in Spain and by the second half of the seventeenth century was widespread in Mexico.

The villancicos as a whole (with the exception of those written entirely in Latin or dealing with fine points of learning or theology) were characterized by a religiosity adjusted to the mentality of the common people. In tone they varied from simple doctrinal seriousness to infectious merriment. The humor arose from the spoofing of recognizable social types of the day and the reproduction of their dialects or jargon. The range of comical or picturesque types covered by Sor Juana is wide: student showoffs dropping snippets of Latin after every other phrase, bickering sacristans, Portuguese speaking their Lusitanian Spanish, toughs spouting thieves' slang, Indians speaking Nahuatl, and blacks their purportedly African tongues—all of them, and Basques as well, colorfully maltreating the Spanish language.

Sor Juana displays endless resourcefulness in varying the subject matter. It includes the liberal arts (rhetoric, music, astronomy, geometry), penmanship and metrics, physics (the four elements), and gardening (flowers and herbs). Mary appears now as a swan, now as a lady of great learning, now as a shepherdess. Earth vies with heaven and flowers battle stars. The dances of "Saint John of Lima" and "The Wool Carder" turn up here too, along with popular *seguidillas,* as graceful as those to which Bizet's Carmen will one day dance, and boisterous *jácaras* celebrating exploits of underworld heroes. The present selection includes several echoes of the Song of Songs; Sor Juana is particularly fond of the motif "I am black but comely." We watch the Virgin's Assumption into Heaven through the eyes of two black slaves, "Guinean queens," and through those of Indians. There are lullabies for the Christ Child. The special grace and beauty of the villancicos written for the day of Saint Catherine of Alexandria point to strong sisterly feelings on Sor Juana's part. Clearly she saw analogues to her own situation, especially in Catherine's persecution for brilliance of mind and her besting of assembled sages in a contest of wits.

In addition to writing in the popular vein of her villancicos, Sor Juana produced for the feast of Corpus Christi three *autos sacramentales,* one-act plays in celebration of the Eucharist. One of these, *The Divine Narcissus,* ranks among the masterpieces of this dramatic kind, which by her day had a tradition of long standing in the Hispanic world. The form had been brought to perfection by Sor Juana's immediate precursor, Calderón, whose play *Eco y Narciso* probably attracted her to the subject.

The action of *The Divine Narcissus,* divided into five tableaux and fifteen scenes, is slight; the doctrinal content, however, though fundamentally orthodox, is handled with considerable originality. Sor Juana surpasses Calderón both in intellectual subtlety and in the delicacy of her lyricism, which here reaches a peak of fluid expressiveness. Throughout, she blends with remarkable smoothness the classical pastoral tradition, Catholic sacramental theology, reminiscences of the Song of Songs and other books of the Bible, echoes of secular Spanish poetry and even of hermetic writings. The six selections chosen for this anthology seek to provide some idea of this richness.

*I*N HER *Reply to Sor Philothea,* Sor Juana mentions "a trifle called *The Dream*" as the only work she ever wrote for herself rather than at the behest of others. Although this is an overstatement, the personal significance she attaches to *First Dream* is telling. The work is an intellectual apologia, no doubt more difficult than the autobiographical *Reply to Sor Philothea* yet just as compelling and no less revealing. For all the apparent objectivity of its third-person account of a flight of the spirit, Sor Juana undoubtedly has *First Dream* in mind when, in the *Reply to Sor Philothea,* she tells of the "freedom and lack of restraint" with which "the constant activity of my brain" proceeds when she is asleep. Though Sor Juana's references are mostly to the soul, in effect this is a dream of the mind; it is decidedly less spiritual than cerebral. There are no mystic overtones and the few doctrinal or scriptural allusions are purely tangential. Significantly, at the peak of the soul's ascent, rather than submerging selfhood in the Godhead, it directs its gaze inward, first at the spark of the divine within itself, then at the reflection within it of God's immense creation.

First Dream is such in more than one sense. It is purportedly the account of an actual dream recalled in waking hours and related from a standpoint beyond that of the individual dreamer, one which takes in the sleep enveloping the dream as well as the dream itself. (The same Spanish word, *sueño,* means both sleep and dream.) *First Dream* is such also in the sense that it is the vision of an unrealizable aspiration. A further dimension is hinted at in the designation "first" which, though apparently not Sor Juana's, was added to the title when the poem was first printed in the second volume of her works (Seville, 1692). The adjective points to the fact that nearly half of the poem, everything subsequent to the account of the soul's thwarted attempt at intuitive universal understanding, is given over to its ensuing cogitations as it ponders the pros and cons of undertaking a second flight. We are there introduced into the speaker's most prized intimacy, the workshop of her mind, where thought swings in pendular fashion between the resolve to try again and the fear of a second failure. The bolder course is prevailing when sleep and dream are interrupted by the coming of day before the soul has had a chance to act. The protagonist is now expressly linked to a subjective self, which speaks of "my mind" and "my thought," and is perhaps also alluded to ambiguously in the Spanish text when the subject of verbs—I? it?—is left unexpressed (as it cannot be in English). In the very last line of the poem the narrating voice is for the only time indisputably identified as that of a woman—again only in the Spanish. This line thus functions as an author's signature. The poem itself, dealing as it does with the "sexless" soul, had had no need or occasion to allude to the author's femininity. By not doing so until the very end, it demonstrates that her pen's creation is indistinguishable from that of a man.

As the plenary confession of the faculty of mind and as the mature summation of the intellectual adventure of a lifetime, the poem weaves into its fabric an extraordinary range of scholastic and philosophical readings and of literary and rhetorical culture. As modern scholarship has demonstrated, Sor Juana has at her fingertips the long literary tradition of the philosophically revealing dream, from Cicero's *Dream of Scipio* onward, with such accompanying topoi as the struggle of night and day, sleep's universal dominion, sleep as the image of death, and the deceptiveness of dreams. That repercussions of the hermetic tradition of the Renaissance had reached Sor Juana is evident in, among other passages, the extensive one on the pyramids and their esoteric significance. (One wonders if the first word of the poem—"Pyramidal"—is not already pointing, however obliquely, in this direction.)

The lack of a formal education, though deplored by Sor Juana, had the compensatory effect, in throwing her on her own resources, of fostering both vast intellectual ambition and the self-reliance needed to pursue it; both might have been inhibited by a more systematic and supervised training. It is to the celebration of the surge of mind, despite a clear-eyed acknowledgment of inevitable ultimate frustration, that *First Dream* is ultimately addressed. The poem is seeded with imagery of conflict, especially of light against dark, lucidity against obscurity and even obscurantism. If, on the soul's reaching the peak of its ascent, the limit of its powers is signaled by an inversion of such imagery—the dark becomes a refuge from the dazzlement of the light—the upward impulse is still not checked. The climactic emblem of Sor Juana's aspiring mind is Phaethon—struck down by Zeus's dazzling lightning bolt yet, by his demonstration of "ambitious mettle," "causing wings to sprout for further flight" in those spurred by his example, those who see his glory in his impulse toward the light, not his defeat in the inability of his eyes to sustain its rays.

First Dream, like the *Reply to Sor Philothea*, at times expressly evinces (within the limitations imposed by her milieu) the spirit of inquiry which I have called prescientific. Sor Juana speaks of "taking endless pains . . . with observant / empirical attention . . . / in experiments performed on animals" and acknowledges the immense difficulties of "the task of investigating Nature." She is fascinated by the optics of the recently invented magic lantern, whose mechanism is evoked toward the end of the poem as the vehicle of a simile illustrative of the operations of the phantasms of the brain. The simile is protracted well beyond its immediate illustrative function out of sheer interest on Sor Juana's part in noting the distances required by "the science of perspective / and confirmed in its [the shadow's] true measurements / by a number of experiments."

We touch here on one of the major difficulties of the poem for modern readers: the lack of proportion between the tenuous narrative thread recounting the experience of the dreaming mind and the weight of rhetoric and erudition that it sustains. Sor Juana denies herself no opportunity to string along this thread excursuses which begin as illustrative similes but turn into what even to a contemporaneous reader must have appeared as digressions, at times proliferating into subdigressions. Writing for her own delectation, Sor Juana has not hesitated to turn the poem into a treasure house for the "things of beauty" with which she stocks her mind (to recall poem 28 again). As her first editor expressly notes, she is "imitating Góngora." She has adapted to her own ends rhetorical and stylistic techniques of Góngora's "Soledades" (Solitudes), poems descriptive of land- and seascapes in which the aimlessness of a human figure's wanderings is translated into a series of loosely linked tableaux in which he figures as onlooker.

With Sor Juana, however, it is reflections of the sublunary world and the superlunary universe that the soul contemplates from its lofty vantage point. Though the images of the immense mechanism prove devastating to its "beautiful intellectual eyes," Sor Juana may be seen as anticipating T. S.

Eliot's assemblage of "fragments I have shored against my ruins." She has preserved in the compartments of her major poem, to linger over as long as her pen desires, a few of the many things that have caught the mind's eye: nuggets of myth from Ovid's *Metamorphoses;* lore of natural history from Pliny; repercussions and sometimes rhythmic echoes of Roman poetry. She dwells in fond detail on atmospherics and cosmology, on the physiological and psychological functioning of the human organism, the interaction of sense, mind, and spirit, using terms and concepts passed down to Saint Thomas from Aristotle and Galen. She passes in review the great chain of being; she pauses at length over those two of the seven wonders of the ancient world, the Lighthouse at Alexandria and the Pyramids of Egypt, that speak to her interest in optics, physics, and geometry. At times she indulges in reflections on law or public policy; at times there are parentheses with a moral or even an aesthetic coloration. Yet even in the latter case—descriptions of the brook and the flowers—Sor Juana's figures of comparison—similes, metaphors—are used rhetorically rather than poetically. They are introduced by way of illustration or explanation, not as a means of expressing what cannot otherwise be conveyed. The soul may be likened at one moment to a person recoiling in shock, at the next, to a ship running aground. This discursive use of imagery, together with the employment of metrical verse rather than prose as an expository vehicle for abstract thought (a practice prolonged by the Jesuits in their "scientific" Latin poetry well into the eighteenth century), constitutes a hurdle which modern readers must surmount if they are to appreciate this unique product of Sor Juana's pen. The reward will justify the effort.

To an age in which knowledge is expanding vertiginously even as it splinters into a thousand specializations, the very thought of encompassing the whole range of knowledge in one sweep is chimerical. Even in Sor Juana's age, and particularly in her circumstances, such an effort required boundless intellectual energy and titanic courage. It is hard to gauge the moral repercussions of the epistemological rebuff that the effort suffers. To what extent did intellectual disheartenment impair Sor Juana's self-confidence and render her more vulnerable to pressures exerted from without against the independence of her mind? Although continuing investigation may shed new light on this question, nothing will reduce the radiance of Sor Juana's stand in favor of the human spirit's right to unimpeded growth in an age which, like our own, was far from taking that right for granted.

Poems

48

*Respondiendo a un caballero del Perú, que le envió unos
barros diciéndole que se volviese hombre*

Señor: para responderos
todas las musas se eximen,
sin que haya, ni aun de limosna,
una que ahora me dicte;
　y siendo las nueve hermanas
madres del donaire y chiste,
no hay, oyendo vuestros versos,
una que chiste ni miste.
　Apolo absorto se queda
tan elevado de oírle
que para aguijar el carro
es menester que le griten.
　Para escucharlo el Pegaso
todo el aliento reprime,
sin que mientras lo recitan
tema nadie que relinche.
　Para, contra todo el orden,
de sus cristales fluxibles
los gorjeos Helicona,
los murmurios Aganipe:
　porque sus murmurios viendo,
todas las musas coligen
que, de vuestros versos, no
merecen ser aprendices.

The Convent and the Court

1

Replying to a gentleman from Peru who had sent her some small clay vessels, telling her she should become a man

Sir, in reply to your note,
no help at all is at hand.
No Muse dictates a word,
none is disposed to be bland.

No, not one of those nine,
mothers of wit, jest, and joke,
dares respond to your verse
with even the feeblest croak.

Apollo himself is struck dumb.
See how he stops in his tracks.
To keep him spurring his steeds,
why, he has to be shouted at.

Pegasus, holding his breath,
hangs on each word you say.
Just let him hear you recite,
and, be certain, he won't neigh.

Against all reason and rhyme,
Helicon cries "Whoa!"
to her fluxible, crystalline gurgles;
Aganip, to her burbling flow,

lest it should dawn on the Muses,
as the springs go babbling away,
that in view of the verse you write,
they might as well call it a day.

Apollo: As god of poetry, Apollo is leader of the Muses.

Helicon, Aganip (Aganippe): Springs on Mount Helicon, sacred to the Muses and emblematic of poetic inspiration.

Apolo suelta la vara
con que los compases rige,
porque reconoce, al veros,
que injustamente preside.

Y así, el responderos tengo
del todo por imposible,
si compadecido acaso
vos no tratáis de inflüirme.

Sed mi Apolo, y veréis que
(como vuestra luz me anime)
mi lira sonante escuchan
los dos opuestos confines.

Mas, ¡oh, cuánto poderosa
es la invocación humilde,
pues ya, en nuevo aliento, el pecho
nuevo espíritu concibe!

De extraño ardor inflamado,
hace que incendios respire;
y como de Apolo, de
Navarrete se reviste.

Nuevas sendas al discurso
hace que elevado pise,
y en nuevos conceptos hace
que él a sí mismo se admire.

Balbuciente con la copia,
la lengua torpe se aflige:
mucho ve, y explica poco;
mucho entiende, y poco dice.

Pensaréis que estoy burlando:
pues mirad, que el que me asiste
espíritu no está a un
dedo de que profetice.

Mas si es querer alabaros
tan reservado imposible,
que en vuestra pluma no más
puede parecer factible,

¿de qué me sirve emprenderlo,
de qué intentarlo me sirve,
habiendo plumas que en agua
sus escarmientos escriben?

Dejo ya vuestros elogios
a que ellos solos se expliquen:
pues los que en sí sólo caben,
consigo sólo se miden.

Apollo drops the baton
that measures out his beat,
forced as he is to admit
he can never hope to compete.

And so, replying to you
is simply out of the question—
or maybe you'd help me out
with some sublime suggestion?

Just be my Apollo and see,
while enlightening me with your light,
how the ends of the world lend ear
as I take my lyrely flight.

Oh, all the power that dwells
in the humblest invocation!
Already new breath swells my chest,
new spirits infuse inspiration.

Inflamed by a strange new ardor,
my breast is a conflagration.
Navarrete no less than Apollo
inspires exhilaration.

Uplifted, my mind now moves
on paths leading higher and higher.
It breaks forth in new conceits
(which it's not the last to admire).

Stammering, stuttering, my tongue
flounders in disarray;
seeing much, it explains very little;
grasping much, it has little to say.

You will think I'm pulling your leg,
but hold on, and I'll make you see
that the spirit that flows in my veins
is a stone's throw from prophecy.

Yet if, for singing your praise,
no power on earth will do,
if your feather-pen alone
is worthy to celebrate you,

why should I make the attempt,
why throw to the winds all caution,
especially when feathers are known
to have written their lessons in water?

So I'll leave it up to your praise
to drink to its own health,
since whoever is his own model
has no other rule than self,

Navarrete: Name of the "gentleman from Peru," otherwise unidentified.

Y paso a estimar aquellos
hermosamente sutiles
búcaros, en quien el arte
hace al apetito brindis:
    barros en cuyo primor
ostenta soberbio Chile,
que no es la plata, no el oro,
lo que tiene más plausible,
    pues por tan baja materia
hace que se desestimen
doradas copas que néctar
en sagradas mesas sirven.
    Bésoos las manos por ellos,
que es cierto que tanto filis
tienen los barros que juzgo
que sois vos quien los hicisteis.
    Y en el consejo que dais,
yo os prometo recibirle
y hacerme fuerza, aunque juzgo
que no hay fuerzas que entarquinen:
    porque acá Sálmacis falta,
en cuyos cristales dicen
que hay no sé qué virtud de
dar alientos varoniles.
    Yo no entiendo de esas cosas;
sólo sé que aquí me vine
porque, si es que soy mujer,
ninguno lo verifique.
    Y también sé que, en latín,
sólo a las casadas dicen
úxor, o mujer, y que
es común de dos lo virgen.
    Con que a mí no es bien mirado
que como a mujer me miren,
pues no soy mujer que a alguno
de mujer pueda servirle;
    y sólo sé que mi cuerpo,
sin que a uno u otro se incline,
es neutro, o abstracto, cuanto
sólo el alma deposite.

and I'll turn to lauding those vessels
wrought to the subtlest delight,
wherein the prowess of art
salutes the appetite.
    Vessels so rarely attractive,
whereon Chile is proud to reveal
that neither in silver nor gold
does she lodge her greatest appeal,
    since, using such lowly material,
she undermines the splendor
of the gods' own golden goblets
from which they sip their nectar.
    I kiss your hands for these gifts,
so delicate in their shaping
as to leave no room for doubt
that your hand was in at their making.
    Regarding the advice you proffer,
I'll take it as part of the bargain
and do myself violence, although
no violence can make me a Tarquin.
    Hereabouts there's no spring of Salmacis,
whose crystalline waters, I'm told,
possessed some magic or other
from which masculine powers flowed.
    Such things are not my concern;
with one thought I came to this spot:
to be rid of those who'd inquire
whether I am a woman or not.
    In Latin it's just of the married
that *uxor*, or woman, is said.
A virgin has no sex at all—
or indeed she has both, being unwed.
    So the man who looks upon me
as a woman, shows want of respect,
since one embracing my state
is foreclosed to the other sex.
    Of one thing I'm sure: that my body
disinclined to this man or that,
serves only to house the soul—
you might call it neuter or abstract.

Tarquin: Properly Sextus, son of Tarquinius Superbus and legendary
violator of Lucretia and cause of her suicide.

Salmacis: The waters of this spring had the power to change a person's
sex, though not the power Sor Juana suggests, since they changed
Hermaphroditus from a male to a bisexual.

Y dejando esta cuestión
para que otros la ventilen,
porque en lo que es bien que ignore.
no es razón que sutilice,
    generoso perüano
que os lamentáis de infelice,
¿qué Lima es la que dejasteis,
si acá la *lima* os trajisteis?
    Bien sabéis la ley de Atenas
con que desterró a Arístides:
que aun en lo bueno, es delito
el que se singularice.
    Por bueno lo desterraron
y a otros varones insignes;
porque el exceder a todos
es delito irremisible.
    El que a todos se aventaja,
fuerza es que a todos incite
a envidia, pues él lucir
a todos juntos impide.
    Al paso que la alabanza
a uno para blanco elige,
a ese mismo paso trata
la envidia de perseguirle.
    A vos de Perú os destierran
y nuestra patria os admite,
porque nos da el cielo acá
la dicha que allá despiden.
    Bien es que vuestro talento
diversos climas habite:
que los que nacen tan grandes,
no sólo para sí viven.

50

En que responde la poetisa, con la discreción que acostum-
bra (al conde de la Granja, que le había escrito el romance
«A vos, mejicana musa»...)

    Allá va, aunque no debiera
    (incógnito señor mío),
    la respuesta de portante
    a los versos de camino.

And leaving this question aside
as more fit for others to probe—
since it's wrong to apply my mind
to things I shouldn't know—

rest assured, my generous stranger,
you've not left lustrous Lima behind
when your homesick heart can emote in
a style so Peruvianly refined.

Well you know that Athenian law
which of old banished Aristides:
it held excess, even of good,
a crime past all abiding.

He was exiled for being a good man
like others who have stood out,
since the most unforgivable crime
is to place people's stature in doubt.

Envy pursues the superior
perforce. They're always dismayed
when people charge that their brilliance
puts everyone else in the shade.

The moment a chorus of praise
settles on one among many,
that very moment he's doomed
to become a target for envy.

Peru has condemned you to exile,
whereas here we hope you'll remain:
thus Heaven sees fit to grant us
the favor that others disdain.

It's only fit that your talent
should dwell in more climates than one,
for those who are born to such greatness
cannot live for themselves alone.

2

*In which the poet, with her usual show of wit, answers the Count of
La Granja*

Here comes, although it shouldn't
(my incognito Don)
an ambling, rambling answer
to the verse you sent along.

Aristides: The banishment of Aristides, one of the Athenian commanders
at Marathon in 490 b.c., lacks basis in fact.

Count of La Granja: Antonio de Oviedo y Rueda, a Spanish man of letters
who settled in Peru, known primarily as a religious poet.

No debiera: porque cuando
se oculta el nombre, es indicio
que no habéis querido ser
hombre de nombre conmigo;

por lo cual, fallamos que
fuera muy justo castigo,
sin perdonaros por pobre,
dejaros por escondido.

Pero el diablo del romance
tiene, en su oculto artificio,
en cada copla una fuerza
y en cada verso un hechizo.

Tiene un agrado tirano
que, en lo blando del estilo,
el que suena como ruego
apremia como dominio.

Tiene una virtud de quien
el vigor penetrativo
se introduce en las potencias,
sin pasar por los sentidos.

Tiene una altiva humildad,
que con estruendo sumiso
se rinde, para triunfar
con las galas de rendido.

Tiene qué sé yo qué yerbas,
qué conjuros, qué exorcismos,
que ni las supo Medea
ni Tesalia las ha visto.

Tiene unos ciertos sonsaques,
instrumentos atractivos,
garfios del entendimiento
y del ingenio gatillos

que al raigón más encarnado
del dictamen más bien fijo
que haya, de callar, harán
salir la muela y el grito.

Por esto, como forzada,
sin saber lo que me digo,
os respondo, como quien
escribe sin albedrío.   ll. 1–44

Why do I say it shouldn't?
Why, a man who hides his name,
when it comes to being acknowledged
has forfeited all claim.

Wherefore this court decrees
as a fitting penalty
that you remain ignored
in your anonymity.

Still, in that fiendish ballad
some mystery must dwell:
each quatrain has hidden powers,
each line exerts a spell.

Despotically appealing,
in style all smooth and bland,
what passes for entreaty
turns out to be command.

Whatever the power may be,
evading all defenses
it goes straight to the head,
short-circuiting the senses.

Arrogantly humble,
clamorously submissive,
surrendering in triumph,
that pseudo-obsequious missive

must know some herb or other,
some charm or countercharm
that would make Medea jealous,
cause Thessaly alarm.

With cunning powers of wheedling—
instruments of attraction,
angling hooks for the wits,
levers to aid extraction—

it seizes the embedded root
of a will determined never
to utter a peep, and yanks
will and shriek out together.

Therefore, under duress,
not knowing what's happened to me,
I answer as anyone must
whose will is no longer free.

Medea: The legendary sorceress of awesome powers who figures in the tale of the Argonauts, in Thessaly and elsewhere.

19

*Puro amor, que ausente y sin deseo de indecencias, puede
sentir lo que el más profano*

Lo atrevido de un pincel,
Filis, dio a mi pluma alientos:
que tan gloriosa desgracia
más causa corrió que miedo.

   Logros de errar por tu causa
fue de mi ambición el cebo;
donde es el riesgo apreciable
¿qué tanto valdrá el acierto?

   Permite, pues, a mi pluma
segundo arriesgado vuelo,
pues no es el primer delito
que le disculpa el ejemplo.   ll. 1–12

   . . . . .

   de ti, peregrina Filis?,
cuyo divino sujeto
se dio por merced al mundo,
se dio por ventaja al cielo;

   en cuyas divinas aras,
ni sudor arde sabeo,
ni sangre se efunde humana,
ni bruto se corta cuello,

   pues del mismo corazón
los combatientes deseos
son holocausto poluto,
son materiales afectos,

   y solamente del alma
en religiosos incendios
arde sacrificio puro
de adoración y silencio.   ll. 41–56

   . . . . .

   Yo, pues, mi adorada Filis,
que tu deidad reverencio,
que tu desdén idolatro
y que tu rigor venero:

   bien así, como la simple
amante que, en tornos ciegos,
es despojo de la llama
por tocar el lucimiento;

3

A pure love, however distant, eschewing all unseemliness, may feel whatever the most profane might feel

Phyllis, a brush's boldness
emboldens my feather-pen:
that brush's glorious failure
engenders hope, not fear.
    Risking error in your cause
sufficed to spur me on.
When risk becomes so precious,
what value has mere success?
    So do allow this quill
to risk another flight,
since, having offended once,
it otherwise has no leave.
. . . . .

You, O exquisite Phyllis,
such a heavenly creature,
grace's gift to the world,
heaven's very perfection.
    On your most hallowed altars
no Sheban gums are burnt,
no human blood is spilt,
no throat of beast is slit,
    for even warring desires
within the human breast
are a sacrifice unclean,
a tie to things material,
    and only when the soul
is afire with holiness
does sacrifice glow pure,
is adoration mute.
. . . . .

I, my dearest Phyllis,
who revere you as divine,
who idolize your disdain,
and venerate your rigor;
    I, like the hapless lover
who, blindly circling and circling,
on reaching the glowing core,
falls victim to the flame;

Sheban gums: Incense distilled from the gum of trees in Sheba, a part of
Arabia.

como el niño que, inocente,
aplica incauto los dedos
a la cuchilla, engañado
del resplandor del acero,

y herida la tierna mano,
aún sin conocer el yerro,
más que el dolor de la herida
siente apartarse del reo;

cual la enamorada Clicie
que, al rubio amante siguiendo,
siendo padre de las luces,
quiere enseñarle ardimientos;

como a lo cóncavo el aire,
como a la materia el fuego,
como a su centro las peñas,
como a su fin los intentos;

bien como todas las cosas
naturales, que el deseo
de conservarse, las une
amante en lazos estrechos...

Pero ¿para qué es cansarse?
Como a ti, Filis, te quiero;
que en lo que mereces, éste
es solo encarecimiento.

Ser mujer, ni estar ausente,
no es de amarte impedimento;
pues sabes tú que las almas
distancia ignoran y sexo.   II. 77–112
. . . . .

¿Puedo yo dejar de amarte
si tan divina te advierto?
¿Hay causa sin producir?
¿Hay potencia sin objeto?

Pues siendo tú el más hermoso,
grande, soberano exceso
que ha visto en círculos tantos
el verde torno del tiempo,

¿para qué mi amor te vio?
¿Por qué mi fe te encarezco,
cuando es cada prenda tuya
firma de mi cautiverio?

I, like the innocent child,
who, lured by the flashing steel,
rashly runs a finger
along the knife-blade's edge;
    who, despite the cut he suffers,
is ignorant of the source
and protests giving it up
more than he minds the pain;
    I, like adoring Clytie,
gaze fixed on golden Apollo,
who would teach him how to shine—
teach the father of brightness!
    I, like air filling a vacuum,
like fire feeding on matter,
like rocks plummeting earthward,
like the will set on a goal—
    in short, as all things in Nature,
moved by a will to endure,
are drawn together by love
in closely knit embrace . . .
    But, Phyllis, why go on?
For yourself alone I love you.
Considering your merits,
what more is there to say?
    That you're a woman far away
is no hindrance to my love:
for the soul, as you well know,
distance and sex don't count.
    . . . . .

    How could I fail to love you,
once I found you divine?
Can a cause fail to bring results,
capacity go unfulfilled?
    Since you are the acme of beauty,
the height of all that's sublime—
that Time's green axle-tree
beholds in its endless turning—
    can you wonder my love sought you out?
Why need I stress that I'm true,
when every one of your features
betokens my enslavement?

Clytie: This blond nymph enamored of Apollo was transformed into the
sunflower (helianthus), which turns toward him all day long.

Vuelve a ti misma los ojos
y hallarás, en ti y en ellos,
no sólo el amor posible,
mas preciso el rendimiento,
    entre tanto que el cuidado,
en contemplarte suspenso,
que vivo asegura sólo
en fe de que por ti muero.   ll. 169–188

82

*Expresa su respeto amoroso: dice el sentido en que llama
suya a la señora virreina marquesa de la Laguna*

Divina Lysi mía:
perdona si me atrevo
a llamarte así, cuando
aun de ser tuya el nombre no merezco.
    A esto, no osadía
es llamarte así, puesto
que a ti te sobran rayos,
si en mí pudiera haber atrevimientos.
    Error es de la lengua,
que lo que dice imperio
del dueño, en el dominio,
parezcan posesiones en el siervo.
    Mi rey, dice el vasallo;
mi cárcel, dice el preso;
y el más humilde esclavo,
sin agraviarlo, llama suyo al dueño.
    Así, cuando yo mía
te llamo, no pretendo
que juzguen que eres mía,
sino sólo que yo ser tuya quiero.
    Yo te vi; pero basta:
que a publicar incendios
basta apuntar la causa,
sin añadir la culpa del efecto.
    Que mirarte tan alta,
no impide a mi denuedo;
que no hay deidad segura
al altivo volar del pensamiento.
    Y aunque otras más merezcan,
en distancia del cielo
lo mismo dista el valle
más humilde que el monte más soberbio,

Turn your eyes toward yourself
and you'll find in yourself and in them
not only occasion for love
but compulsion to surrender.
    Meanwhile my tender care
bears witness I only live
to gaze at you spellbound and sigh,
to prove that for you I die.

4

*She expresses her loving respect, explaining what she means when she says
Her Ladyship the Vicereine, Marquise de la Laguna, belongs to her*

My divine Lysis:
do forgive my daring,
if so I address you,
unworthy though I am to be known as yours.
    I cannot think it bold
to call you so, well knowing
you've ample thunderbolts
to shatter any overweening of mine.
    It's the tongue that misspeaks
when what is called dominion—
I mean, the master's rule—
is made to seem possession by the slave.
    The vassal says: my king;
my prison, the convict says;
and any humble slave
will call the master his without offense.
    Thus, when I call you mine,
it's not that I expect
you'll be considered such—
only that I hope I may be yours.
    I saw you—need more be said?
To broadcast a fire,
telling the cause suffices—
no need to apportion blame for the effect.
    Seeing you so exalted
does not prevent my daring;
no god is ever secure
against the lofty flight of human thought.
    There are women more deserving,
yet in distance from heaven
the humblest of valleys
seems no farther than the highest peak.

En fin, yo de adorarte
el delito confieso;
si quieres castigarme,
este mismo castigo será premio.

91

Excusándose de un silencio, en ocasión de un precepto
para que lo rompa

Pedirte, señora, quiero
de mi silencio perdón,
si lo que ha sido atención
le hace parecer grosero.

Y no me podrás culpar
si hasta aquí mi proceder,
por ocuparse en querer,
se ha olvidado de explicar.

Que en mi amorosa pasión
no fue descuido, ni mengua,
quitar el uso a la lengua
por dárselo al corazón.

Ni de explicarme dejaba:
que, como la pasión mía
acá en el alma te vía,
acá en el alma te hablaba.

Y en esta idea notable
dichosamente vivía,
porque en mi mano tenía
el fingirte favorable.

Con traza tan peregrina
vivió mi esperanza vana,
pues te pudo hacer humana
concibiéndote divina.

¡Oh, cuán loca llegué a verme
en tus dichosos amores,
que, aun fingidos, tus favores
pudieron enloquecerme!

¡Oh, cómo, en tu sol hermoso
mi ardiente afecto encendido,
por cebarse en lo lucido,
olvidó lo peligroso!

Perdona, si atrevimiento
fue atreverme a tu ardor puro;
que no hay sagrado seguro
de culpas de pensamiento.

In sum, I must admit
to the crime of adoring you;
should you wish to punish me,
the very punishment will be reward.

5

Excusing herself for silence, on being summoned to break it

My lady, I must implore
forgiveness for keeping still,
if what I meant as tribute
ran contrary to your will.

Please do not reproach me
if the course I have maintained
in the eagerness of my love
left my silence unexplained.

I love you with so much passion,
neither rudeness nor neglect
can explain why I tied my tongue,
yet left my heart unchecked.

The matter to me was simple:
love for you was so strong,
I could see you in my soul
and talk to you all day long.

With this idea in mind,
I lived in utter delight,
pretending my subterfuge
found favor in your sight.

In this strange, ingenious fashion,
I allowed the hope to be mine
that I still might see as human
what I really conceived as divine.

Oh, how mad I became
in my blissful love of you,
for even though feigned, your favor
made all my madness seem true!

How unwisely my ardent love,
which your glorious sun inflamed,
sought to feed upon your brightness,
though the risk of your fire was plain!

Forgive me if, thus emboldened,
I made bold with that sacred fire:
there's no sanctuary secure
when thought's transgressions conspire.

De esta manera engañaba
la loca esperanza mía,
y dentro de mí tenía
todo el bien que deseaba.

Mas ya tu precepto grave
rompe mi silencio mudo;
que él solamente ser pudo
de mi respeto la llave.

Y aunque el amar tu belleza
es delito sin disculpa,
castígueseme la culpa
primero que la tibieza.

No quieras, pues, rigurosa,
que, estando ya declarada,
sea de veras desdichada
quien fue de burlas dichosa.

Si culpas mi desacato,
culpa también tu licencia;
que si es mala mi obediencia,
no fue justo tu mandato.

Y si es culpable mi intento,
será mi afecto precito,
porque es amarte un delito
de que nunca me arrepiento.

Esto en mis afectos hallo,
y más, que explicar no sé;
mas tú, de lo que callé,
inferirás lo que callo.

77

Que explican un ingenioso sentir de ausente y desdeñado

Me acerco y me retiro:
¿quién sino yo hallar puedo
a la ausencia en los ojos
la presencia en lo lejos?

Del desprecio de Filis,
infelice, me ausento.
¡Ay de aquel en quien es
aun pérdida el desprecio!

Tan atento la adoro
que, en el mal que padezco,
no siento sus rigores
tanto como el perderlos.

Thus it was I kept indulging
these foolhardy hopes of mine,
enjoying within myself
a happiness sublime.

But now, at your solemn bidding,
this silence I herewith suspend,
for your summons unlocks in me
a respect no time can end.

And, although loving your beauty
is a crime beyond repair,
rather the crime be chastised
than my fervor cease to dare.

With this confession in hand,
I pray, be less stern with me.
Do not condemn to distress
one who fancied bliss so free.

If you blame me for disrespect,
remember, you gave me leave;
thus, if obedience was wrong,
your commanding must be my reprieve.

Let my love be ever doomed
if guilty in its intent,
for loving you is a crime
of which I will never repent.

This much I descry in my feelings—
and more that I cannot explain;
but you, from what I've not said,
may infer what words won't contain.

6

Lines that cleverly disclose the feelings of one absent and disdained

I approach, and I withdraw:
who but I could find
absence in the eyes,
presence in what's far?

From the scorn of Phyllis,
now, alas, I must depart.
One is indeed unhappy
who misses even scorn!

So caring is my love
that my present distress
minds hard-heartedness less
than the thought of its loss.

No pierdo, al partir, sólo
los bienes que poseo,
si en Filis, que no es mía,
pierdo lo que no pierdo.

¡Ay de quien un desdén
lograba tan atento,
que por no ser dolor
no se atrevió a ser premio!

Pues viendo, en mi destino,
preciso mi destierro,
me desdeñaba más
porque perdiera menos.

¡Ay! ¿Quién te enseñó, Filis,
tan primoroso medio:
vedar a los desdenes
el traje del afecto?

A vivir ignorado
de tus luces, me ausento
donde ni aun mi mal sirva
a tu desdén de obsequio.

79

Consuelos seguros en el desengaño

Ya, desengaño mío,
llegasteis al extremo
que pudo en vuestro ser
verificar el serlo.

Todo lo habéis perdido;
mas no todo, pues creo
que aun a costa es de todo
barato el escarmiento.

No envidiaréis de amor
los gustos lisonjeros:
que está un escarmentado
muy remoto del riesgo.

El no esperar alguno
me sirve de consuelo;
que también es alivio
el no buscar remedio.

En la pérdida misma
los alivios encuentro:
pues si perdí el tesoro,
también se perdió el miedo.

Leaving, I lose more
than what is merely mine:
in Phyllis, never mine,
I lose what can't be lost.

Oh, pity the poor person
who aroused such kind disdain
that to avoid giving pain,
it would grant no favor!

For, seeing in my future
obligatory exile,
she disdained me the more,
that the loss might be less.

Oh, where did you discover
so neat a tactic, Phyllis:
denying to disdain
the garb of affection?

To live unobserved
by your eyes, I now go
where never pain of mine
need flatter your disdain.

7

Sure consolation in disillusion

Disillusionment,
this is the bitter end,
this proves you're rightly called
the end of illusion.

You've made me lose all,
yet no, losing all
is not paying too dear
for being undeceived.

No more will you envy
the allurements of love,
for one undeceived
has no risk left to run.

It's some consolation
to be expecting none:
there's relief to be found
in seeking no cure.

In loss itself
I find assuagement:
having lost the treasure,
I've nothing to fear.

No tener qué perder
me sirve de sosiego;
que no teme ladrones,
desnudo, el pasajero.

Ni aun la libertad misma
tenerla por bien quiero:
que luego será daño
si por tal la poseo.

No quiero más cuidados
de bienes tan inciertos,
sino tener el alma
como que no la tengo.

61

Pinta la proporción hermosa de la Excelentísima Señora
condesa de Paredes, con otra de cuidados, elegantes esdrú-
julos, que aún le remite desde Méjico a su Excelencia

Lámina sirva el cielo al retrato,
Lísida, de tu angélica forma:
cálamos forme el sol de sus luces;
sílabas las estrellas compongan.

Cárceles tu madeja fabrica:
Dédalo que sutilmente forma
vínculos de dorados Ofires,
Tíbares de prisiones gustosas.

Hécate, no triforme, mas llena,
pródiga de candores asoma;
trémula no en tu frente se oculta,
fúlgida su esplendor desemboza.

Círculo dividido en dos arcos,
pérsica forman lid belicosa;
áspides que por flechas disparan,
víboras de halagüeña ponzoña.

Lámparas, tus dos ojos, febeas
súbitos resplandores arrojan:
pólvora que, a las almas que llega,
tórridas, abrasadas transforma.

Having nothing to lose
brings peace of mind:
one traveling without funds
need not fear thieves.
    Liberty itself
for me is no boon:
if I hold it such,
it will soon be my bane.
    No more worries for me
over boons so uncertain:
I will own my very soul
as if it were not mine.

8

*She paints the shapely proportions of the Most Excellent Countess de
Paredes in lines sent to Her Excellency from Mexico*

May Heaven serve as plate for the engraving
portraying, Lysis, your angelic figure;
may the sun turn its beams into quills,
may all the stars compose their syllables.
    Your skein of locks is as a prison-house,
a Cretan labyrinth that twists and curls
in webbings of golden Ophirs,
in Tibbars of fair prison-cells.
    Hecate full, not triple-shaped,
lavishing white light, comes forth;
not masked, but radiant steadily,
she sheds her brightness from your brow.
    Two bow-shaped arcs, a semicircle each,
form warlike Persian weaponry,
dispatching asps instead of arrows,
vipers that flatter venomously.
    Lamps of Phoebus, your two eyes
flash sudden beams of brilliance—
gunpowder turning every soul they strike
into a flaming Torrid Zone.

Ophirs: Mentioned in the Old Testament as a gold-producing region,
Ophir stands here metonymically for gold.

Tibbars: Gold dust from Central Africa.

Hecate: The powerful triform moon-goddess, worshiped as Hecate or
Persephone in the underworld, Diana or Artemis on earth, and Selenē or
Luna in the heavens.

Límite de una y otra luz pura,
último, tu nariz judiciosa,
árbitro es entre dos confinantes,
máquina que divide una y otra.
    Cátedras del abril, tus mejillas,
clásicas dan a mayo, estudiosas:
métodos a jazmines nevados,
fórmula rubicunda a las rosas.
    Lágrimas del aurora congela,
búcaro de fragancias, tu boca:
rúbrica con carmines escrita,
cláusula de coral y de aljófar.
    Cóncavo es, breve pira, en la barba,
pórfido en que las almas reposan:
túmulo les eriges de luces,
bóveda de luceros las honra.
    Tránsito a los jardines de Venus,
órgano es de marfil, en canora
música, tu garganta, que en dulces
éxtasis aun al viento aprisiona.
    Pámpanos de cristal y de nieve,
cándidos tus dos brazos, provocan
Tántalos, los deseos ayunos:
míseros, sienten frutas y ondas.
    Dátiles de alabastro tus dedos,
fértiles de tus dos palmas brotan,
frígidos si los ojos los miran,
cálidos si las almas los tocan.
    Bósforo de estrechez tu cintura,
cíngulo ciñe breve por zona;
rígida, si de seda, clausura,
músculos nos oculta ambiciosa.
    Cúmulo de primores tu talle,
dóricas esculturas asombra:
jónicos lineamientos desprecia,
émula su labor de sí propia.
    Móviles pequeñeces tus plantas,
sólidos pavimentos ignoran;
mágicos que, a los vientos que pisan,
tósigos de beldad inficionan.
    Plátano tu gentil estatura,
flámula es, que a los aires tremola:
ágiles movimientos, que esparcen
bálsamo de fragantes aromas.

Placing limits on those pure lights,
your nose in all its rectitude
makes peace between twin abutters,
sets bounds to keep them apart.

Your cheeks are April's lecture halls,
with classic lessons to impart to May:
recipes for making jasmine snowy,
formulas for redness in the rose.

In your mouth Aurora's chill tears
are kept in a many-scented vase;
its rubric is written in carmine,
its clause penned in coral and pearl.

A small pyre hollowed out of porphyry
glows on your chin, a resting-place for souls.
You build them there a catafalque of lights,
vaulted with stars to sing their praise.

A passageway to Venus' gardens,
your throat is as an ivory organ
whose music melodiously ensnares
the very wind in bonds of ecstasy.

Tendrils of crystal and of snow,
your two white arms incite desires doomed
to barrenness, like those of Tantalus:
thirst unslaked by water, fruitless hunger.

Your fingers are alabaster dates
springing in abundance from your palms,
frigid if the eye beholds them,
torrid if the soul should touch them.

Your waist, a straitened Bosphorus,
a cord encircles like a girdling Zone—
confinement strict, albeit silken,
ambitiously concealing muscles.

Your figure shines with every grace,
leaving Doric sculpture in the shade,
disdaining the aligned Ionic shaft,
fashioned after self alone.

Mobilely minute, your feet
are unaware of solid pavements,
injecting beauty's magic toxins
in every wind where they alight.

Your slender form, like the banana plant,
light as a streamer, flutters in the breeze,
its agile motion scattering abroad
a balm of aromatic fragrances.

Aurora's chill tears: The morning dew.
  girdling Zone: *Zonē* in Greek means both girdle and a zone of the earth

Índices de tu rara hermosura,
rústicas estas líneas son cortas;
cítara solamente de Apolo,
méritos cante tuyos, sonora.

126

En un anillo retrató a la señora condesa de Paredes;
dice por qué

Este retrato que ha hecho
copiar mi cariño ufano,
es sobrescribir la mano
lo que tiene dentro el pecho:
que, como éste viene estrecho
a tan alta perfección,
brota fuera la afición;
y en el índice la emplea,
para que con verdad sea
índice del corazón.

127

Al mismo intento

Éste, que a la luz más pura
quiso imitar la beldad,
representa su deidad,
mas no copia su hermosura.
En él, mi culto asegura
su veneración mayor;
mas no muestres el error
de pincel tan poco sabio,
que para Lysi es agravio
el que para mí es favor.

89

Al retrato de una decente hermosura, la marquesa
de la Laguna

Acción, Lysi, fue acertada
el permitir retratarte,
pues ¿quién pudiera mirarte,
si no es estando pintada?

Even to suggest your peerless beauty,
these rustic lines of mine will never do.
Apollo's resonant lyre must be plucked
to sing your praise in tones befitting you.

9

Having had a portrait of Her Ladyship, the Countess de Paredes,
painted on a ring, she tells why

This portrait, which love's dedication
caused to be copied here,
is the hand's indication
of all the breast holds dear.
For such extreme perfection
the breast offered little space,
hence the overflow of affection
on the index has found a place,
which finger by grace of art
is index of the heart.

10

On the same subject

This portrait was hoping to catch
a beauty divinely bright;
divinity it caught aright
but beauty it could not match.
In it my worship has secured
the goal of its veneration,
but the faulty brush's creation
has left Lysis' beauty obscured.
Thus piety places its trust
in a portrait to beauty unjust.

11

On the portrait of a decorous beauty, the Marquise de la Laguna

Lysis, you were well advised
to let your portrait be done,
for, except in painted colors,
your beauty is harmless to none.

Como de Febo el reflejo
es tu hermoso rosicler,
que para poderlo ver
lo miran en un espejo.
    Así, en tu copia, advertí
que el que llegare a mirarte
se atreverá a contemplarte
viendo que estás tú sin ti.
    Pues aun pintada, severa
esa belleza sin par,
muestra que para matar
no te has menester entera:
    pues si el resplandor inflama
todo lo que deja ciego,
fuera aventurar el fuego
desautorizar la llama.
    Que en tu dominio absoluto,
por más soberano modo,
para sujetarlo todo
basta con un substituto.
    Pues ¿qué gloria en la conquista
del mundo pudiera haber
si te costara el vencer
la indecencia de ser vista?
    Porque aunque siempre se venza,
como es victoria tan baja,
conseguida con ventaja,
más es que triunfo, vergüenza;
    pues la fuerza superior
que se emplea en un rendido,
es disculpa del vencido
y afrenta del vencedor.
    No es la malla y el escudo
seña del valor subido,
porque un pecho muy vestido
muestra un corazón desnudo;
    y del muy armado, infiero
que, con recelo y temor,
se desnuda del valor
cuando se viste de acero.
    Y así era hacer injusticia
a tu decoro y grandeza
si triunfara tu belleza
donde basta tu noticia.

As with the shafts of Phoebus,
the fair flush of your complexion
admits no closer approach
than a mirror's reflection.

Thus in your portrait it seemed,
without risk to life or health,
one might contemplate your beauty
since you'd not be present yourself.

But even in reproduction,
beauty so greatly desired
offers proof that for slaying victims
no presence of yours is required;

for if a mere glimmer proves blinding
and leaves its victim a shell,
why bring the full fire into play?
The glimmer will do just as well.

Surely the lordly procedure,
when sway is absolute,
for extending one's dominion,
is through a substitute.

For what glory could accrue,
though the world were your demesne,
from a conquest that entailed
condescending to be seen?

Though victory be always yours,
achieved in a manner so tame—
conceding no handicap—
it brings less triumph than shame.

Whenever superior force
is vented on those who give in,
it justifies their surrender
and humiliates those who win.

The shield and coat-of-mail
in valor have no part:
an overarmed breast is a sign
that points to a naked heart.

A man so armed, be assured,
only fear and trembling can feel;
he divests himself of valor
when he dons his armor of steel.

And thus it would not be fair
or fitting to your perfection
if your beauty should win the day,
instead of its mere reflection.

Amor, hecho tierno Apeles,
en tan divina pintura,
para pintar tu hermosura
hizo las flechas pinceles.

Mira si matará verte
formada tan homicida:
que es cada línea una herida
y cada rasgo una muerte.

Y no fue de Amor locura
cuando te intentó copiar:
pues quererte eternizar
no fue agraviar tu hermosura;

que estatua, que a la beldad
se le erige por grandeza,
si no copia la belleza,
representa la deidad.

Pues es rigor, si se advierte,
que, en tu copia singular,
estés capaz de matar
e incapaz de condolerte.

¡Oh tú, bella copia dura,
que ostentas tanta crueldad,
concédete a la piedad
o niégate a la hermosura!

¿Cómo, divino imposible,
siempre te muestras, airada,
para dar muerte, animada;
para dar vida, insensible?

¿Por qué, hermosa pesadumbre,
de una humilde voluntad,
ni dejas la libertad
ni aceptas la servidumbre?

Pues porque en mi pena entienda
que no es amarte servicio,
violentas al sacrificio
y no agradeces la ofrenda.

Tú despojas de la vida
y purgas la sinrazón,
por la falta de intención,
del delito de homicida.

En tan supremo lugar
exenta quieres vivir,
que aun no te tiene el rendir
la costa de despreciar.

Love, turned youthful Apelles,
to carry out his conception,
fashioned brushes from arrows
and painted you to perfection.

No wonder it's fatal to see you:
it's homicide you evoke,
with a wound in every line
and death in every stroke.

Love knew what he was about:
it did not insult your beauty
to perpetuate your likeness;
it was merely doing love's duty.

When beauty is seen in sculpture,
her nature is not traduced;
though herself beyond imitation,
her deity is reproduced.

Inevitably it follows,
with a copy uniquely fair,
that you're capable of killing
and incapable of care.

O lovely, hard-hearted copy,
don't assume so cruel a mien:
allow yourself to take pity
or keep your beauty unseen!

Why is it, heavenly puzzle,
that you're always so irate,
giving death such precedence,
giving life so little weight?

Whence, oh beautiful torment,
so perplexing an attitude,
neither freeing a humble servant
nor accepting her servitude?

To show my unfortunate self
that my love will never be suffered,
you reject the sacrifice
and refuse the tribute offered.

You deprive a person of life
and assert there's no cause for alarm,
since killing was not your intent
and you never meant any harm.

Occupying so lofty a station,
you still would remain exempt,
denying one who surrenders
even a show of contempt.

Desprecia siquiera, dado
que aun eso tendrán por gloria;
porque el desdén ya es memoria
y el desprecio ya es cuidado.

Mas ¿cómo piedad espero
si descubro, en tus rigores,
que con un velo de flores
cubres una alma de acero?

De Lysi imitas las raras
facciones; y en el desdén
¿quién pensara que también
su condición imitaras?

¡Oh Lysi, de tu belleza
contempla la copia dura,
mucho más que en la hermosura
parecida en la dureza!

Vive, sin que el tiempo ingrato
te desluzca; y goza, igual,
perfección de original
y duración de retrato.

103

Esmera su respetuoso amor hablando a un retrato

Copia divina, en quien veo
desvanecido al pincel,
de ver que ha llegado él
donde no pudo el deseo;
alto, soberano empleo
de más que humano talento;
exenta de atrevimiento,
pues tu beldad increíble,
como excede a lo posible,
no la alcanza el pensamiento.

¿Qué pincel tan soberano
fue a copiarte suficiente?
¿Qué numen movió la mente?
¿Qué virtud rigió la mano?
No se alabe el arte, vano,
que te formó peregrino:
pues en tu beldad convino,
para formar un portento,
fuese humano el instrumento,
pero el impulso, divino.

Deign at least to show scorn:
it will not be so hard to bear,
for disdain betrays concern
and contempt acknowledges care.
    But why do I hope for pity,
when your harshness can only reveal
that beneath a veil of flowers
you have hidden a soul of steel?
    Lysis' exquisite features
you've managed to catch without strain;
your feat is greater still
in capturing her disdain.
    O Lysis, behold your beauty
in harsh likeness recreated;
yes, more than your loveliness,
it's your harshness that's imitated!
    Live on, and may thankless time
never tarnish you: may you thrive
original in perfection,
as portrait, ever alive.

12

She adds luster to her respectful love as she addresses a portrait

Godlike copy, in you the brush
was overcome with pride,
for it found itself in regions
to human desire denied;
a talent more than human
was there its matchless guide.
Beyond reach of human daring,
a beauty in you was caught
hitherto unimaginable,
foreclosed even to thought.
    Whose was that peerless brush
that could rise to copying you?
What power could stir the mind?
What strength the hand renew?
Let art not vainly boast
that such a feat could do.
In fashioning this marvel
your loveliness required,
to aid a human instrument,
an impulse God-inspired.

Tan espíritu te admiro,
que cuando deidad te creo,
hallo el alma que no veo
y dudo el cuerpo que miro.
Todo el discurso retiro,
admirada en tu beldad:
que muestra con realidad,
dejando el sentido en calma,
que puede copiarse el alma.
que es visible la deidad.

Mirando perfección tal
cual la que en ti llego a ver,
apenas puedo creer
que puedes tener igual;
y a no haber original
de cuya perfección rara
la que hay en ti se copiara,
perdida por tu afición,
segundo Pigmalïón,
la animación te impetrara.

Toco, por ver si escondido
lo viviente en ti parece:
¿posible es, que de él carece
quien roba todo el sentido?
¿Posible es que no ha sentido
esta mano que le toca,
y a que atiendas te provoca
a mis rendidos despojos?
¿Que no hay luz en esos ojos?
¿Que no hay voz en esa boca?

Bien puedo formar querella,
cuando me dejas en calma,
de que me robas el alma
y no te animas con ella;
y cuando altivo atropella
tu rigor, mi rendimiento,
apurando el sufrimiento,
tanto tu piedad se aleja
que se me pierde la queja
y se me logra el tormento.

Tal vez, pienso que piadoso
respondes a mi afición;
y otras, teme el corazón
que te esquivas desdeñoso.
Ya alienta el pecho, dichoso,
ya infeliz al rigor muere;

In you I see pure spirit.
Your deity I extol,
for I doubt the body I see
and discover the invisible soul.
Wonderstruck at your beauty,
my thoughts soar out of control.
Tranquilizing the senses,
you offer confirmation
that the brush can copy the soul,
deity admit imitation.

Seeing your every perfection,
admiring your rare technique,
it is hard indeed to believe
you are anything but unique.
Were no original found,
no model toward which you might strive,
in my passionate love for you,
my pleading would surely contrive—
Pygmalion-like in insistence—
that the gods should bring you alive.

I touch you in disbelief:
will no life in you react?
Could a portrait steal breath away,
yet not with breath interact?
I find it beyond belief
that it felt no touch in fact,
that to my pleas for favor
my hand summoned no replies,
that no voice came forth from this mouth,
no light shone from these eyes.

I've ample cause for complaint,
as you rob me of soul and sense,
that you've not at least let the soul
give you life in recompense;
and as your hardness of heart,
unmoved by my lack of defense,
increases the pain I suffer,
far from displaying compassion,
with every complaint I utter,
you torment me in crueler fashion.

While at times I fancy your pity
responds to my love's protestation,
at others my heart is afraid
your disdain will not brook supplication.
Hope now leaps up in my breast,
now it dies in desperation.

pero, como quiera, adquiere
la dicha de poseer,
porque, al fin, en mi poder
serás lo que yo quisiere.
    Y aunque ostentes el rigor
de tu original, fïel,
a mí me ha dado el pincel
lo que no puede el amor.
Dichosa vivo al favor
que me ofrece un bronce frío:
pues aunque muestres desvío,
podrás, cuando más terrible,
decir que eres impasible,
pero no que no eres mío.

102

Décimas que acompañaron un retrato enviado
a una persona

A tus manos me traslada
la que mi original es,
que aunque copiada la ves,
no la verás retratada:
en mí toda transformada,
te da de su amor la palma;
y no te admire la calma
y silencio que hay en mí,
pues mi original por ti
pienso que está más sin alma.
    De mi venida envidioso
queda, en mi fortuna viendo
que él es infeliz sintiendo,
y yo, sin sentir, dichoso.
En signo más venturoso,
estrella más oportuna
me asiste sin duda alguna;
pues que, de un pincel nacida,
tuve ser con menos vida,
pero con mejor fortuna.
    Mas si por dicha, trocada
mi suerte, tú me ofendieres,
por no ver que no me quieres
quiero estar inanimada.
Porque el de ser desamada
será lance tan violento

No matter—one triumph is mine:
the possession I take of you,
for, once in my hands, you become
whatever I make of you.
    And, choose as you will to display
your original's hardness of heart,
the brush has granted to me
what love refused to impart:
a painted metal's favor,
if none from its counterpart.
For, though you remain aloof,
even when most malign,
you can only show indifference,
you can't say that you're not mine.

13

Lines accompanying a portrait sent to a certain person

My original, a woman,
sends me on to you;
though here you see her copied,
her feelings still are true.
Though converted into me,
her love remains your due.
Don't wonder at my silence:
What word can portrait say?
Her own is deeper still
since you took her soul away.
    Envying my move to you,
she cannot help but see
how unhappy awareness makes her,
how happy unawareness, me.
The more beneficent star,
the more benevolent sign,
surely presides over me:
for, though born of color and line
and less alive than she,
a better lot is mine.
    But if you prove unreceptive—
for fortune can be unkind—
I'd rather have no life at all,
no feeling in soul or mind,
than know myself unloved,
torture so hard to bear,

que la fuerza del tormento
llegue, aun pintada, a sentir:
que el dolor sabe infundir
almas para el sentimiento.

   Y si te es, faltarte aquí
el alma, cosa importuna,
me puedes tú infundir una
de tantas como hay en ti:
que como el alma te di,
y tuyo mi ser se nombra,
aunque mirarme te asombra
en tan insensible calma,
de este cuerpo eres el alma
y eres cuerpo de esta sombra.

195

*A la Excma. Sra. condesa de Paredes, marquesa de la Laguna,
enviándole estos papeles que Su Excia. le pidió y que pudo
recoger Soror Juana de muchas manos, en que estaban no
menos divididos que escondidos, como tesoro, con otros que
no cupo en el tiempo buscarlos ni copiarlos*

El hijo que la esclava ha concebido,
dice el derecho que le pertenece
al legítimo dueño que obedece
la esclava madre, de quien es nacido.

   El que retorna el campo agradecido,
opimo fruto, que obediente ofrece,
es del señor, pues si fecundo crece,
se lo debe al cultivo recibido.

   Así, Lysi divina, estos borrones
que hijos del alma son, partos del pecho,
será razón que a ti te restituya;

   y no lo impidan sus imperfecciones,
pues vienen a ser tuyos de derecho
los conceptos de una alma que es tan tuya.

that even a soul formed of paint
could never remain unaware,
for pain has ways of reviving
the power of souls to care.

    And, should it irk you that here
I'm soulless, as portraits will be,
take just one soul of the many
within you and lend it to me,
for when I gave you my soul,
and made you my life's trustee,
although you may find it surprising
to see me here lifeless and staid,
I made you the soul of this body
and the body of this shade.

14

*To that most excellent lady, the Countess de Paredes, on sending
manuscripts of verse that she wished retrieved from their possessors*

    The child the slave girl has conceived
becomes acknowledged property
of the rightful lord and master
whom the mother serves in fealty.

    That harvest which a grateful earth
in plentiful obedience yields,
the owner's is whose mind was set
on wresting fruits from barren fields.

    Just so, fair Lysis, these poor scrawls—
soul's children, offspring of the heart—
revert to you, to be your own.

    No hindrance may their failings be,
since thoughts of one entirely yours
are rightly yours and yours alone.

169

Fabio: en el ser de todos adoradas
son todas las beldades ambiciosas;
porque tienen las aras por ociosas
si no las ven de víctimas colmadas.

Y así, si de uno solo son amadas,
viven de la fortuna querellosas,
porque piensan que más que ser hermosas
constituye deidad el ser rogadas.

Mas yo soy en aquesto tan medida,
que en viendo a muchos, mi atención zozobra,
y sólo quiero ser correspondida

de aquel que de mi amor réditos cobra;
porque es la sal del gusto el ser querida:
que daña lo que falta y lo que sobra.

170

*De amor, puesto antes en sujeto indigno, es enmienda
blasonar del arrepentimiento*

Cuando mi error y tu vileza veo,
contemplo, Silvio, de mi amor errado,
cuán grave es la malicia del pecado,
cuán violenta la fuerza de un deseo.

A mi mesma memoria apenas creo
que pudiese caber en mi cuidado
la última línea de lo despreciado,
el término final de un mal empleo.

Yo bien quisiera, cuando llego a verte,
viendo mi infame amor, poder negarlo;
mas luego la razón justa me advierte

Vicarious Love

15

She demonstrates that in love a single attachment is reasonable and desirable

Fabio, what pretty women covet most
is worship from every man who comes along.
Altars are strictly useless in their eyes
unless the weight of victims makes them groan.
  Therefore, should one man only pay them court,
they'll protest to Fortune they've been cheated,
convinced the gist of being a deity
lies not in beauty but in being entreated.
  Yet, prizing moderation in such matters,
for throngs of suitors I've a strong distaste.
I only wish to grant my love's increase
  to one who feels it cannot be replaced.
Love's delicacy consists in being loved;
one pinch too much or little spoils love's taste.

16

To make amends for choosing an unworthy object of love, one must make public confession of one's mistake

Silvio, that I could err and place my love
in one as vile as you has made me see
how heavy a weight sin's evil is to bear,
how harsh desire's vehemence can be.
  Sometimes I think my memory deceives:
how can it be that I in truth did care
for one embodying traits I most despise,
whose every word of love conceals a snare?
  Dearly I wish whenever my eyes behold you
that I could deny a love so badly flawed;
yet, with a moment's thought, I realize

que sólo se remedia en publicarlo:
porque del gran delito de quererte,
sólo es bastante pena, confesarlo.

6

Con que, en sentidos afectos, prelude al dolor
de una ausencia

Ya que para despedirme,
dulce idolatrado dueño,
ni me da licencia el llanto
ni me da lugar el tiempo,
    háblente los tristes rasgos,
entre lastimosos ecos,
de mi triste pluma, nunca
con más justa causa negros.
    Y aun ésta te hablará torpe
con las lágrimas que vierto,
porque va borrando el agua
lo que va dictando el fuego.
    Hablar me impiden mis ojos;
y es que se anticipan ellos,
viendo lo que he de decirte,
a decírtelo primero.
    Oye la elocuencia muda
que hay en mi dolor, sirviendo
los suspiros de palabras,
las lágrimas de conceptos.
    Mira la fiera borrasca
que pasa en el mar del pecho,
donde zozobran, turbados,
mis confusos pensamientos.
    Mira cómo ya el vivir
me sirve de afán grosero;
que se avergüenza la vida
de durarme tanto tiempo.
    Mira la muerte, que esquiva
huye porque la deseo;
que aun la muerte, si es buscada,
se quiere subir de precio.
    Mira cómo el cuerpo amante,
rendido a tanto tormento,
siendo en lo demás cadáver,
sólo en el sentir es cuerpo.

there is no cure save bruiting it abroad.
For crimes of love admit no expiation
save to confess and face humiliation.

17

In which, with deep feeling, she foresees the pain
of separation

Kept from saying farewell,
sweet love, my only life,
by unremitting tears,
by unrelenting time,
   these strokes must speak for me,
amidst my echoing sighs,
sad penstrokes never yet
more justly colored black.
   Their speech perforce is blurred
by tears that well and drop,
for water quickly drowns
words conceived in flame.
   Eyes forestall the voice,
foreseeing, as they do,
each word I plan to speak
and saying it themselves.
   Heed the eloquent silence
of sorrow's speech and catch
words that breathe through sighs,
conceits that shine through tears.
   Behold the raging storm
that rocks my bosom's sea:
engulfed, my thoughts capsize,
bewildered and confused.
   Behold my life reduced
to wretchedness and toil
and see the shame life feels
at clinging to me still.
   Just look at fickle death
fleeing when I pursue,
for even death, besought,
will sell itself more dear.
   Behold my loving flesh
surrendering when racked:
in all else but a corpse;
in suffering, body still.

Mira cómo el alma misma
aun teme, en su ser exento,
que quiera el dolor violar
la inmunidad de lo eterno.
    En lágrimas y suspiros,
alma y corazón a un tiempo,
aquél se convierte en agua
y ésta se resuelve en viento.
    Ya no me sirve de vida
esta vida que poseo,
sino de condición sola
necesaria al sentimiento.

211

Que expresan sentimientos de ausente

Amado dueño mío,
escucha un rato mis cansadas quejas,
pues del viento las fío,
que breve las conduzca a tus orejas,
si no se desvanece el triste acento
como mis esperanzas en el viento.
    Óyeme con los ojos,
ya que están tan distantes los oídos,
y de ausentes enojos
en ecos, de mi pluma mis gemidos;
y ya que a ti no llega mi voz ruda,
óyeme sordo, pues me quejo muda.
    Si del campo te agradas,
goza de sus frescuras venturosas,
sin que aquestas cansadas
lágrimas te detengan, enfadosas;
que en él verás, si atento te entretienes,
ejemplos de mis males y mis bienes.
    Si al arroyo parlero
ves, galán de las flores en el prado,
que, amante y lisonjero,
a cuantas mira intima su cuidado,
en su corriente mi dolor te avisa
que a costa de mi llanto tiene risa.
    Si ves que triste llora
su esperanza marchita, en ramo verde,
tórtola gemidora,
en él y en ella mi dolor te acuerde,
que imitan, con verdor y con lamento,
él mi esperanza y ella mi tormento.

See how my very soul,
inviolate though it be,
yet fears lest grief invade
the precincts everlasting.
    Tears and sighs dissolve
my heart and soul together,
the soul reducing to wind,
turning the heart to water.
    Senseless to me as life
is this life I maintain;
the only sense it knows
is nourishment for pain.

18

Expressing the pangs of separation

Belovèd of my life,
listen a moment to the weary lament
I cast upon the wind
that it may sooner reach your ears,
provided nothing leads its notes astray,
like all my hopes the wind has borne away.
    Hear me with eyes alone,
since ears are out of hearing's farthest reach,
hear how my pen, with moans,
echoes separation's bitterest pangs
and, since you cannot catch my raucous tune,
hear me unhearing, hear a pain gone mute.
    If Nature pleases you,
delight in the happy freshness of the land,
letting no tears of mine,
wearisome and intrusive, interfere;
in the country you will find, if you look close,
signs that reveal my joys and sorrows both.
    See how the brook laughs on,
wooing every flower in the meadow,
caressing each one tenderly,
speaking its love for everything in bloom:
then let its current tell you of my plight,
of how my tears have paid for its delight.
    See how the turtledove
laments the withering of her fondest hope,
perched on the leafy bough,
and let the bough and bird together recall—
the green-leaved bough, the mourning of the dove—
my hope now sacrificed to hopeless love.

Si la flor delicada,
si la peña, que altiva no consiente
del tiempo ser hollada,
ambas me imitan, aunque variamente,
ya con fragilidad, ya con dureza,
mi dicha aquélla y ésta mi firmeza.

Si ves el ciervo herido
que baja por el monte, acelerado,
buscando, dolorido,
alivio al mal en un arroyo helado,
y sediento al cristal se precipita,
no en el alivio, en el dolor me imita.

Si la liebre encogida
huye medrosa de los galgos fieros,
y por salvar la vida
no deja estampa de los pies ligeros,
tal mi esperanza, en dudas y recelos,
se ve acosada de villanos celos.

Si ves el cielo claro,
tal es la sencillez del alma mía;
y si, de luz avaro,
de tinieblas se emboza el claro día,
es con su obscuridad y su inclemencia
imagen de mi vida en esta ausencia.

Así que, Fabio amado,
saber puedes mis males sin costarte
la noticia cuidado,
pues puedes de los campos informarte;
y pues yo a todo mi dolor ajusto,
saber mi pena sin dejar tu gusto.   ll. 1–60
. . . . .

Ven, pues, mi prenda amada:
que ya fallece mi cansada vida
de esta ausencia pesada;
ven, pues: que mientras tarda tu venida,
aunque me cueste su verdor enojos,
regaré mi esperanza con mis ojos.   ll. 85–90

70

Endechas que discurren fantasías tristes de un ausente

Prolija Memoria,
permite siquiera
que por un instante
sosieguen mis penas.

See how the tender blossom,
the crag whose loftiness will not be scaled
by tread of passing time—
the one so frail, the other so unyielding—
are both my emblems, though each differently:
the one is bliss, the other constancy.
    See how the wounded hart
goes streaking down the mountainside,
desperate to find relief
in icy currents of swift water brooks;
behold his thirsty plunge into the stream:
his wounds, not their relief, like mine will seem.
    See how the cowering hare
flies panic-stricken from the savage hounds;
racing to save her life,
she leaves no imprint of her bounding flight:
just so my hope, amid distrust and doubt,
by ruthless jealousy is put to rout.
    See how the sky when clear
mirrors my soul in all its guilelessness;
how, when its light is dimmed
by dismal pall of cloudy overcast,
its very darkness and inclemency
portray my state when you depart from me.
    Dear Fabio, thus it is
that you may learn of my full misery
with ease, when you so choose:
you only need to ask the countryside:
each thing there speaks only of my sadness;
you'll learn my plight at no cost to your gladness.
    . . . . .

    Return, beloved one;
my weary life is suffering decline
from absence so prolonged.
Return, but if you stay away,
although my hope is fed by tears of pain,
I'll keep it green till you return again.

19

Doleful lines relating the sad fantasies of one absent

    Insidious memory,
    grant some surcease;
    an instant only
    let me suffer in peace.

Afloja el cordel
que, según aprietas,
temo que reviente
si das otra vuelta.

Mira que si acabas
con mi vida, cesa
de tus tiranías
la triste materia.
. . . . .

Yo ya sé que es frágil
la naturaleza
y que su constancia
sola es no tenerla.

Sé que la mudanza
por puntos, en ella
es de su ser propio
caduca dolencia.

Pero también sé
que ha habido firmeza;
que ha habido excepciones
de la común regla.

Pues ¿por qué la suya
quieres tú que sea,
siendo ambas posibles,
de aquélla y no de ésta?

Mas, ¡ay!, que ya escucho
que das por respuesta
que son más seguras
las cosas adversas.

Con estos temores,
en confusa guerra,
entre muerte y vida
me tienes suspensa.

Ven a algún partido
de una vez, y acepta
permitir que viva
o dejar que muera.   ll. 77–104

78

*Expresa, aun con expresiones más vivas, el sentimiento que
padece una mujer amante de su marido muerto*

Agora que conmigo
sola en este retrete
por pena, o por alivio,
permite Amor que quede;

Loosen the rope,
don't twist so tight;
with one turn more
life will take flight.
    If you snuff out my life,
you'll find, for your pains,
there's no hunting to do
where no quarry remains.
    . . . . .

    Well I know how frail
Nature's nature must be
since she's constant only
in inconstancy.
    I know well that to change
with each second fleeting
is the flaw innate
in her very being.
    Yet well I know too
that change is not all,
that exceptions exist
to the common rule.
    So, Memory, for once,
dwell on constancy;
from inconstancy's hold
let Nature be free.
    But alas, I can hear
your ready reply:
that the surest things
are those we'd deny.
    Plaguing me thus
with relentless care,
you keep life hanging
by a single hair.
    Come, make up your mind,
cease to vacillate:
have I leave to live
or must death be my fate?

20

*She expresses feelingly the pain a loving wife suffers at her husband's
death*

    Now that love at last
allows me the chance
to grieve or be soothed
in quiet seclusion,

agora, pues, que hurtada
estoy, un rato breve,
de la atención de tantos
ojos impertinentes,

salgan del pecho, salgan
en lágrimas ardientes,
las represadas penas
de mis ansias crüeles.

Afuera, ceremonias
de atenciones corteses,
alivios afectados,
consuelos aparentes.

Salga, el dolor, de madre,
y rompa vuestras puentes
del raudal de mi llanto
el rápido torrente.

. . . . .

¡En fin, murió mi esposo!
Pues, ¿cómo, indignamente,
yo la suya pronuncio
sin pronunciar mi muerte?

¿Él sin vida, y yo animo
este compuesto débil?
¿Yo con voz, y él difunto?
¿Yo viva, cuando él muere?

No es posible; sin duda
que, con mi amor aleves,
o la pena me engaña
o la vida me miente.

Si él era mi alma y vida,
¿cómo podrá creerse
que sin alma me anime,
que sin vida me aliente?

¿Quién conserva mi vida,
o de adónde le viene
aire con que respire,
calor que la fomente?

Sin duda que es mi amor
el que en mi pecho enciende
estas señas, que en mí
parecen de viviente.

Y como, en un madero
que abrasa el fuego ardiente,
nos parece que luce
lo mismo que padece;

now that for a space
my life is withdrawn
from the constant stare
of inquisitive eyes,
    let the pain held back
in my anguished breast
issue forth at last
in scalding tears.
    Etiquette be forgone,
and solicitude,
superfluous assuagement,
would-be consolation.
    Let grief overflow
and the swift rush of tears
sweep such bridges away
with impetuous force.
    . . . . .

    My husband, in short, is dead.
Can I be so unworthy
as to mention his death
and not proclaim my own?
    He lifeless—while I still enliven
this feeble bodily frame?
I discoursing, and he deceased?
I alive when he is dead?
    It cannot be. Without a doubt,
my grief either deceives me
or life itself is lying:
either way, my love is betrayed.
    If he was my heart and soul,
could anyone believe
that I am alive with no soul,
that I can breathe with no heart?
    Who keeps my life going
and where does it find
the air for breathing,
the heart's needed warmth?
    It must be my love
that kindles in my breast
these hollow displays
of apparent life.
    And, as when a log
blazes up aflame,
we see only the glow,
we overlook the pain;

y cuando el vegetable
humor en él perece,
nos parece que vive
y no es sino que muere:
  así yo, en las mortales
ansias que el alma siente,
me animo con las mismas
congojas de la muerte.

ll. 41–76

84

*En que describe racionalmente los efectos irracionales
del amor*

Este amoroso tormento
que en mi corazón se ve,
sé que lo siento, y no sé
la causa por que lo siento.
  Siento una grave agonía
por lograr un devaneo,
que empieza como deseo
y para en melancolía.
  Y cuando con más terneza
mi infeliz estado lloro,
sé que estoy triste e ignoro
la causa de mi tristeza.
  Siento un anhelo tirano
por la ocasión a que aspiro;
y cuando cerca la miro,
yo misma aparto la mano,
  porque, si acaso se ofrece,
después de tanto desvelo,
la desazona el recelo
o el susto la desvanece.
  Y si alguna vez sin susto
consigo tal posesión,
cualquiera leve ocasión
me malogra todo el gusto.
  Siento mal del mismo bien
con receloso temor,
y me obliga el mismo amor
tal vez a mostrar desdén.

ll. 1–28

and thus, when the sap
appears most alive,
in truth it is drawing
its dying breath;
   so I, when my soul
is in agony,
revive with the very
death pangs I feel.

21

In which she describes rationally the irrational effects
of love

   That my heart is suffering
from love pangs is plain,
but less clear by far
is the cause of its pain.
   To make fancy come true
my poor heart strains
but, thwarting desire,
only gloom remains.
   And when most I plead
and lament my plight,
though I see my sadness,
its cause escapes sight.
   I yearn for the chance
to which I aspire,
yet when it impends,
I shrink from desire,
   lest, sensing at hand
that longed-for day,
my misgivings spoil it,
fear drive it away.
   And if, reassured,
I clasp it tight,
with the slightest pretext,
all pleasure takes flight.
   My timid misgivings
turn boon into bane
and for love's very sake,
I must show disdain!

164

En que satisface un recelo con la retórica del llanto

Esta tarde, mi bien, cuando te hablaba,
como en tu rostro y tus acciones vía
que con palabras no te persuadía,
que el corazón me vieses deseaba;
   y Amor, que mis intentos ayudaba,
venció lo que imposible parecía:
pues entre el llanto, que el dolor vertía,
el corazón deshecho destilaba.
   Baste ya de rigores, mi bien, baste;
no te atormenten más celos tiranos
ni el vil recelo tu quietud contraste
   con sombras necias, con indicios vanos.
pues ya en líquido humor viste y tocaste
mi corazón deshecho entre tus manos.

165

Que contiene una fantasía contenta con amor decente

Detente, sombra de mi bien esquivo,
imagen del hechizo que más quiero,
bella ilusión por quien alegre muero,
dulce ficción por quien penosa vivo.
   Si al imán de tus gracias, atractivo,
sirve mi pecho de obediente acero,
¿para qué me enamoras lisonjero
si has de burlarme luego fugitivo?
   Mas blasonar no puedes, satisfecho,
de que triunfa de mí tu tiranía:
que aunque dejas burlado el lazo estrecho
   que tu forma fantástica ceñía,
poco importa burlar brazos y pecho
si te labra prisión mi fantasía.

22

In which she allays misgivings with the rhetoric of tears

Speaking to you, belovèd, this afternoon,
I could see by your gestures and doubting air
that words were unavailing to convince you,
and I longed to have you see my heart laid bare.
Then Love, reading my mind, came to my aid
and achieved what I thought no one could do:
he distilled my broken heart until it flowed
and swelled the stream of tears wept over you.
So, beloved, put an end to harshness now,
jealous torments will cease if you command,
and doubts no longer trouble your peace of mind
    with needless gloom, with insubstantial shams,
since, in that flood of tears, you saw and touched
my broken heart within your very hands.

23

Which contains a fantasy satisfied with a love befitting it

Semblance of my elusive love, hold still—
image of a bewitchment fondly cherished,
lovely fiction that robs my heart of joy,
fair mirage that makes it joy to perish.
Since already my breast, like willing iron,
yields to the powerful magnet of your charms,
why must you so flatteringly allure me,
then slip away and cheat my eager arms?
Even so, you shan't boast, self-satisfied,
that your tyranny has triumphed over me,
evade as you will arms opening wide,
    all but encircling your phantasmal form:
in vain shall you elude my fruitless clasp,
for fantasy holds you captive in its grasp.

384

Encomiástico poema a los años de la Excma. Señora Condesa de Galve

MÚSICA . . . Pues una mensura mesma,
aunque a diversos sentidos
determinada, demuestra
la Armonía a los oídos
y a los ojos la Belleza.
 Limitados los sentidos
juzgan mensuras diversas
en los objetos sensibles;
y así dan la diferencia
entre lo que ven o escuchan,
lo que gustan o que tientan.
Mas el alma, allá en abstracto,
conoce con evidencia
que es una proporción misma,
aunque distinta parezca,
aquella que al gusto halaga
o que al tacto lisonjea,
la que divierte a los ojos
o la que al oído suena.
 Pongo un ejemplo vulgar.
En una línea se asientan
la mitad, la tercia parte,
la cuarta, la quinta y sexta,
de que usa la Geometría.
Redúcese esto a materia
grave, y quiere ponderarse
en balanzass, donde sea
árbitro juez el fiel
que su cuantidad nivela.
Elígese un cuerpo grave,

What Is Music?

24

From the encomiastic poem for the birthday of Her Excellency, the Countess de Galve

MUSIC ... A single measuring rod,
though adapted to the modes
of different senses, demonstrates
Harmony to the ears
and Beauty to the eyes.
   Their limitations cause the senses
to posit diverse dimensions
in the objects they perceive:
thus differences result
between the seen or heard
or what is touched or tasted.
But the soul, which deals abstractly,
has ways of knowing
there is but one proportion,
different as it may appear,
whether it appeal to taste
or flatter touch,
whether it delight the eye
or sound in the ear.
   Here's an everyday example:
Place along a line
a half, a third,
a quarter, fifth, and sixth—
fractions geometry uses.
Convert these into solids
and proceed to weigh them
on a balance with a needle
to serve as arbiter
and even out the scales.
Choose an object of some weight

y de la misma manera
que se dividió la línea,
se proporcionan las pesas.
Y éstas, si quieren, después
armónicamente suenan,
como en la de los martillos
tan repetida experiencia.
  No es otra cosa lo Hermoso
que una proporción que ordena
bien unas partes con otras:
pues no bastara ser bellas
absolutamente, si
relativa no lo fueran.
Destemplado un instrumento,
(aunque tenga la madera
más apta para el sonido;
aunque las más finas cuerdas
se le pongan; y en fin, aunque
en la forma y la materia
se apure el primor del Arte),
como sin concierto suena,
más que deleita, disgusta;
más que acaricia, atormenta.
  Así, la Beldad no está
sólo en que las partes sean
excesivamente hermosas,
sino en que unas a otras tengan
relativa proporción.
Luego nada representa
a la Belleza mejor
que la Música . . .   ll. 180–240

and in like fashion
to the line's divisions,
set out the counterweights.
These may then be made
to sound in harmony
as in that very common
experiment with the hammer.
   The Beautiful is simply
proportion which aligns
each part with all the rest;
since beauty absolute
could never be sufficient,
it must be relative as well.
An instrument untuned
(though made of a wood
most given to resonance,
though fitted out
with slenderest strings,
though in form and matter
the object of Art's fond care)
would sound without concent,
not please but cause displeasure,
torture and not caress.
   Thus Beauty is not only
surpassing loveliness
in each single part
but also proportion kept
by each to every other.
Hence nothing represents
Beauty half so well
as Music . . .

experiment: In *El Melopeo y maestro. Tratado de música teórica y práctica* (The
Musicmaker and Master: Treatise on Theoretical and Practical Music) of
Pietro Cerone (Naples, 1613), a work studied and annotated by Sor Juana,
the "experiment with the hammers" is related at length (p. 228) in
explanation of the discovery of the proportional relationships of musical
intervals.

56

Traigo conmigo un cuidado,
y tan esquivo que creo
que, aunque sé sentirlo tanto,
aun yo misma no lo siento.

Es amor; pero es amor
que, faltándole lo ciego,
los ojos que tiene, son
para darle más tormento.

El término no es *a quo*,
que causa el pesar que veo:
que siendo el término el bien,
todo el dolor es el medio.

Si es lícito, y aun debido
este cariño que tengo,
¿por qué me han de dar castigo
porque pago lo que debo?

¡Oh cuánta fineza, oh cuántos
cariños he visto tiernos!
Que amor que se tiene en Dios
es calidad sin opuestos.

De lo lícito no puede
hacer contrarios conceptos,
con que es amor que al olvido
no puede vivir expuesto.

Yo me acuerdo, ¡oh nunca fuera!,
que he querido en otro tiempo
lo que pasó de locura
y lo que excedió de extremo;

mas como era amor bastardo,
y de contrarios compuesto,
fue fácil desvanecerse
de achaque de su ser mesmo.

Divine Love

25

In which she expresses the effects of Divine Love and proposes to die loving, despite the risk

There's something disturbing me,
so subtle, to be sure,
that though I feel it keenly,
it's not hard to endure.

It's love, but love, for once,
without a blindfold—whence
whoever sees his eyes,
feels torture the more intense.

It's not from their terminus a quo
that my sufferings arise,
for their terminus is the Good;
it's in distance that suffering lies.

If this emotion of mine
is proper—indeed, is love's due—
why must I be chastised
for paying what I owe?

Oh, all the consideration,
the tenderness I have seen:
when love is placed in God,
nothing else can intervene.

From what is legitimate
it cannot deviate;
no risk of being forgotten
need it ever contemplate.

I recall—were it not so—
a time when the love I knew
went far beyond madness even,
reached excesses known to few,

but being a bastard love,
built on warring tensions,
it simply fell apart
from its own dissensions.

Mas ahora, ¡ay de mí!, está
tan en su natural centro,
que la virtud y razón
son quien aviva su incendio.

Quien tal oyere, dirá
que, si es así, ¿por qué peno?
Mas mi corazón ansioso
dirá que por eso mesmo.

¡Oh humana flaqueza nuestra,
a donde el más puro afecto
aun no sabe desnudarse
del natural sentimiento!

Tan precisa es la apetencia
que a ser amados tenemos,
que, aun sabiendo que no sirve,
nunca dejarla sabemos.

Que corresponda a mi amor,
nada añade; mas no puedo,
por más que lo solicito,
dejar yo de apetecerlo.

Si es delito, ya lo digo;
si es culpa, ya la confieso;
mas no puedo arrepentirme,
por más que hacerlo pretendo.

Bien ha visto, quien penetra
lo interior de mis secretos,
que yo misma estoy formando
los dolores que padezco.

Bien sabe que soy yo misma
verdugo de mis deseos,
pues muertos entre mis ansias,
tienen sepulcro en mi pecho.

Muero, ¿quién lo creerá?, a manos
de la cosa que más quiero,
y el motivo de matarme
es el amor que le tengo.

Así alimentando, triste,
la vida con el veneno,
la misma muerte que vivo
es la vida con que muero.

Pero valor, corazón:
porque en tan dulce tormento,
en medio de cualquier suerte
no dejar de amar protesto.

But oh, being now directed
to the goal true lovers know,
through virtue and reason alone
it must stronger and stronger grow.

    Therefore one might inquire
why it is I still languish.
My troubled heart would reply:
what makes my joy makes my anguish.

    Yes, from human weakness,
in the midst of purest affection,
we still remain a prey
to natural dejection.

    To see our love returned
is so insistent a craving
that even when out of place,
we still find it enslaving.

    It means nothing in this instance
that my love be reciprocated;
yet no matter how hard I try,
the need persists unabated.

    If this is a sin, I confess it,
if a crime, I must avow it;
the one thing I cannot do
is repent and disallow it.

    The one who has power to probe
the secrets of my breast,
has seen that I am the cause
of my suffering and distress.

    Well he knows that I myself
have put my desires to death—
my worries smother them,
their tomb is my own breast.

    I die (who would believe it?)
at the hands of what I love best.
What is it puts me to death?
The very love I profess.

    Thus, with deadly poison
I keep my life alive:
the very death I live
is the life of which I die.

    Still, take courage, heart:
when torture becomes so sweet,
whatever may be my lot,
from love I'll not retreat.

2

*Acusa la hidropesía de mucha ciencia, que teme inútil aun
para saber y nociva para vivir*

Finjamos que soy feliz,
triste pensamiento, un rato;
quizá podréis persuadirme,
aunque yo sé lo contrario:
    que pues sólo en la aprehensión
dicen que estriban los daños,
si os imagináis dichoso
no seréis tan desdichado.
    Sírvame el entendimiento
alguna vez de descanso,
y no siempre esté el ingenio
con el provecho encontrado.
    Todo el mundo es opiniones
de pareceres tan varios
que lo que el uno que es negro,
el otro prueba que es blanco.
    A unos sirve de atractivo
lo que otro concibe enfado;
y lo que éste por alivio,
aquél tiene por trabajo.
    El que está triste, censura
al alegre de liviano;
y el que está alegre, se burla
de ver al triste penando.
    Los dos filósofos griegos
bien esta verdad probaron:
pues lo que en el uno risa,
causaba en el otro llanto.

The Self, the World

26

She condemns the bloatedness of much learning, which she considers useless even as knowledge and harmful for living

For a little while, sad Thought,
let's pretend I've a happy lot.
You may actually convince me,
though now I'm convinced I do not.

In feeling apprehension
they say the trouble lies:
if you'll only feel you're happy,
you needn't be otherwise.

Let my intelligence serve,
for once, as a source of comfort.
Must wit forever remain
an enemy to profit?

The world is full of opinions
of what is or is not true;
whatever is black for one
will be white in another's view.

What one man finds attractive
will make another recoil;
while what brings one man relief,
another rejects as toil.

The man who is sad condemns
the cheerful man as inane,
while the cheerful are greatly amused
when they hear the sad complain.

Those two old thinkers of Greece
were always of opposite cheer:
what split the one with laughter
reduced the other to tears.

Two old thinkers: Democritus and Heraclitus—prototypes, respectively, of
a laughing outlook on the world and a tearful one.

Célebre su oposición
ha sido por siglos tantos,
sin que cuál acertó, esté
hasta agora averiguado;   ll. 1–32
. . . . .

Si es mío mi entendimiento,
¿por qué siempre he de encontrarlo
tan torpe para el alivio,
tan agudo para el daño?
El discurso es un acero
que sirve por ambos cabos:
de dar muerte, por la punta;
por el pomo, de resguardo.
Si vos, sabiendo el peligro,
queréis por la punta usarlo,
¿qué culpa tiene el acero
del mal uso de la mano?
No es saber, saber hacer
discursos sutiles, vanos;
que el saber consiste sólo
en elegir lo más sano.
Especular las desdichas
y examinar los presagios
sólo sirve de que el mal
crezca con anticiparlo.
En los trabajos futuros,
la atención, sutilizando,
más formidable que el riesgo
suele fingir el amago.
¡Qué feliz es la ignorancia
del que, indoctamente sabio,
halla de lo que padece,
en lo que ignora, sagrado!
No siempre suben seguros
vuelos del ingenio osados,
que buscan trono en el fuego
y hallan sepulcro en el llanto.
También es vicio el saber,
que si no se va atajando,
cuando menos se conoce
es más nocivo el estrago;
y si el vuelo no le abaten,
en sutilezas cebado,
por cuidar de lo curioso
olvida lo necesario.   ll. 57–96
. . . . .

The centuries since their time
have echoed their difference of view,
but no one can ever decide
which opinion is false, which true.
    . . . . .

If my wits are mine alone,
why must they always be
inept at doing me good,
adroit at harming me?
    Reason, just like a sword,
can be wielded at either end:
the blade, to wound to the death;
the hilt, to provide defense.
    If, well aware of the danger,
you insist on using the blade,
how can you blame the sword
for a choice you yourself have made?
    It's no wisdom to use one's mind
for subtle but hollow display:
true wisdom simply consists
in choosing the sounder way.
    To deal in portents of trouble
and ominous speculation
will only compound disaster
with a burden of expectation.
    When it dwells on imagined troubles,
the mind is all tribulation;
later on, it will find real danger
less frightening than anticipation.
    How happy in his unknowing
is the man unlettered yet wise,
who finds relief from suffering
in what no knowledge supplies.
    The boldest flights of wit
will be buffeted by the wind;
though aspiring to thrones of fire,
in tombs of tears they will end.
    Learning is one more vice.
Unless deterred, its ambition,
when the learned least expect,
will lead them straight to perdition.
    If its course is not deflected,
on subtleties learning feeds,
impertinently inquisitive,
indifferent to genuine needs.
    . . . . .

¿Qué loca ambición nos lleva
de nosotros olvidados?
Si es para vivir tan poco,
¿de qué sirve saber tanto?

¡Oh, si como hay de saber,
hubiera algún seminario
o escuela donde a ignorar
se enseñaran los trabajos,

qué felizmente viviera
el que, flojamente cauto,
burlara las amenazas
del influjo de los astros!

Aprendamos a ignorar,
Pensamiento, pues hallamos
que cuanto añado al discurso,
tanto le usurpo a los años.   ll. 129–144

145

*Procura desmentir los elogios que a un retrato de la poetisa
inscribió la verdad, que llama pasión*

Este, que ves, engaño colorido,
que del arte ostentando los primores,
con falsos silogismos de colores
es cauteloso engaño del sentido;

éste, en quien la lisonja ha pretendido
excusar de los años los horrores,
y venciendo del tiempo los rigores
triunfar de la vejez y del olvido,

es un vano artificio del cuidado,
es una flor al viento delicada,
es un resguardo inútil para el hado:

es una necia diligencia errada,
es un afán caduco y, bien mirado,
es cadáver, es polvo, es sombra, es nada.

146

*Quéjase de la suerte: insinúa su aversión a los vicios,
y justifica su divertimiento a las musas*

En perseguirme, mundo, ¿qué interesas?
¿En qué te ofendo, cuando sólo intento
poner bellezas en mi entendimiento
y no mi entendimiento en las bellezas?

What mad ambition drives us
to forget ourselves, to our grief?
What use is all our learning,
when human life is so brief?

What we need is a seminar
with no other aim than showing
not the ways of human learning
but the comforts of not knowing.

Exempt from need for caution,
taking pleasure in all things,
we'd scoff at whatever threats
the stars' influence brings.

Thought, let's learn not to know,
since so plainly it appears
that whatever we add to our minds
we take away from our years.

27

*She disavows the flattery visible in a portrait of herself, which she calls
bias*

These lying pigments facing you,
with every charm brush can supply
set up false premises of color
to lead astray the unwary eye.

Here, against ghastly tolls of time,
bland flattery has staked a claim,
defying the power of passing years
to wipe out memory and name.

And here, in this hollow artifice—
frail blossom hanging on the wind,
vain pleading in a foolish cause,

poor shield against what fate has wrought—
all efforts fail and in the end
a body goes to dust, to shade, to nought.

28

*She complains of her lot, suggesting her aversion to vice and
justifying her resort to the Muses*

World, in hounding me, what do you gain?
How can it harm you if I choose, astutely,
rather to stock my mind with things of beauty,
than waste its stock on every beauty's claim?

Yo no estimo tesoros ni riquezas;
y así, siempre me causa más contento
poner riquezas en mi pensamiento
que no mi pensamiento en las riquezas.
    Y no estimo hermosura que, vencida,
es despojo civil de las edades,
ni riqueza me agrada fementida,
    teniendo por mejor, en mis verdades,
consumir vanidades de la vida
que consumir la vida en vanidades.

149

*Encarece de animosidad la elección de estado durable hasta
la muerte*

Si los riesgos del mar considerara,
ninguno se embarcara; si antes viera
bien su peligro, nadie se atreviera
ni al bravo toro osado provocara.
    Si del fogoso bruto ponderara
la furia desbocada en la carrera
el jinete prudente, nunca hubiera
quien con discreta mano lo enfrenara.
    Pero si hubiera alguno tan osado
que, no obstante el peligro, al mismo Apolo
quisiese gobernar con atrevida
    mano el rápido carro en luz bañado,
todo lo hiciera, y no tomara sólo
estado que ha de ser toda la vida.

150

*Muestra sentir que la baldonen por los aplausos
de su habilidad*

¿Tan grande, ¡ay hado!, mi delito ha sido
que, por castigo de él o por tormento,
no basta el que adelanta el pensamiento,
sino el que le previene al oído?
    Tan severo en mi contra has procedido,
que me persuado, de tu duro intento,
a que sólo me diste entendimiento
porque fuese mi daño más crecido.

Costliness and wealth bring me no pleasure;
the only happiness I care to find
derives from setting treasure in my mind,
and not from mind that's set on winning treasure.

I prize no comeliness. All fair things pay
to time, the victor, their appointed fee
and treasure cheats even the practiced eye.

Mine is the better and the truer way:
to leave the vanities of life aside,
not throw my life away on vanity.

29

She ponders the choice of a way of life
binding until death

If men weighed the hazards of the sea,
none would embark. If they foresaw
the dangers of the ring, rather than taunt
the savage bull, they'd cautiously withdraw.

If the horseman should prudently reflect
on the headlong fury of the steed's wild dash,
he'd never undertake to rein him in
adroitly, or to wield the cracking lash.

But were there one of such temerity
that, facing undoubted peril, he still planned
to drive the fiery chariot and subdue

the steeds of Apollo himself with daring hand,
he'd stop at nothing, would not meekly choose
a way of life binding a whole life through.

30

She shows distress at being abused for the applause
her talent brings

Fate, was my crime of such enormity
that, to chastise me or torment me more,
beyond that torture which the mind foresees,
you whisper you have yet more harm in store?

Pursuing me with such severity,
you make your heartlessness only too plain:
when you bestowed this gift of mind on me,
you only sought to aggravate my pain.

Dísteme aplausos, para más baldones;
subir me hiciste, para penas tales;
y aun pienso que me dieron tus traiciones
penas a mi desdicha desiguales,
porque, viéndome rica de tus dones,
nadie tuviese lástima a mis males.

147

*En que da moral censura a una rosa, y en ella
a sus semejantes*

Rosa divina que en gentil cultura
eres, con tu fragante sutileza,
magisterio purpúreo en la belleza,
enseñanza nevada a la hermosura.
    Amago de la humana arquitectura,
ejemplo de la vana gentileza,
en cuyo ser unió naturaleza
la cuna alegre y triste sepultura.
    ¡Cuán altiva en tu pompa, presumida,
soberbia, el riesgo de morir desdeñas,
y luego desmayada y encogida
    de tu caduco ser das mustias señas,
con que con docta muerte y necia vida
viviendo engañas y muriendo enseñas!

151

Sospecha crueldad disimulada, el alivio que la esperanza da

Diuturna enfermedad de la esperanza,
que así entretienes mis cansados años
y en el fiel de los bienes y los daños
tienes en equilibrio la balanza;
    que siempre suspendida, en la tardanza
de inclinarse, no dejan tus engaños
que lleguen a excederse en los tamaños
la desesperación o confïanza:
    ¿quién te ha quitado el nombre de homicida?
Pues lo eres más severa, si se advierte
que suspendes el alma entretenida;
    y entre la infausta o la felice suerte,
no lo haces tú por conservar la vida,
sino por dar más dilatada muerte.

Bringing me applause, you stirred up envy's ire.
Raising me up, you knew how hard I'd fall.
No doubt it was your treachery saddled me
    with troubles far beyond misfortune's call,
that, seeing the store you gave me of your blessings,
no one would guess the cost of each and all.

31

*In which she visits moral censure on a rose, and in it, on fellow
humans*

Rose, celestial flower finely bred,
you offer in your scented subtlety
crimson instruction in everything that's fair,
snow-white sermons to all beauty.
    Semblance of our human shapeliness,
portent of proud breeding's doom,
in whose being Nature chose to link
a joyous cradle and a joyless tomb.
    How haughtily you broadcast in your prime
your scorn of all suggestion you must die!
Yet how soon as you wilt and waste away,
    your withering brings mortality's reply.
Wherefore with thoughtless life and thoughtful death,
in dying you speak true, in life you lie.

32

She suspects that the relief Hope gives is cruelty in disguise

Hope, long-lasting fever of men's lives,
constant beguiler of my weary years,
you keep the needle of the balance poised
at the still center between joys and fears.
    You hover at the midpoint, disinclined
to move this way or that, lest your deceit
allow too free a hand to either state:
unbounded confidence, abject defeat.
    Who was it claimed you never killed a man?
That you're a slayer anyone can tell
from the suspense in which you keep the soul
    poised between lucky and unlucky chance.
Nor is it true your aim is multiplying
our days on earth: it's to protract our dying.

152

Verde embeleso de la vida humana,
loca esperanza, frenesí dorado,
sueño de los despiertos intrincado,
como de sueños, de tesoros vana;
    alma del mundo, senectud lozana,
decrépito verdor imaginado;
el hoy de los dichosos esperado
y de los desdichados el mañana:
    sigan tu sombra en busca de tu día
los que, con verdes vidrios por anteojos,
todo lo ven pintado a su deseo;
    que yo, más cuerda en la fortuna mía,
tengo en entrambas manos ambos ojos
y solamente lo que toco veo.

157

Refiere con ajuste, y envidia sin él, la tragedia
de Píramo y Tisbe

De un funesto moral la negra sombra,
de horrores mil y confusiones llena,
en cuyo hueco tronco aun hoy resuena
el eco que doliente a Tisbe nombra,
    cubrió la verde matizada alfombra
en que Píramo amante abrió la vena
del corazón, y Tisbe de su pena
dio la señal que aun hoy al mundo asombra.
    Mas viendo del Amor tanto despecho,
la Muerte, entonces de ellos lastimada,
sus dos pechos juntó con lazo estrecho.
    ¡Mas, ay de la infeliz y desdichada
que a su Píramo dar no puede el pecho
ni aun por los duros filos de una espada!

189

En la muerte de la excelentísima Señora Marquesa de Mancera

Mueran contigo, Laura, pues moriste,
los afectos que en vano te desean,
los ojos a quien privas de que vean
hermosa luz que a un tiempo concediste.

33

On the same subject

Green allurement of our human life,
mad Hope, wild frenzy gold-encrusted,
sleep of the waking full of twists and turns
for neither dreams nor treasures to be trusted;
    soul of the world, new burgeoning of the old,
fantasy of blighted greenery,
day awaited by the happy few,
morrow which the hapless long to see:
    let those pursue your shadow's beckoning
who put green lenses in their spectacles
and see the world in colors that appeal.
    Myself, I'll act more wisely toward the world:
I'll place my eyes right at my fingertips
and only see what my two hands can feel.

34

With some retouches and with envy, she relates the tragedy of Pyramus
and Thisbe

A dismal mulberry tree's black shade
where shadowy dreads stir dolefully
and in whose hollow trunk there still resounds
an echo calling Thisbe soulfully,
    covered the dappled greensward of a lawn
where amorous Pyramus pierced his breast
and bled away, and Thisbe showed her grief
by an act with which the world is still impressed.
    But seeing Love behave so atrociously,
Death pitied them and bound their chests
in one tight knot together dotingly.
    Oh, surely a fate far more to be deplored
is that poor woman's who can't bind her breast
to her Pyramus' own with so much as a sword!

35

On the death of that most excellent lady, the Marquise de Mancera

Let them die with you, Laura, now you are dead,
these longings that go out to you in vain,
these eyes on whom you once bestowed
a lovely light never to gleam again.

Muera mi lira infausta en que influiste
ecos, que lamentables te vocean,
y hasta estos rasgos mal formados sean
lágrimas negras de mi pluma triste.
   Muévase a compasión la misma muerte
que, precisa, no pudo perdonarte;
y lamente el amor su amarga suerte,
   pues si antes, ambicioso de gozarte,
deseó tener ojos para verte,
ya le sirvieran sólo de llorarte.

51

En reconocimiento a las inimitables plumas de la Europa,
que hicieron mayores sus obras con sus elogios
(que no se halló acabado)

¿Cuándo, númenes divinos,
dulcísimos cisnes, cuándo
merecieron mis descuidos
ocupar vuestros cuidados?
   ¿De dónde a mí tanto elogio?
¿De dónde a mí encomio tanto?
¿Tanto pudo la distancia
añadir a mi retrato?
   ¿De qué estatura me hacéis?
¿Qué coloso habéis labrado,
que desconoce la altura
del original lo bajo?
   No soy yo la que pensáis,
sino es que allá me habéis dado
otro ser en vuestras plumas
y otro aliento en vuestros labios,
   y diversa de mí misma
entre vuestras plumas ando,
no como soy, sino como
quisisteis imaginarlo.
   A regiros por informes,
no me hiciera asombro tanto,
que ya sé cuánto el afecto
sabe agrandar los tamaños.
   Pero si de mis borrones
visteis los humildes rasgos,
que del tiempo más perdido
fueron ocios descuidados,

Let this unfortunate lyre that echoes still
to sounds you woke, perish calling your name,
and may these clumsy scribblings represent
black tears my pen has shed to ease its pain.
    Let Death himself feel pity, and regret
that, bound by his own law, he could not spare you,
and Love lament the bitter circumstance
    that if once, in his desire for pleasure,
he wished for eyes that they might feast on you,
now weeping is all those eyes could ever do.

36

*To the matchless pens of Europe, whose praises only enhanced her
works. Lines found unfinished.*

When, divine geniuses,
O sweetest swans, tell me when
my trifles ever deserved
to occupy your attention?
    Why such praise of me?
How explain such panegyrics?
Has distance really the power
to magnify my likeness?
    What view can you have of my stature,
to go and build a Colossus
whose lofty height ignores
the poor original's lowness?
    I am not at all what you think.
What you've done is attribute to me
a different nature with your pens,
a different talent with your lips.
    Borne on your feather-pens' plumes,
my flight is no longer mine;
it's not as you like to imagine,
not what your fancy depicts.
    Were you judging by word of mouth,
I would not be so astonished.
To be partial, after all,
means to magnify sizes at will.
    But you've actually seen those scrawls,
those quite unpretentious drafts
that occupied a few moments
of idle and carefree time,

¿qué os pudo mover a aquellos
mal merecidos aplausos?
¿Así puede a la verdad
arrastrar lo cortesano?

　¿A una ignorante mujer,
cuyo estudio no ha pasado
de ratos, a la precisa
ocupación mal hurtados;

　a un casi rústico aborto
de unos estériles campos,
que el nacer en ellos yo,
los hace más agostados;

　a una educación inculta,
en cuya infancia ocuparon
las mismas cogitaciones
el oficio de los ayos,

　se dirigen los elogios
de los ingenios más claros
que en púlpitos y en escuelas
el mundo venera sabios?

　¿Cuál fue la ascendente estrella
que, dominando los astros,
a mí os ha inclinado, haciendo
lo violento voluntario?

　¿Qué mágicas infusiones
de los indios herbolarios
de mi patria, entre mis letras
el hechizo derramaron?

　¿Qué proporción de distancia,
el sonido modulando
de mis hechos, hacer hizo
cónsono lo destemplado?

　¿Qué siniestras perspectivas
dieron aparente ornato
al cuerpo compuesto sólo
de unos mal distintos trazos?

　¡Oh cuántas veces, oh cuántas,
entre las ondas de tantos
no merecidos loores,
elogios mal empleados;

　oh cuántas, encandilada
en tanto golfo de rayos,
o hubiera muerto Faetonte
o Narciso peligrado,

so how can you be moved
to this undeserved applause?
Can courtesy play so loose
with simple truthfulness?

How can an ignorant woman
with only a moment or two
to snatch for her own pursuits
while giving duty its due,

a practically rustic creature
miscarried by barren fields—
themselves made all the more fallow
by giving birth to me—

how can a lack of schooling,
an infancy self-taught
in which my own cogitations
had to play the tutor's part,

be recipient of the praise
of the most distinguished wits,
esteemed by the whole world as sages,
the light of schools and pulpits?

What star was in the ascendent,
holding sway over heavenly bodies,
to have thus inclined you to me
and made duress seem free will?

What kind of sorcerer's brew
did the Indians inject—
the herb-doctors of my country—
to make my scrawls cast this spell?

What intervals caused by distance
could modulate the sound
of my works, and harmonize
something so wholly discordant?

What left-handed perspective
gave an apparent decorum
to a body consisting solely
of lines drawn helter-skelter?

How often, how very often
amidst the billowing clouds
of so much unwarranted praise—
eulogy so misapplied—

how often I would have been dazzled
by the glitter of light-struck seas,
only, like Phaethon, to drown
or to risk my life like Narcissus,

Phaethon: Son of Apollo, whose attempt to drive his father's chariot
brought him to a disastrous end, struck down by a thunderbolt of Zeus.

a no tener en mí misma
remedio tan a la mano,
como conocerme, siendo
lo que los pies para el pavo!
   Vergüenza me ocasionáis
con haberme celebrado,
porque sacan vuestras luces
mis faltas más a lo claro.
   Cuando penetrar el sol
intenta cuerpos opacos,
el que piensa beneficio
suele resultar agravio:
   porque densos y groseros,
resistiendo en lo apretado
de sus tortüosos poros
la intermisión de los rayos,
   y admitiendo solamente
el superficial contacto,
sólo de ocasionar sombras
les sirve lo iluminado.
   Bien así, a la luz de vuestros
panegíricos gallardos,
de mis obscuros borrones
quedan los disformes rasgos.
   Honoríficos sepulcros
de cadáveres helados,
a mis conceptos sin alma
son vuestros encomios altos:
   elegantes panteones,
en quienes el jaspe y mármol
regia superflua custodia
son de polvo inanimado.
   Todo lo que se recibe
no se mensura al tamaño
que en sí tiene, sino al modo
que es del recipiente vaso.
   Vosotros me concebisteis
a vuestro modo, y no extraño
lo grande: que esos conceptos
por fuerza han de ser milagros.
   La imagen de vuestra idea
es la que habéis alabado;
y siendo vuestra, es bien digna
de vuestros mismos aplausos.

had I not possessed within me
a remedy unfailing:
knowing myself was my cure,
as his ugly feet are the peacock's.

Despite your eulogizing,
you've made me feel ashamed
because your brilliance projects
my flaws in high relief.

Whenever the sun attempts
to penetrate opaque bodies,
though he wants to be beneficial,
he ends by showing up faults,

because, being dense and crude,
the compact bodies resist
with their clogged misshapen pores
the entrance of his rays,

and, since superficial contact
is all they ever allow,
any light shining upon them
will merely give rise to shadows.

Just so, under the glare
of your courtly panegyrics,
the smudges and heavy strokes
of my pen all stand exposed.

Tombs of stately grandeur
for stone-cold corpses—
such are your high-sounding praises
to my spiritless conceits:

elegant pantheons
finished in marble and jasper,
custodials too regal
for a handful of lifeless dust.

Whatever is received
acquires its dimensions
not from actual size
but from the vessel receiving.

The conception you hold of me
is proportionate to yourselves.
No wonder it's grand: your concepts
are miracles, pure and simple.

Your praises have been lavished
on an image of your idea;
being yours, it surely deserves
the tribute of your applause.

ugly feet: The peacock's ugly feet were proverbial as a caution against
vanity.

Celebrad ese, de vuestra
propia aprehensión, simulacro,
para que en vosotros mismos
se vuelva a quedar el lauro.

Si no es que el sexo ha podido
o ha querido hacer, por raro,
que el lugar de lo perfecto
obtenga lo extraordinario;

mas a esto solo, por premio
era bastante el agrado,
sin desperdiciar conmigo
elogios tan empeñados.

Quien en mi alabanza viere
ocupar juicios tan altos,
¿qué dirá, sino que el gusto
tiene en el ingenio mando?...

Celebrate that likeness
of what you have apprehended
and let the laurel wreath
be restored to your own brows.

Might it be the surprise of my sex
that explains why you are willing
to allow an unusual case
to pass itself off as perfection?

If so, the pleasure you've brought me
suffices by way of reward,
with no need to waste on me
such serious applause.

One who found such lofty wits
in praising me so benign,
could only conclude that they'd let
the heart overrule the mind . . .

92

*Arguye de inconsecuentes el gusto y la censura de los
hombres que en las mujeres acusan lo que causan*

Hombres necios que acusáis
a la mujer sin razón,
sin ver que sois la ocasión
de lo mismo que culpáis:
   si con ansia sin igual
solicitáis su desdén,
¿por qué queréis que obren bien
si las incitáis al mal?

Combatís su resistencia
y luego, con gravedad,
decís que fue liviandad
lo que hizo la diligencia.

Parecer quiere el denuedo
de vuestro parecer loco,
al niño que pone el coco
y luego le tiene miedo.

Queréis, con presunción necia,
hallar a la que buscáis,
para pretendida, Thais,
y en la posesión, Lucrecia.

¿Qué humor puede ser más raro
que el que, falto de consejo,
él mismo empaña el espejo
y siente que no esté claro?

Con el favor y el desdén
tenéis condición igual,
quejándoos, si os tratan mal,
burlándoos, si os quieren bien.

In a Lighter Vein

37

She demonstrates the inconsistency of men's wishes in blaming women
for what they themselves have caused

Silly, you men—so very adept
at wrongly faulting womankind,
not seeing you're alone to blame
for faults you plant in woman's mind.
    After you've won by urgent plea
the right to tarnish her good name,
you still expect her to behave—
you, that coaxed her into shame.
    You batter her resistance down
and then, all righteousness, proclaim
that feminine frivolity,
not your persistence, is to blame.
    When it comes to bravely posturing,
your witlessness must take the prize:
you're the child that makes a bogeyman,
and then recoils in fear and cries.
    Presumptuous beyond belief,
you'd have the woman you pursue
be Thais when you're courting her,
Lucretia once she falls to you.
    For plain default of common sense,
could any action be so queer
as oneself to cloud the mirror,
then complain that it's not clear?
    Whether you're favored or disdained,
nothing can leave you satisfied.
You whimper if you're turned away,
you sneer if you've been gratified.

Thais: Athenian courtesan who accompanied Alexander on his Asiatic
conquests.

Opinión, ninguna gana;
pues la que más se recata,
si no os admite, es ingrata,
y si os admite, es liviana.

　Siempre tan necios andáis
que, con desigual nivel,
a una culpáis por crüel
y a otra por fácil culpáis.

　¿Pues cómo ha de estar templada
la que vuestro amor pretende,
si la que es ingrata, ofende,
y la que es fácil, enfada?

　Mas, entre el enfado y pena
que vuestro gusto refiere,
bien haya la que no os quiere
y quejaos en hora buena.

　Dan vuestras amantes penas
a sus libertades alas,
y después de hacerlas malas
las queréis hallar muy buenas.

　¿Cuál mayor culpa ha tenido
en una pasión errada:
la que cae de rogada
o el que ruega de caído?

　¿O cuál es más de culpar,
aunque cualquiera mal haga:
la que peca por la paga
o el que paga por pecar?

　Pues ¿para qué os espantáis
de la culpa que tenéis?
Queredlas cual las hacéis
o hacedlas cual las buscáis.

　Dejad de solicitar,
y después, con más razón,
acusaréis la afición
de la que os fuere a rogar.

　Bien con muchas armas fundo
que lidia vuestra arrogancia,
pues en promesa e instancia
juntáis diablo, carne y mundo.

With you, no woman can hope to score;
whichever way, she's bound to lose;
spurning you, she's ungrateful;
succumbing, you call her lewd.

Your folly is always the same:
you apply a single rule
to the one you accuse of looseness
and the one you brand as cruel.

What happy mean could there be
for the woman who catches your eye,
if, unresponsive, she offends,
yet whose complaisance you decry?

Still, whether it's torment or anger—
and both ways you've yourselves to blame—
God bless the woman who won't have you,
no matter how loud you complain.

It's your persistent entreaties
that change her from timid to bold.
Having made her thereby naughty,
you would have her good as gold.

So where does the greater guilt lie
for a passion that should not be:
with the man who pleads out of baseness
or the woman debased by his plea?

Or which is more to be blamed—
though both will have cause for chagrin:
the woman who sins for money
or the man who pays money to sin?

So why are you men all so stunned
at the thought you're all guilty alike?
Either like them for what you've made them
or make of them what you can like.

If you'd give up pursuing them,
you'd discover, without a doubt,
you've a stronger case to make
against those who seek you out.

I well know what powerful arms
you wield in pressing for evil:
your arrogance is allied
with the world, the flesh, and the devil!

160

*Para este soneto burlesco se le dieron a la poetisa los consonantes
forzados en un doméstico solaz*

Aunque eres, Teresilla, tan *muchacha*,
le das quehacer al pobre de *Camacho*,
porque dará tu disimulo un *chacho*
a aquel que se pintare más sin *tacha*.

De los empleos que tu amor *despacha*
anda el triste cargado como un *macho*,
y tiene tan crecido ya el *penacho*
que ya no puede entrar si no se *agacha*.

Estás a hacerle burlas ya tan *ducha*
y a salir de ellas bien estás tan *hecha*,
que de lo que tu vientre *desembucha*

sabes darle a entender, cuando *sospecha*,
que has hecho, por hacer su hacienda *mucha*,
de ajena siembra, suya la *cosecha*.

71

*Para cantar a la música de un tono y baile regional,
que llaman el cardador*

A Belilla pinto
(tengan atención),
porque es de la carda,
por el cardador.

Del pelo el esquilmo,
mejor que Absalón,
se vende por oro
con ser de vellón.

En su frente lisa
Amor escribió,
y dejó las cejas
a plana renglón.

Los ojos rasgados,
de *ábate que voy*,
y luego unas niñas
de *líbrenos Dios*.

38

For this burlesque sonnet the poet was given set rhymes at a private gathering

Tessie, you may be a slip of a thing
but you give your poor Camacho quite a whirl:
the way you cheat on him could make a sire
of purest driven snow or flawless pearl.
    All those easy attentions your love bestows
weigh the wretch down as heavily as a mule.
Those branches on his brow have grown so tall,
he stoops on entering even a vestibule.
    You ply your trade so skillfully by now,
you've grown so expert at concealing fraud,
that when your swollen belly drops its load,
    you've led him to believe, if he has doubts,
that solely to increase his worldly store
you've let him harvest what another sowed.

39

To be sung to the music of a local tune and dance known as "The Wool Carder"

I'll paint Little Liz
—now mind you listen—
to the Wool Carder's tune,
since she's light with her fingers.
    What she lifts from the fleece
might be Absalom's hair,
selling as gold,
though actually gilt.
    On her smooth forehead
Love loves to write.
The eyebrows alone
take up the whole page.
    Those large eyes of hers
say: "Better watch out!"
The pupils declare:
"Heaven forbid."

Absalom's hair: "But in all Israel there was not a man so comely, and so exceedingly beautiful as Absalom . . . And when he polled his hair . . . he weighed the hair of his head at two hundred sicles" (2 Kings [2 Sam.] 14:25–26).

Con tener en todo
tan grande sazón,
sólo las mejillas
se quedan en flor.
    Ámbar es y algalia
la respiración,
y así las narices
andan al olor.
    De los lacticinios
nunca se guardó,
pues siempre en su cuello
se halla requesón.
    Es tan aseada
que, sin prevención,
en sus manos siempre
está el almidón.
    Talle más estrecho
que la condición
de cierta persona
que conozco yo.
    Pie a quien de tan poco
sirve el calzador,
que aun el poleví
tiene por ramplón.
    Éste, de Belilla
no es retrato, no;
ni bosquejo, sino
no más de un borrón.

72

Para otro baile, tono y música regional que llaman
San Juan de Lima

Agrísima Gila,
que en lugar de dar
confites al gusto,
dentera le das:
    por San Juan de Lima
te quiero pintar,
porque entre tus agrios
tengas éste más.
    El ámbar y mirra
en tu pelo está
derretido: mira
si amargo será.

Everything else
is fully ripe:
only her cheeks
are still in bloom.
   Amber and civet
her breath exhales,
and thus her nostrils
are keen on those scents.
   She never refrained
from milk and cheese;
her neck reminds you
of clotted cream.
   So dainty is she
that, upon my word,
her hands are nothing
but snow-white starch.
   As strict of waist
as strict by nature
is a certain person
well known to me.
   Her foot has no need
of any horn;
even wingèd heels
would weigh it down.
   This is not a portrait
of our Little Liz—
not even a sketch:
it's just a draft.

40

*Words to "Saint John of Lima," another local dance, tune, and
accompaniment*

Gila, so tart
that rather than give
the taste buds sweetmeats,
you pucker them up:
   I'll paint you to the tune
of Saint John of Lima.
There's a lime to sharpen
the tartness in you.
   Amber and myrrh
anoint your hair—
small wonder then,
it's so bittersweet.

Tu frente el jazmín
pretende afeitar,
pero al fin se sale
con ello el azahar.

La tinta a tus cejas
el color les da,
con que a alcaparrosa
y agallas sabrán.

Son aceitunados
tus ojos, y están
bien aderezados
de orégano y sal.

Quiso a tus mejillas
teñir un lagar;
mas, como eres niña,
se quedó en agraz.

El carmín más vivo
en tu boca está,
a la vista hermoso
y amargo al gustar.

Tu cándido cuello
tan nevado está,
que sobre el limón
se puso la sal.

De cuajada leche
tus manos serán,
de la que al sereno
se pasó a acedar.

Al coturno de oro
los ojos se van,
mas se experimentan
píldora al tragar.

Si este tu retrato
muy agrio no está,
ponle tú la hiel
de tu natural.

8

Letra para cantar

Hirió blandamente el aire
con su dulce voz Narcisa,
y él le repitió los ecos
por bocas de las heridas.

Jasmine once wanted
to tint your brow
but what prevailed
was lemon flower.

It was ink that gave
your eyebrows color:
that's why they reek
of vitriol and gallnuts.

With your olive eyes
a seasoning comes,
made to order for them:
oregano and salt.

A winepress sought
to stain your cheeks
but you're such a child,
the wine proved too green.

The liveliest scarlet
enlivens your mouth—
lovely to look at,
bitter to taste.

The white of your neck
is such pure driven snow,
it's like lemon rind covered
with crusted salt.

Your hands might be dipped
in curdled milk,
which during the night
turns good and sour.

The gold of your buskin
attracts all eyes,
but then they must swallow
the bitter pill inside.

And if this portrait
isn't acid enough,
just add a dash
of your natural gall.

41

Lines for singing

Narcisa's lovely voice
gently stabbed at the air.
Through the mouths of the
wounds it opened,
the echoing air replied.

De los celestiales ejes
el rápido curso fija,
y en los elementos cesa
la discordia nunca unida.

Al dulce imán de su voz
quisieran, por asistirla,
firmamento ser el móvil,
el sol ser estrella fija.

Tan bella, sobre canora,
que el Amor, dudoso, admira
si se deben sus arpones
a sus ecos o a su vista:

porque tan confusamente
hiere que no se averigua
si está en la voz la hermosura
o en los ojos la armonía.

Homicidas sus facciones
el mortal cambio ejercitan:
voces, que alternan los ojos;
rayos, que el labio fulmina.

¿Quién podrá vivir seguro
si su hermosura divina
con los ojos y las voces
duplicadas armas vibra?

El mar la admira sirena,
y con sus marinas ninfas
le da en lenguas de las aguas
alabanzas cristalinas.

Pero Fabio, que es el blanco
adonde las flechas tira,
así le dijo, culpando
de superfluas sus heridas:

—¡No dupliques las armas,
bella homicida,
que está ociosa la muerte
donde no hay vida!

Her voice stops in their courses
the wheeling celestial axes.
The elements call a truce
in their unrelenting discord.

Magnetized by her voice,
wishing to hear it always,
the firmament longs to be mobile,
the sun to become a fixed star.

Torn between beauty and song,
Love hesitates and wonders
whether he owes his darts
to her singing or her fair looks.

The blending is so complete
that no one can ever be certain
whether beauty is in the voice
or harmony in the eyes.

Those lethal features of hers
effect a mortal exchange:
the eyes dart resonant notes,
the lips shoot withering flames.

Can anyone call himself safe
from beauty so passing fair,
when it's doubly equipped with arms
and wields either eyes or voice?

As siren she dazzles the sea,
which calls its resident mermaids
to sing in tongues of water
the crystalline song of her praise.

But Fabio, being the target
at whom her arrows are aimed,
accused her of being redundant
in wounding, and spoke these words:

Do not wield those twofold weapons,
you beautiful slayer of men:
Death has nothing to do
where life has never been!

celestial axes: The ten concentric spheres of the Ptolemaic system, in
perpetual revolution about Earth.
firmament: The Empyrean, outer, nonrevolving sphere of the fixed stars.

221

Aquella Zagala
del mirar sereno,
hechizo del soto
y envidia del Cielo:
    la que al Mayoral
de la cumbre, excelso,
hirió con un ojo,
prendió en un cabello:
    a quien su Querido
le fué mirra un tiempo,
dándole morada
sus cándidos pechos:
    la que en rico adorno
tiene, por aseo,
cedrina la casa
y florido el lecho:
    la que se alababa
que el color moreno
se lo iluminaron
los rayos Febeos:
    la por quien su Esposo
con galán desvelo
pasaba los valles,
saltaba los cerros:
    la del hablar dulce,
cuyos labios bellos
destilan panales,
leche y miel vertiendo:
    la que preguntaba
con amante anhelo
dónde de su Esposo
pacen los corderos:

Festive Worship: The *Villancicos*

42

That shepherd lass
with eyes so serene,
the charm of the grove,
the envy of Heaven;
  who with just one look
left the head shepherd smitten,
snared the lord of the summit
with a single hair;
  the lass whose Belovèd
was myrrh to her once
when his dwelling place
was between her white breasts;
  she whose refinement
makes her house a bower
with woodwork of cedar
and blossoms for bedding;
  who was proud to say
she was black but comely,
that Phoebus' rays
had scorched her face;
  for whose sake the Bridegroom,
restless with love,
traversed the valleys,
leapt through the hills;
  who speaks so sweetly,
her lovely lips
are honeycomb flowing,
drip honey and milk;
  she who kept asking,
breathless with love,
to what place the Bridegroom
led his flocks to graze;

a quien su Querido,
liberal y tierno,
del Líbano llama
con dulces requiebros,
        por gozar los brazos
de su amante Dueño,
trueca el valle humilde
por el Monte excelso.
        Los pastores sacros
del Olimpo eterno,
la gala le cantan
con dulces acentos;
        pero los del valle,
su fuga siguiendo
dicen presurosos
en confusos ecos:

Estribillo ¡ Al Monte, al Monte, a la Cumbre
corred, volad, Zagales,
que se nos va María por los aires!
¡ Corred, corred, volad, aprisa, aprisa,
que nos lleva robadas las almas y las vidas,
y llevando en sí misma nuestra riqueza,
nos deja sin tesoros el Aldea!

224

*Maitines de la Asunción, México, 1676; del Villancico Octavo,
en forma de ensaladilla*

Los Mejicanos alegres
también a su usanza salen,
que en quien campa la lealtad
bien es que el aplauso campe;
        y con las cláusulas tiernas
del Mejicano lenguaje,
en un Tocotín sonoro
dicen con voces süaves:

Tocotín —Tla ya timohuica,
totlazo Zuapilli,
maca ammo, Tonantzin,
titechmoilcahuíliz.

whose Belovèd calls her
with tender enticement
to Lebanon away,
uttering soft endearments:
   to enjoy the embrace
of her loving Master,
now trades lowly vale
for lofty hill.

   The holy shepherds
of ageless Olympus
lift high her praises
in sweetest tones;
   but those of the valley,
hard on her trail,
hurriedly cry
in a jumble of echoes:

Refrain   To the Hill, to the Hill, to the Summit
hurry, shepherd lads, fly—
Mary is ascending the skies!
Hurry, hurry, fly quick, fly quicker,
our lives, our souls she takes with her,
bears our wealth away in herself
and leaves our village bereft!

43

*Feast of the Assumption, City of Mexico, 1676, from the Eighth
Villancico, a medley*

The joyous Mexicans
come forth as always,
loyal subjects ever
prepared to applaud,
   and in the soft phrases
of the Mexican tongue,
sound with gentle voices
a vibrant Tocotín:

Tocotín   Beloved Lady,
since you're departing,
oh, Mother, please
do not forget us.

Tocotín: A lively Aztec dance with accompanying words and music. The
Nahuatl text has been translated from Sor Juana Inés de la Cruz, *Obras
completas*, ed. Adolfo Méndez Plancarte, 4 vols. (Mexico City: Fondo de
Cultura Económica, 1951–1957), II, 365; hereafter cited as *OC.*

Ma nel in Ilhuícac
huel timomaquítiz,
¿amo nozo quenman
timotlalnamíctiz?
   In moayolque mochtin
huel motilinizque;
tlaca amo, tehuatzin
ticmomatlaníliz.
   Ca mitztlacamati
motlazo Piltzintli,
mac tel, in tepampa
xicmotlatlauhtili.
   Tlaca ammo quinequi,
xicmoilnamiquili
ca monacayotzin
oticmomaquiti.
   Mochichihualayo
oquimomitili,
tla motemictía
ihuan Tetepitzin.
   Ma mopampantzinco
in moayolcatintin,
in itla pohpoltin,
tictomacehuizque.
   Totlatlácol mochtin
tïololquiztizque;
Ilhuícac tïazque,
timitzittalizque:
   in campa cemícac
timonemitíliz,
cemícac mochíhuaz
in monahuatiltzin.

258

*Maitines de la Asunción, México, 1679; del Villancico Octavo,
en forma de ensaladilla*

A la voz del sacristán,
en la iglesia se colaron
dos princesas de Guinea
con vultos azabachados.
   Y mirando tanta fiesta,
por ayudarla cantando,
soltando los cestos, dieron
albricias a los muchachos.

However delighted
with Heaven above,
will you not sometimes
hear how we pine?
    All your faithful
shall rise aloft
unless by your hand
you raise them yourself.
    Since the Son you love
is much in your debt,
entreat him, Mother,
for all your children.
    If he seems unwilling,
remind him gently
how once you gave him
your virginal feeding.
    Recall to his mind
how you suckled him,
how, a babe in arms,
you lulled him to sleep.
    With your intercession,
your unhappy children
will all be made whole
and worthy to serve you.
    All our dreary sins
we will cast aside,
we'll go to Heaven
and see you, Virgin,
    up there where you live
forevermore,
where your commandments
are ever obeyed.

44

*Feast of the Assumption, City of Mexico, 1679, from the Eighth
Villancico, a medley*

At the sacristan's voice
there slipped into the church
two Guinean queens
with faces of jet.
    Seeing the gaiety,
they thought they would help
and, setting baskets down,
sang the boys this song:

Estribillo   1—¡Ha, ha, ha!
2—¡Monan vuchiá¡
He, he, he,
cambulé!
1—¡Gila coro,
    gulungú, gulungú,
    hu, hu, hu!
2—¡Menguiquilá,
    ha, ha, ha!

Coplas   1—Flasica, naquete día
qui tamo lena li glolia,
no vindamo pipitolia,
pueque sobla la aleglía:
que la Señola Malía
a turo mundo la da.
¡Ha, ha, ha! &.
    2—Dejémoso la cocina
y vámoso a turo trote,
sin que vindamo gamote
nin garbanzo a la vizina:
qui arto gamote, Cristina,
hoy a la fieta vendrá.
¡Ha, ha, ha! &.
    1—Ésa sí qui se nomblaba
ecrava con devoción,
e cun turo culazón
a mi Dioso servïaba:
y polo sel buena ecrava
le dieron la libertá.
¡Ha, ha, ha! &.
    2—Mílala como cohete,
qui va subiendo lo sumo;
como valita li humo
qui sale de la pebete:
y ya la estrella se mete,
a donde mi Dioso está.
¡Ha, ha, ha! &.

Ha, ha, ha!
Monan vuchilá!
Hé, hé, hé,
cambulé!
Gila coro,
gulungú, gulungú,
hu, hu, hu!
Menguiquilá,
ha, ha, ha!

Verses   Fanny, this mo'nin'
we's full of glory,
don' le's sell ladyfingers
o' them almon' kisses.
We've sumpin' better:
Mary's fingers to kiss!
Ha, ha, ha . . . !
   Le's get a move on
an' skip the kitchen.
We won' sell no sweet 'taters
o' chick-peas to the gals
'cause plenty of sweet chicks
will be comin' to the fair.
Ha, ha, ha . . . !
   There never was a slave
as devout as that Handmaid
of the Lawd. She done serve Him
with her heart an' soul,
an' fo' bein' sech a good slave,
they natch'ly set her free.
Ha, ha, ha . . . !
   See her there cleavin'
the sky like a rocket,
like a pilla' of smoke
shootin' up from the incense,
sittin' down in the stars
at the right hand of the Lawd.
Ha, ha, ha . . . !

Ha, ha, ha! Monan vuchilá: The refrain is made up of rhythmic African
words.

xxxvii

Maitines de la Asunción, Puebla, 1681, del Villancico Quarto

1—! Afuera, afuera, afuera,
aparta, aparta, aparta,
que trinan los clarines,
que suenan las dulzainas!
   2—Estrellas se despeñan,
Auroras se levantan.
   1—Bajen las luces,
suban fragancias,
cuadrillas de jazmines,
claveles y retamas,
   2—que corren,
      3—que vuelan,
   1—que tiran,
      2—que alcanzan,
   1—con flores,
      2—con brillos,
        3—con rosas,
   1—con llamas.

279

*Maitines de la Purísima Concepción de Nuestra Señora, Puebla,
1689; principio del Villancico Quinto*

Estribillo   ¡Un instante me escuchen,
que cantar quiero
un instante que estuvo
fuera del tiempo!

Coplas   Escúchenme mientras cante,
que poco habrá que sufrir,
pues lo que quiero decir
es solamente un instante.
   Un instante es, de verdad,
pero tan privilegiado,
que fue un instante cuidado
de toda la eternidad.

---

xxxvii: This villancico is attributed to Sor Juana.

45

Feast of the Assumption, Puebla, 1681, from the Fourth Villancico

Fall back, fall back, fall back,
make way, make way, make way,
the bugles are blowing,
the flageolets piping!
　Stars are plunging,
dawns arising.
　Lower the lights,
let fragrances rise,
troops of jasmine,
spice-pinks, and broom,
running,
　flying,
pelting,
　catching,
with flowers,
　with glitter,
with roses,
　with flame.

46

Feast of the Immaculate Conception of Our Lady, Puebla, 1689,
Fifth Villancico, opening lines

Refrain　　Hear me one moment—
I'm all set to sing
of a Moment that stood
outside of time!

Verses　　Hear me as I sing—
you won't find it trying
since what I have to say
will be only a Moment.
　A Moment only,
yet prized so high,
for a Moment the Eternal
hung in suspense.

281

Estribillo   Morenica la esposa está,
            porque el sol en el rostro le da.
Coplas   Aunque en el negro arrebol
negra la esposa se nombra,
no es porque ella tiene sombra,
sino porque le da el sol
de su pureza el crisol,
que el sol nunca se le va.
   ¡Morenica la esposa está,
porque el sol en el rostro le da!
   Comparada la luz pura
de uno y otro, entre los dos,
ante el claro sol de Dios
es morena la criatura;
pero se añade hermosura
mientras más se acerca allá.
   ¡Morenica la esposa está,
porque el sol en el rostro le da!
   Del sol, que siempre la baña,
está abrasada la esposa;
y tanto está más hermosa
cuanto más de él se acompaña:
nunca su pureza empaña,
porque nunca el sol se va.
   ¡Morenica la esposa está,
porque el sol en el rostro le da!
   No de la culpa el horror
hacer pudo efecto tal,
pues ella da la causal
de su encendido color,
añadiendo, por primor,
que eso más gracia le da.
   ¡Morenica la esposa está,
porque el sol en el rostro le da!
   Negra se confiesa; pero
dice que esa negregura
le da mayor hermosura:
pues en el albor primero,
es de la gracia el lucero
el primer paso que da.
   ¡Morenica la esposa está,
porque el sol en el rostro le da!

47

Feast of the Immaculate Conception of Our Lady, Puebla, 1689,
Seventh Villancico

Refrain   Black is the Bride,
         the Sun scorches her face.
Verses   Red clouds swirling dark
         make the Bride think she's black,
         yet there's no shadow in her,
         of pure sunlight no lack.
         The crucible of the Sun
         leaves her purity intact.
          Black is the Bride,
         the Sun scorches her face.
          Placing next to the Bride's
         the Sun's spotless light
         makes the creature look dark
         since God is purest bright.
         Yet, basking in the Sun,
         she grows fairer in men's sight.
          Black is the Bride,
         the Sun scorches her face.
          Bathed in sunlight,
         the Bride burns with his rays,
         growing in fairness
         as she draws near his blaze;
         spotless, without flaw,
         in his unceasing gaze.
          Black is the Bride,
         the Sun scorches her face.
          It was not foul sin
         left her face inflamed.
         Her heightened color
         is easily explained,
         and the grace of her presence
         has thereby but gained.
          Black is the Bride,
         the Sun scorches her face.
          Though she calls herself black,
         her blackness, she shall say,
         makes her the more comely.
         In the first Light of Day,
         it's the Morning Star of Grace
         setting forth on its way.
          Black is the Bride,
         the Sun scorches her face.

Contexto es, y no pequeño,
que, cuanto más se humillaba,
se confesó por esclava;
pero expresó de qué dueño,
protestando el desempeño
de que libre de otro está.
    ¡Morenica la esposa está,
porque el sol en el rostro le da!

283

Nacimiento de Nuestro Señor, Puebla, 1689; final del Villancico Primero

1—Pues está tiritando
amor en el hielo,
y la escarcha y la nieve
me lo tienen preso,
¿quién le acude?
    2—¡El agua!
        3—¡La tierra!
            4—¡El aire!
1—¡No, sino el fuego!
    1—Pues al niño fatigan
sus penas y males,
y a sus ansias no dudo
que alientos le falten,
¿quién le acude?
    2—¡El fuego!
        3—¡La tierra!
            4—¡El agua!
1—¡No, sino el aire!
    1—Pues el niño amoroso
tan tierno se abrasa,
que respira en volcanes
diluvios de llamas,
¿quién le acude?
    2—¡El aire!
        3—¡El fuego!
            4—¡La tierra!
1—¡No, sino el agua!
    1—Si por la tierra el niño
los cielos hoy deja,
y no halla en qué descanse
su cabeza en ella,
¿quién le acude?

On that high occasion,
awed by the angel's word,
she asked how it could be
that she, Handmaid of the Lord,
having never known a man,
could give God's Son to the world.
     Black is the Bride,
the Sun scorches her face.

48

Nativity of Our Lord, Puebla, 1689, First Villancico, concluding
lines

Since Love is shivering
in the ice and cold,
since hoarfrost and snow
have ringed him round,
who will come to his aid?
     Water!
          Earth!
               Air!
No, Fire will!
     Since the Child is assailed
by pains and ills
and has no breath left
to face his woes,
who will come to his aid?
     Fire!
          Earth!
               Water!
No, but Air will!
     Since the loving Child
is so burning hot,
that he breathes a volcanic
deluge of flame,
who will come to his aid?
     Air!
          Fire!
               Earth!
No, Water will.
     Since today the Child
leaves heaven for earth
and finds nowhere to rest
his head in this world,
who will come to his aid?

2—¡El agua!
3—¡El fuego!
4—¡El aire!
1—¡No, mas la tierra!

287

Nacimiento de Nuestro Señor, Puebla, 1689; principio del Villancico Quinto

1—Pues mi Dios ha nacido a penar,
déjenle velar.
2—Pues está desvelado por mí,
déjenle dormir.
  1—Déjenle velar,
que no hay pena, en quien ama,
como no penar.
  2—Déjenle dormir,
que quien duerme, en el sueño
se ensaya a morir.
  1—Silencio, que duerme.
  2—Cuidado, que vela.
  1—¡No le despierten, no!
  2—¡Sí le despierten, sí!
  1—¡Déjenle velar!
  2—¡Déjenle dormir!

312

*Maitines de Santa Catarina de Alejandría, Oaxaca, 1691,
Villancico Primero*

Estribillo Aguas puras del Nilo,
parad, parad,
y no le llevéis
el tributo al Mar,
pues él vuestras dichas
puede envidiar.

Water!
Fire!
Air!
No, but Earth will!

49

Feast of the Nativity, Puebla, 1689, Fifth Villancico, opening lines

> Since my God was born to pain,
> awake he shall remain.
> Since he's wakeful for me,
> let him go to sleep.
> Awake he shall remain:
> there's no pain for a lover
> like not feeling pain.
> Let him go to sleep,
> for the sleeper, in slumber,
> learns how death feels.
> Quiet, he's asleep.
> Careful, he's awake.
> He is not to be wakened!
> He must be waked up!
> Awake he shall remain!
> Let him go to sleep!

50

Saint's Day of Catherine of Alexandria, Oaxaca, 1691, First Villancico

Refrain   Pure waters of the Nile,
subside, subside,
do not carry the tribute
to the seagoing tide:
the sea might rob you
of the joys that abide.

Catherine of Alexandria: Legend holds that during the persecution of
Christians in the early fourth century by the Roman emperor Maximinus,
Saint Catherine enraged him by adjuring him to give up his heathen gods.
Subsequently, she not only bested the pagan scholars he had summoned to
confute her but converted the empress and soldiers sent to reason with
her. Maximinus ordered her body broken on a spiked wheel, which
collapsed at her touch. He then had her beheaded.

¡No, no, no corráis,
pues ya no podéis
aspirar a más!
¡Parad, parad!

Coplas   Sosiega, Nilo undoso,
tu líquida corriente;
tente, tente,
párate a ver gozoso
la que fecundas, bella,
de la tierra, del Cielo, Rosa, Estrella.
    Tu corriente oportuna,
que piadoso moviste,
viste, viste,
que de Moisés fue cuna,
siendo arrullo a su oído
la onda, la espuma, el tumbo y el sonido.
    Más venturoso ahora
de abundancia de bienes,
tienes, tienes
la que tu margen dora
Belleza, más lozana
que Abigaíl, Esther, Raquel, Susana.
    La hermosa Catarina,
que la gloria Gitana
vana, vana,
elevó a ser Divina,
y en las virtudes trueca
de Débora, Jael, Judith, Rebeca.
    No en frágil hermosura,
que aprecia el loco abuso,
puso, puso
esperanza segura,
bien que excedió su cara
la de Ruth, Bethsabé, Thamar y Sara.
    A ésta, Nilo sagrado,
tu corriente sonante
cante, cante,
y en concierto acordado
tus ondas sean veloces
sílabas, lenguas, números y voces.

No, no, flow no more—
you could not have desired
greater joy than these joys;
subside, subside.

Verses   Billowy Nile,
slow your current down,
stay still, stay still,
let your joy be crowned
with the Rose of the earth and Heaven's Star,
whose lifestream you are.
    How hushed was the measure
your awed current kept,
as it flowed past the rushes
where Moses slept
and lulled his sleep well
with foam and wave, ripple and swell.
    More fortunate now
in your plentiful store,
you've a beauty to show
who adorns your shore
with more bountiful manna
than Abigail, Esther, Rachel, Susannah.
    Beautiful Catherine,
who made Egypt's glory,
so hollow before,
a Heavenly story,
whose virtues are hailed
by Deborah, Judith, Rebecca, and Jael.
    She fastened no hopes
on fragile beauty,
much prized by the world
and still so futile,
yet of face she was fairer
than Ruth, Bathsheba, Tamar, and Sarah.
    To her, sacred Nile,
may the sound of your flowing
be as a song
in harmony growing
till your water rejoices
in syllables, tongues, measures, and voices.

316

Estribillo Venid, Serafines
venid a mirar
una Rosa que vive
cortada, más;
   y no se marchita,
antes resucita
al fiero rigor,
porque se fecunda
con su propio humor.
   Y así, es beneficio
llegarla a cortar:
¡venid, Jardineros,
venid a mirar
una Rosa que vive
cortada, más!

Coplas Contra una tierna Rosa
mil cierzos conjuran:
¡oh qué envidiada vive,
con ser breve la edad de la hermosura!
   Porque es bella la envidian,
porque es docta la emulan:
¡oh qué antiguo en el mundo
es regular los méritos por culpas!
   De girantes cuchillas
en el filo, aseguran
a un aliento mil soplos,
a un solo corazón inmensas puntas.
   Contra una sola vida
tantas muertes procuran;
que es el rencor cobarde,
y no se aseguraba bien con una.
   Mas no ve la ignorante,
ciega, malvada astucia,
que el suplicio en que pena,
sabe hacer Dios el carro donde triunfa.
   Cortesana en sus filos
la máquina rotunda,
sólo es su movimiento
mejorar Catarina de fortuna.

51

Saint's Day of Catherine of Alexandria, Oaxaca, 1691, from the Fifth Villancico

Refrain   Seraphim, come,
come here and ponder
a Rose that, when cut,
lives all the longer.
    So far from wilting,
it will be revived
when cruelly tortured,
be fructified
by its own sweet moisture:
    And thus to cut it
renews the wonder.
Gardeners, come,
come here and ponder
a Rose that, when cut,
lives all the longer.

Verses   Against one frail Rose
a thousand storm winds plot.
Sheer envy is its lot,
though one brief span is all the life it knows.
    Men envy the Rose its beauty,
its wiseness they resent.
Far too long the world has known
that virtue attracts sin as complement.
    Thus they guarantee
that the slash of whirling knives
from one breath will draw a thousand,
give one heart thorns to pierce a thousand lives.
    Rancor, ever a coward,
is afraid of a simple death:
to snuff out a single life,
it finds a thousand ways to stifle breath.
    But wily, witless evil
is blind and cannot see
that the wicked torturer's wheel
is destined for the chariot of victory.
    Thus, the whirling instrument,
considerate in its blades,
makes its every revolution
one more song in glorious Catherine's praise.

No extraña, no, la Rosa
las penetrantes púas,
que no es nuevo que sean
pungente guarda de su pompa augusta.

322

Maitines de Santa Catarina de Alejandría, Oaxaca, 1691,
Villancico Onceno

1—Un prodigio les canto.
   2—¿Qué, qué, qué, qué, qué?
1—Esperen, aguarden, que yo lo diré.
   2—¿Y cuál es? ¡Diga aprisa, que ya rabio por saber!
1—Esperen, aguarden, que yo lo diré.

Coplas Érase una Niña,
como digo a usté,
cuyos años eran,
ocho sobre diez.
Esperen, aguarden,
que yo lo diré.
   Ésta (qué sé yo,
cómo pudo ser),
dizque supo mucho,
aunque era mujer.
Esperen, aguarden,
que yo lo diré.
   Porque, como dizque
dice no sé quién,
ellas sólo saben
hilar y coser ...
Esperen, aguarden,
que yo lo diré.
   Pues ésta, a hombres grandes
pudo convencer;
que a un chico, cualquiera
lo sabe envolver.
Esperen, aguarden,
que yo lo diré.
   Y aun una Santita
dizque era también,
sin que le estorbase
para ello el saber.
Esperen, aguarden,
que yo lo diré.

The Rose can hardly find it new
to feel the piercing barbs,
since every rose since time began
has made the prickly thorns its regal guards.

52

Saint's Day of Catherine of Alexandria, Oaxaca, 1691, Eleventh Villancico

I've a strange thing to sing you.
  What is it now? What?
If you'd hush up, I'd tell you.
  What is it? Hurry, I'm dying to know.
If you'd hush up, I'd tell you.

Verses   There once was a girl—
you'll see who I mean—
whose years had reached
the age of eighteen.
If you'd just hush up,
my meaning you'd glean.
  This girl (don't ask how
'cause here words fail)
knew a lot, so they say,
though she *was* female.
If you'd just hush up,
you'd hear my tale.
  Now people are always
saying ... you know ...
that all girls can do
is spin and sew.
If you'd just hush up
and not fuss so.
  But her, she could argue
with grown men and win,
so kids couldn't lick her
to save their skin.
If you'd just hush up
and not butt in.
  The makings of sainthood
was in her, they say;
even knowing so much
didn't get in her way.
If you'd just hush up
and let me say.

Pues como Patillas
no duerme, al saber
que era Santa y Docta,
se hizo un Lucifer.
Esperen, aguarden,
que yo lo diré.

   Porque tiene el Diablo
esto de saber,
que hay mujer que sepa
más que supo él.
Esperen, aguarden,
que yo lo diré.

   Pues con esto, ¿qué hace?
Viene, y tienta a un Rey,
que a ella la tentara
a dejar su Ley.
Esperen, aguarden,
que yo lo diré.

   Tentóla de recio;
mas ella, pardiez,
se dejó morir
antes que vencer.
Esperen, aguarden,
que yo lo diré.

   No pescuden más,
porque más no sé,
de que es Catarina,
para siempre. Amén.

Now when word reached Old Nick,
who don't shut an eye,
she's so holy and smart
he made like he'd die.
If you'd just hush up,
I'll tell you why.

Because if there's one thing
drives the Devil up a tree,
it's hearing of a woman
who's smarter than he.
If you'd just hush up
and let me be.

So what does he do?
Goes and urges a King
to tempt her in her faith
and demand she give in.
If you'd just keep still
and not butt in.

His terrible threats
didn't make a dent:
she would sooner die
than ever relent.
If you'd just hush up
and let me end.

No more questions now
'cause all I can say
is that Catherine will live
forever and a day.
You needn't hush up,
I've had my say.

From *The Divine Narcissus*

The cast of *The Divine Narcissus* includes Narcissus (Christ), Human Nature, Grace, Paganism, Synagogue, Echo (Fallen Angelic Nature, that is, Satan), and Pride and Self-Love, companions of Satan. In the introductory scene Human Nature listens to Synagogue and Paganism, whose singing, accompanied by choruses, extols the beauty of God and Narcissus, respectively. Human Nature points out their limitations, summoning them to collaborate with her as she brings out "with allegorical colors that body forth ideas" the full revelation behind their restricted vision. The Human Letters of Paganism will supply the story of Narcissus and the pastoral framework; Synagogue, in her Divine Letters, the substance of the idea of the Incarnation glimpsed by her prophets and psalmists.

As the play proceeds, Human Nature laments the "turbid waters" of guilt that distort her image and separate her from the Divine Narcissus. She announces her intention to seek a spring that will wash her clean and reveal Narcissus to her. Echo appears with Pride and Self-Love, and, in a skillful fusing of the classical and biblical myths, Sor Juana has her relate her attempt to marry Narcissus and become his equal, and his utter rejection. This changed her love to hate and has caused her to take out her spite by thwarting Human Nature's impulse to assume Echo's desired place in Narcissus' affections, as well as by keeping Human Nature so disfigured by "the turbid waters of sin" that Narcissus will be unable to recognize and love his own likeness in her.

Narcissus now appears (Second Tableau) on a mountaintop, which Echo ascends. She tempts him, in a passage filled with echoes both of the third temptation of Christ by Satan (Matt. 4:8–11) and of the topos of proffered rural riches stemming from Polyphemus' courtship of Galatea in Theocritus and Ovid. (The first selection.)

The setting of the Third Tableau is a landscape of meadow and woods with a Fountain at one end. Human Nature laments, in language reminiscent of the Bride's in the Song of Songs, the fruitlessness of her age-old quest of Narcissus. (The second selection translates the first part of her soliloquy.) Grace appears and reveals that the impulse of Human Nature to seek out Narcissus has brought Human Nature closer to her, since she is the Dawn to Narcissus' Sun. To be actually embraced by her, Human Nature must make herself deserving of Grace by drawing near to the Immaculate waters of the Fountain—the Fountain Sealed—the lifegiving waters which have flowed forever from Paradise and which, through Esther, prefigure Mary, Full of Grace, conceived without sin. At the Fountain, Grace and Human Nature hide in the greenery to await Narcissus when he comes to quench his burning thirst. Human Nature calls upon the Fountain to reflect her image, so that Narcissus may fall in love with it. Narcissus appears as the Good Shepherd and laments the loss of his favorite sheep. (The third selection is the first part of the lament.)

In the Fourth Tableau, Narcissus looks into the Fountain and is entranced by the beauty and brilliance of the image reflected there—not merely his own, as in the myth, but Human Nature's as well, since she is already reflected in him. (This development is original with Sor Juana. Narcissus speaks his love in the fourth selection.) Echo appears, but when she seeks to express her jealousy and frustrated rage to Pride and Self-Love, she can only blurt out the last syllables of their questions. The same thing occurs as she listens to Narcissus voicing the boundless unconsummated passion which has subjected his immortality to the terrible suffering of human love. He expresses his agony in a sonnet that marks his death. (The fifth selection.)

In the final Tableau, Human Nature calls upon nymphs and shepherds to grieve with her. (The sixth selection is the opening of her lament.) Her anguish is compounded by the thought that he died because of her. But Grace appears and assures Human Nature that he is alive. Narcissus now appears, freshly appareled. To Echo's resolve to ensnare Human Nature, Narcissus replies that, in the sacraments, he has provided medicines to protect her Soul. A Chalice with a Host appears as a flower beside the Fountain; Human Nature and Grace embrace; and the work ends in a eucharistic hymn.

De Cuadro segundo, Escena V

Eco   Bellísimo Narciso,
que a estos humanos valles,
del monte de tus glorias
las celsitudes traes:
    mis pesares escucha,
indignos de escucharse,
pues ni aun en esto esperan
alivio mis pesares.
    Eco soy, la más rica
pastora de estos valles;
bella decir pudieran
mis infelicidades.
    Mas desde que severo
mi beldad despreciaste,
las que canté hermosuras
ya las lloro fealdades.
    Pues tú mejor conoces
que los claros imanes
de tus ojos arrastran
todas las voluntades,
    no extrañarás el ver
que yo venga a buscarte,
pues todo el mundo adora
tus prendas celestiales.
    Y así, vengo a decirte
que ya que no es bastante
a ablandar tu dureza
mi nobleza y mis partes,
    siquiera por ti mismo
mires interesable
mis riquezas, atento
a tus comodidades.
    Pagarte intento, pues
no será disonante
el que venga a ofrecerte
la que viene a rogarte.
    Y pues el interés
es en todas edades
quien del amor aviva
las viras penetrantes,
    tiende la vista a cuanto
alcanza a divisarse
desde este monte excelso
que es injuria de Atlante.

From the Second Tableau, Scene V

ECHO   Most beautiful Narcissus,
from your mountain of glory,
you bring loftiness down
to these human valleys:
    hear my unhappy tale,
though such is my distress
that even in the telling
my pain will not lessen.
    I am Echo, the richest
shepherd maid of these dales;
for the gift of my beauty
in unhappiness I pay.
    For you met this beauty
with a look of contempt.
That I now find it ugly
is my song's lament.
    You are surely aware
that those bright-shining lodestars
of your eyes can allure
the freest of lovers.
    Thus it will not surprise you
to find Echo on bended knee,
for your heavenly endowments
place the world at your feet.
    Listen then to my plea:
Since my station and name
have proved unavailing
to soften your disdain,
    won't you stop and consider
your own welfare? Don't ignore
the riches I offer,
the ease they afford.
    I propose to enrich you.
To support my petition,
to strengthen my plea,
I bring a proposition.
    Now, since time began,
self-interest—it's well known—
has been love's surest means
to drive his darts home,
    so let your gaze take in
all the land it surveys
from this lofty summit
that leaves Atlas in the shade.

Mira aquestos ganados
que, inundando los valles,
de los prados fecundos
las esmeraldas pacen.

Mira en cándidos copos
la leche, que al cuajarse,
afrenta los jazmines
de la aurora que nace.

Mira, de espigas rojas,
en los campos formarse
pajizos chamelotes
a las olas del aire.

Mira de esas montañas
los ricos minerales,
cuya preñez es oro,
rubíes y diamantes.

Mira, en el mar soberbio,
en conchas congelarse
el llanto de la aurora
en perlas orientales.

Mira de esos jardines
los fecundos frutales,
de especies diferentes
dar frutos admirables.

Mira con verdes pinos
los montes coronarse:
con árboles que intentan
del cielo ser gigantes.

Escucha la armonía
de las canoras aves
que en coros diferentes
forman dulces discantes.

Mira de uno a otro polo
los reinos dilatarse,
dividiendo regiones
los brazos de los mares,
    y mira cómo surcan
de las veleras naves
las ambiciosas proas
sus cerúleos cristales.

Mira entre aquellas grutas
diversos animales:
a unos, salir feroces;
a otros, huir cobardes.

See, into the valleys
those streams of cattle pour
to graze on the emeralds
that stud each valley floor.

See, like drifts of snow,
the curdled milk in jars
puts the jasmine to shame
with which dawn snuffs out stars.

See red-gold ears of grain
sending billows everywhere
like waves of watered silk
stirred by waves of the air.

Behold the rich ores
those swelling mountains hold:
how they teem with diamonds,
glow with rubies and gold.

See in the leaping ocean
how the dawn's welling tears
are congealed in conch shells
and turn into pearls.

See, in those gardens,
how the fruit trees flourish;
behold the broad range
of rich fruits they nourish.

See how green crowns of pine
on high summits endeavor
to repeat the exploit
of the giants storming heaven.

Listen to the music
of all those singing birds.
In all of their choirs
sweet descants are heard.

See from pole to pole
realms spread far and wide.
Behold the many regions
which arms of sea divide,

and see the ambitious prows
of those swift-sailing ships—
how they cleave in their passage
the azure's crystal drift.

See amid those grottos
creatures of every sort,
some timidly fleeing,
some bursting fiercely forth.

Todo, bello Narciso,
sujeto a mi dictamen,
son posesiones mías,
son mis bienes dotales.
Y todo será tuyo,
si tú con pecho afable
depones lo severo
y llegas a adorarme.

De Cuadro tercero, Escena VI

NATURALEZA　De buscar a Narciso fatigada,
HUMANA　sin permitir sosiego a mi pie errante
ni a mi planta cansada
que tantos ha ya días que vagante
examina las breñas
sin poder encontrar más que las señas,
　a este bosque he llegado donde espero
tener noticias de mi bien perdido;
que si señas confiero,
diciendo está del prado lo florido,
que producir amenidades tantas,
es por haber besado ya sus plantas.
　¡Oh, cuántos días ha que he examinado
la selva flor a flor, y planta a planta,
gastando congojado
mi triste corazón en pena tanta,
y mi pie fatigando, vagabundo,
tiempo, que siglos son; selva, que es mundo!
　Díganlo las edades que han pasado,
díganlo las regiones que he corrido,
los suspiros que he dado,
de lágrimas los ríos que he vertido,
los trabajos, los hierros, las prisiones
que he padecido en tantas ocasiones.
　Una vez, por buscarle, me toparon
de la ciudad las guardas, y atrevidas,
no sólo me quitaron
el manto, mas me dieron mil heridas
los centinelas de los altos muros,
teniéndose de mí por mal seguros.
　¡Oh ninfas que habitáis este florido
y ameno prado, ansiosamente os ruego
que si acaso al querido
de mi alma encontrareis, de mi fuego
le noticiéis, diciendo el agonía
con que de amor enferma el alma mía!

All this, fair Narcissus,
is mine to dispose of;
these are my possessions,
they accompany my love.
    All is yours to enjoy
if you cease to be cold,
put severity aside
and love me heart and soul.

Third Tableau, Scene VI

HUMAN   Worn out with searching for Narcissus,
NATURE   granting my wandering foot no respite,
my tired steps no rest,
as all day long now, for so many days,
they trudged the barren rocky places,
unable to find more than passing traces:
    at last I've come upon this wood in hope
here to have word of my lost treasure.
For surely this is no lie:
this meadow is declaring in its bloom
that all the loveliness I here descry
came from his footfalls' kiss as he passed by.
    Oh, all these many days, how I have searched
the woodland, flower by flower, plant by plant,
eating my heart away
in utmost tribulation,
while my poor, roving footsteps erred
through centuries of time, woods broad as world!
    To this the ages passing testify,
the regions of the world I have traversed,
the sighs that I have heaved,
the flowing streams of tears my eyes have shed,
the toils, the chains, the prison bars
that left me branded with a thousand scars.
    The watchmen who went about the city
once found me as I sought him.
Not only did the keepers of the walls
despoil me of my veil—
they also smote me countless times,
as if in payment for unnumbered crimes.
    O nymphs who dwell amidst the bloom
that covers this fair meadow,
I charge you earnestly that if perchance
you come on the Belovèd of my soul,
you tell him of the agony I feel
in this sick soul which he alone can heal!

Si queréis que os dé señas de mi amado,
rubicundo esplendor le colorea
sobre jazmín nevado;
por su cuello, rizado Ofir pasea;
los ojos, de paloma que enamora
y en los raudales transparentes mora.

Mirra olorosa de su aliento exhala;
las manos son al torno, y están llenas
de jacintos, por gala,
o por indicio de sus graves penas:
que si el jacinto es *Ay*, entre sus brillos
ostenta tantos *Ayes* como anillos.

Dos columnas de mármol, sobre basas
de oro, sustentan su edificio bello;
y en delicias no escasas
suavísimo es, y ebúrneo, el blanco cuello;
y todo apetecido y deseado.
Tal es, ¡oh ninfas!, mi divino Amado.

Entre millares mil es escogido;
y cual granada luce sazonada
en el prado florido,
entre rústicos árboles plantada,
así, sin que ningún zagal le iguale,
entre todos los otros sobresale.

Decidme dónde está el que mi alma adora,
o en qué parte apacienta sus corderos,
o hacia dónde —a la hora
meridiana— descansan sus luceros,
para que yo no empiece a andar vagando
por los rediles, que lo voy buscando.

De Cuadro tercero, Escena VIII

(Llegan las dos a la fuente; pónese la NATURALEZA *entre las ramas,
y con ella la* GRACIA, *de manera que parezca que se miran; y sale
por otra parte* NARCISO, *con una honda, como pastor, y canta el último verso de cada una de las coplas, y lo demás representa.)*

NARCISO   Ovejuela perdida,
de tu dueño olvidada,
¿adónde vas errada?
Mira que dividida
de mí, también te apartas de tu vida.

If you would know of my Belovèd's looks,
his skin is flushed with ruddiness aglow
against a whiteness as of snowy jasmine.
Rippling Ophir blows about his neck,
his eyes are as the eyes of doves
that dwell by crystal waters with their loves.
    His breath, like lilies, drops sweet-smelling myrrh,
his hands, so finely wrought,
glisten with hyacinths, not for display
but as a token of his bitter pangs,
for if the hyacinth cries out in pain
as many AI's as rings his hands sustain.
    Two marble columns set
in fine gold sockets shore his handsome frame;
his throat, as white as ivory,
displays abounding charms.
Ah, lovely altogether,
oh nymphs, is my beloved ever.
    Among ten thousand he is chiefest
and, as the ripe pomegranate planted
on the flowering meadow
stands out among the rude surrounding trees,
so he, surpassing all the other swains,
in his unrivaled splendor reigns.
    Tell me where he is whom my soul loves,
where he feeds his lambs,
and where he lays him down to rest ·
at the noontide hour.
For why should I be one who turns aside
by the folds where flocks of other swains abide?

From the Third Tableau, Scene VIII

(Grace and Human Nature draw close to the Fountain; Human Nature stations herself behind the branches, as does Grace, so that they seem to be looking at each other. Narcissus enters another way, with a sling, in shepherd's dress; he sings the last line of each verse, acting out the rest.)

NARCISSUS   Poor little lost sheep,
              forgetful of your Master,
              where can you be straying?
              When you depart from me,
              it's life you leave behind, will you not see?

Hyacinth: Hyacinthos, a youth beloved by Apollo, was accidentally killed by a discus thrown by the god. The flower into which he was turned is covered with florets in the form of the Greek letters AI, a cry of pain. The hyacinths of Narcissus' hands are the wounds of the crucified Christ.

Por las cisternas viejas
bebiendo turbias aguas,
tu necia sed enjaguas,
y con sordas orejas,
de las aguas vivíficas te alejas.
En mis finezas piensa:
verás que, siempre amante,
te guardo vigilante,
te libro de la ofensa,
y que pongo la vida en tu defensa.
De la escarcha y la nieve
cubierto, voy siguiendo
tus necios pasos, viendo
que ingrata no te mueve
ver que dejo por ti noventa y nueve.
Mira que mi hermosura
de todas es amada,
de todas es buscada,
sin reservar criatura,
y sólo a ti te elige tu ventura.
Por sendas horrorosas
tus pasos voy siguiendo,
y mis plantas hiriendo
de espinas dolorosas
que estas selvas producen, escabrosas.
Yo tengo de buscarte;
y aunque tema perdida,
por buscarte, la vida,
no tengo de dejarte,
que antes quiero perderla por hallarte.

De Cuadro cuarto, Escena IX

*(Todo esto ha de haber dicho llegando hacia la fuente, y llegando
a ella, la mira y dice:)*

NARCISO   Llego; mas ¿qué es lo que miro?
¿Qué soberana hermosura
afrenta con su luz pura
todo el celestial zafiro?
Del sol el luciente giro,
en todo el curso luciente,
que da desde ocaso a oriente,
no esparce en signos y estrellas
tanta luz, tantas centellas
como da sola esta fuente.

Drinking stagnant waters
out of ancient cisterns,
you slake your foolish thirst,
while, deaf to your mistake,
the spring of living waters you forsake.
Call to mind my favors:
you'll see how lovingly
I watch over you
to free you of offense,
laying down my life in your defense.
Covered with frost and snow,
I leave the flock behind,
to follow your foolish steps;
still you spurn this love of mine,
though for you I've left the other ninety-nine.
Consider that my beauty,
beloved of every creature,
desired by them all—
by every single one—
has set its heart on winning you alone.
Down paths through briary wastes,
I follow where you've trod,
I brave these rugged woods
until my feet are torn,
are stabbed and pierced by every passing thorn.
Still, I shall seek you out
and, even if in the search
I risk my very life,
yours I shall not disown:
to find you I would sooner lose my own.

Fourth Tableau, Scene IX

*(Setting as in Scene VIII, but with the Fountain center stage and Narcissus looking
into it.)*

NARCISSUS Here at last—but what greets my eyes?
What surpassing beauty is this,
beside whose purest light
the whole celestial sphere turns pale?
The glistening band of the sun
in all his shining course
from Occident to Orient
will never shed in signs and stars
a light like this, will never flash
as bright as this one Fount.

Cielo y tierra se han cifrado
a componer su arrebol:
el cielo con su farol,
y con sus flores el prado.
La esfera se ha trasladado
toda, a quererla adornar;
pero no, que tan sin par
belleza, todo el desvelo
de la tierra, ni del cielo,
no la pudieran formar.

Recién abierta granada
sus mejillas sonrosea;
sus dos labios hermosea
partida cinta rosada,
por quien la voz delicada,
haciendo al coral agravio,
despide el aliento sabio
que así a sus claveles toca;
leche y miel vierte la boca,
panales destila el labio.

Las perlas que en concha breve
guarda, se han asimilado
al rebaño, que apiñado
desciende en copos de nieve;
el cuerpo, que gentil mueve,
el aire a la palma toma;
los ojos, por quien asoma
el alma, entre su arrebol
muestran, con luces del sol,
benignidad de paloma.

Terso el bulto delicado,
en lo que a la vista ofrece,
parva de trigo parece,
con azucenas vallado;
de marfil es torneado
el cuello, gentil coluna.
No puede igualar ninguna
hermosura a su arrebol:
escogida como el sol
y hermosa como la luna.

Con un ojo solo, bello,
el corazón me ha abrasado;
el pecho me ha traspasado
con el rizo de un cabello.

Heaven and earth joined hands
to form this burst of brilliance,
heaven supplying the beacon,
the meadow giving the bloom.
The sky came down entire
in eagerness to adorn it.
But no, for beauty so peerless
could never have been devised
by all the loving care
of heaven and earth combined.
     A pomegranate newly opened
blushes over the cheeks.
A scarlet ribbon parted
makes the two lips fair,
and through them the slender voice
that choirs would gladly own
comes forth in fine-tuned breath,
grazing, as it passes, those fragrant pinks.
Honey and milk are under the tongue;
from the lips fall drops of honeycomb.
     Those pearls a small shell holds
resemble, for all the world,
a flock of sheep new-shorn
descending the slopes like snowflakes.
The gracefully swaying body
moves with the palm tree's motion.
The sparkle of the eyes,
through which the soul looks forth,
discloses in their sunbeams
the gentleness of the dove.
     The smoothly fashioned figure
offers itself to the eyes
as a stack of wheat set about
with soft madonna lilies.
The neck is a slender column
of ivory finely wrought.
Never has there been beauty
to match that warming glow,
unique as the sun at noon
and beautiful as the moon.
     With but one of those lovely eyes
my heart has been set afire.
With a single twist of the hair
my breast has been transfixed.

¡Abre el cristalino sello
de ese centro claro y frío,
para que entre el amor mío!
Mira que traigo escarchada
la crencha de oro, rizada,
con las perlas del rocío.

   ¡Ven, Esposa, a tu querido;
rompe esa cortina clara:
muéstrame tu hermosa cara,
suene tu voz a mi oído!
¡Ven del Líbano escogido,
acaba ya de venir,
y coronaré el Ofir
de tu madeja preciosa
con la corona olorosa
de Amaná, Hermón y Sanir!

De Cuadro cuarto, Escena XII

NARCISO   Mas ya el dolor me vence. Ya, ya llego
al término fatal por mi querida:
que es poca la materia de una vida
para la forma de tan grande fuego.

   Ya licencia a la muerte doy: ya entrego
el alma, a que del cuerpo la divida,
aunque en ella y en él quedará asida
mi deidad, que las vuelva a reunir luego.

   Sed tengo: que el amor que me ha abrasado,
aun con todo el dolor que padeciendo
estoy, mi corazón aún no ha saciado.

   ¡Padre! ¿Por qué en un trance tan tremendo
me desamparas? Ya está consumado.
¡En tus manos mi espíritu encomiendo!

Break the crystalline seal
on the clear, cold glass of this fountain
and allow my love to enter.
See how my golden curls
are overspread with hoar-frost,
are wet with dewy pearls.
   Come, my Spouse, to your Lover,
rend that clear curtain,
make your countenance seen,
let me hear your voice in my ear!
Come with me from Lebanon;
ah, if only you come,
I will place a crown on the Ophir
of your precious locks—
even the sweet-smelling crown
of Amana, Sanir, and Hermon!

From the Fourth Tableau, Scene XII

NARCISSUS   But pain now conquers me. For my Belovèd's sake
I have reached the fated point in time.
How far the matter of a life falls short
of a fire's form as vast as this of mine!
   To death my spirit I deliver now
with leave to sever it from flesh,
although my deity yet will cleave
to both, conjoining them afresh.
   I thirst, for my heart remains unsated,
despite the heavy pain I have to bear,
by the flames my love has fanned.
O Father, why, in my frightful hour of care,
hast Thou forsaken me? It is finished now.
My spirit I commend into Thy hand.

Amana, Sanir, and Hermon: "Come from Libanus [Lebanon], my spouse,
come from Libanus, come; thou shalt be crowned from the top of Amana,
from the top of Sanir and Hermon, from the dens of the lions, from the
mountains of the leopards" (Song of Songs 4:8).

De Cuadro quinto, Escena XIV

(Retíranse a un lado; y sale la NATURALEZA *llorando, y todas las* NINFAS *y* PASTORES, *y* MÚSICA *triste.)*

NATURALEZA   Ninfas habitadoras
HUMANA   de estos campos silvestres,
   unas en claras ondas
   y otras en troncos verdes;
    pastores, que vagando
   estos prados alegres,
   guardáis con el ganado
   rústicas sencilleces:
    de mi bello Narciso,
   gloria de vuestro albergue,
   las dos divinas lumbres
   cerró temprana muerte:
    ¡sentid, sentid mis ansias;
   llorad, llorad su muerte!

MÚSICA   ¡Llorad, llorad su muerte!

NATURALEZA   Muerte le dio su amor;
HUMANA   que de ninguna suerte
   pudiera, sino sólo
   su propio amor vencerle.
    De mirar su retrato,
   enamorado muere;
   que aun copiada su imagen,
   hace efecto tan fuerte:
    ¡sentid, sentid mis ansias;
   llorad, llorad su muerte!

MÚSICA   ¡Llorad, llorad su muerte!

NATURALEZA   Ver su malogro, todo
HUMANA   el universo siente:
   las peñas se quebrantan,
   los montes se enternecen;
    enlútase la luna,
   los polos se estremecen,
   el sol su luz esconde,
   el cielo se obscurece.
    ¡Sentid, sentid mis ansias;
   llorad, llorad su muerte!

MÚSICA   ¡Llorad, llorad su muerte!

NATURALEZA   El aire se encapota,
HUMANA   la tierra se conmueve,
   el fuego se alborota,
   el agua se revuelve.

From the Fifth Tableau, Scene XIV

(Enter Human Nature weeping, and all the nymphs and shepherds. Sad music.)

HUMAN NATURE	Nymphs, all you who dwell
	in this sylvan setting,
	some in clear waters,
	in green trunks others;
	    Shepherds, you who roam
	these happy meadows,
	keeping, with your flocks,
	your simple rustic ways:
	    those two heavenly lights
	of my fair Narcissus,
	glory of your retreat,
	are quenched by early death.
	    Oh, come and share my sorrow,
	lament, lament His death!

MUSIC	Lament, lament His death!

HUMAN NATURE	It was His love that killed Him,
	for nothing else beside
	the very love of His own
	could ever overcome Him.
	    Through gazing at His likeness,
	He falls in love and dies,
	for His image, even copied,
	wields almighty power.
	    Oh, come and share my sorrow,
	lament, lament His death!

MUSIC	Lament, lament His death!

HUMAN NATURE	The universe entire grieves
	beholding His sad end:
	rocks are rent asunder,
	mountains melt with pain;
	    the moon puts on mourning,
	the poles are shaken,
	the sun hides his light,
	the heavens are darkened.
	    Oh, come and share my sorrow,
	lament, lament His death!

MUSIC	Lament, lament His death!
HUMAN NATURE	Air is hung with cloud, Earth's depths are stirred, Fire leaps about, Waters boil and swirl.

Abren opacas bocas
los sepulcros patentes,
para dar a entender
que hasta los muertos sienten.
¡Sentid, sentid mis ansias;
llorad, llorad su muerte!

MÚSICA   ¡Llorad, llorad su muerte!
NATURALEZA   Divídese del templo
HUMANA   el velo reverente,
dando a entender que ya
se rompieron sus leyes.
El universo todo,
de su beldad doliente,
capuz funesto arrastra,
negras bayetas tiende.
¡Sentid, sentid mis ansias;
llorad, llorad su muerte!

MÚSICA   ¡Llorad, llorad su muerte!

Graves open wide
their gaping mouths,
making plain to all
the distress of the dead.
Oh, come and share my sorrow,
lament, lament His death!
MUSIC　Lament, lament His death!
HUMAN　The veil of the temple
NATURE　is rent in twain,
that all may behold
the breaking of its laws.
The universe entire,
grieving for His beauty,
trails a cloak of mourning,
hangs black baize in grief.
Oh, come and share my sorrow,
lament, lament His death!
MUSIC　Lament, lament His death!

A Prose Summary
First Dream

The shadow of night mounted from earth, aspiring to reach heaven, whose distant stars scorned its bellicosity. It could not even penetrate to the far—the convex—side of the sphere of the moon and had to be content with fouling the zone of air surrounding the earth. There at least it imposed silence, allowing at most the muffled calls of night birds, such as the owl—Nyctimene—who perversely consumes the olive oil that feeds holy lamps in churches. It also allowed the cry of bats, once sisters punished for being disrespectful to Bacchus and now so afraid of the light that they envelop themselves in a denser darkness within the darkness of night. Along with the screech owl—Ascalaphus—these birds droned on in a sluggish, discordant, sleep-inducing chorus that made Night's summons to inviolate silence and repose easy for every creature of land and sea, not excluding the kingfisher—Halcyon—to obey.

In their inaccessible mountain caves the animals of the wild, the ferocious as well as the timid, were reduced by Nature to a common state of slumber. Even the open-eyed lion, king of beasts, was only feigning wakefulness, while the sensitive stag—Actaeon—through his sleep caught the faintest sounds and nervously twitched his ears. In their well-hidden nests the birds were likewise slumbering—all but the eagle, who takes seriously his royal obligations as king of them all and adopts a special posture in order to stay awake. This never-ending obligation of vigilance may explain the circularity, characterized by no beginning or end, of the crown worn by the king.

The time of silence was drawing to a close, the night was half over, and the limbs, worn out from their daily tasks, were sunk in deep sleep. They were fatigued not only by bodily exertion but exhausted by pleasure—for even a pleasant object constantly before the senses tires them, whence Nature is always shifting weight from one side of the scale to the other, as her needle logs all the activity of the complex clockwork of the universe. The slumber of the limbs had thus released the senses temporarily from what must be considered labor, however much loved, and the senses had succumbed to sleep, which, as Death's image, always eventually wins out over humble and powerful alike, over pope and peasant, over the emperor whose palace the Danube mirrors and the poor rustic.

The soul, free of her daytime task of governing the body, and half detached from it, pays limbs and bones their wages in the form of the heat that characterizes all things living, from the plant upward. The body, like a corpse with a soul, shows, like a clock, languid but well-regulated signs of life in the pulsing of the arteries.

The human clock, the heart, and its ally, the lungs, give unimpeachable testimony of ongoing life. The latter, like a bellows or a magnet for the wind, by expanding and contracting the neck, draw in and warm cool air, but this last, in retaliation for being expelled, keeps carrying off traces of heat, whose cumulative loss will one day result in death. The senses, by their silence, dispute the evidence of heart and lung that life persists; so does the silent tongue.

The stomach, efficient manufacturer of heat and its impartial distributor to the limbs (she gives to each according to its need), records precisely on her natural dial the amount she deems appropriate to each, of the chyle distilled by continuous heat from ingested food. A well-meaning but imprudent or arrogant intercessor, the food has to pay for rashly interposing itself between the stomach's heat and the humid radical by having its substance repeatedly eaten away by the latter. Though no forge of Vulcan, the stomach, through its heat, was sending to the brain vapors arising from the four well-tempered humors—blood, phlegm, yellow bile, and black bile—moist but clear enough not to cloud (as they usually do) the images which the "common" sense supplies to the image-making sense and the latter passes along to the memory to store. The humors even allowed the fantasy freely to combine images of its own. In this it operated like the huge mirror, round as the moon, atop the ancient lighthouse of Alexandria on Pharos Island, which reflected ships great distances at sea. The fantasy reflected not only likenesses of things existing here below, but those of things unseen, of purely mental constructs and spiritual essences, which she displayed to the soul.

The latter was absorbed in delighted contemplation of the spark of divinity God had implanted in her. Considering herself almost free of the bonds of body that always hold her back and interfere with the flight of intellect that plumbs the universe or ponders the well-regulated courses of the stars (not to be confused with the culpable, unhinging, and self-defeating pursuit of an astrology which would read men's future), she imagined herself on the crest of a mountain so high that it dwarfs even the Atlas, which towers over all others, and reduces the always serene summit of Olympus to less than a foothill. Indeed the clouds which wreathe the heights of earth's tallest volcano, a giant goading heaven to war, would be merely a rough and constantly disintegrating sash or girdle of this mountain envisaged by the soul.

If the mountain is thought of in three zones, even the lowest was beyond the reach of the highest flight of eagle. One might compare this mountain to the two giant Pyramids of Memphis in Egypt. The latter, which served the Ptolemies as both tomb and glorious boast exceeding any Fame could make, were so artfully constructed that the eye could not follow their upward-receding shapes to the top, but fell back disoriented from their sunbathed and completely shadeless slopes. Blind Homer, be he poet or historian—from whose heroic poems not one line could be removed as superfluous any more than Jove's thunderbolt or Hercules' club could be taken from them—Homer sees the Pyramids as mere outward concretizations of the inner shape the spirit's movement assumes. Pyramidal, like the upward thrust of flame, is the mind's ascent toward the Prime Mover—God, at once center of universal aspiration and circumference delimiting limitless essences.

Add to these two artificial mountains, the Pyramids, that blasphemous Tower of Babel whose destruction led to the diversifying of the universal language of mankind. Even so the lofty pyramid of mind atop which the soul found herself would immeasurably outstrip them all, for she seemed to have risen above her very self and entered a new sphere. She, supreme creature among all on earth, let the unobstructed and unlimited vision of her intellect range over all creation, but if her eyes might conceivably take in such an immense assemblage, it overwhelmed her understanding, which recoiled.

The eyes, however, overreached and tried to direct their gaze straight into the sun, though no line of vision is strong enough for this. For her trouble, she incurred tears, as did Icarus when he drowned in the sea of his self-pity. The mind had already drawn back, overcome as much by the multiplicity of the densely packed phenomena as by the various features of each. Unable to settle on any one thing, it tried to encompass everything and ended up dulled and undiscerning in the face of all the species that stretched incomprehensibly along the revolving axis of the universe from pole to pole, whether as integral and functioning components or as refining details.

If one who has been a long time in the dark is suddenly exposed to bright light, its very brilliance will blind him, for his eyes will have grown unaccustomed to sunlight. He will use his hands to protect his faltering eyes, affording them the very shade that, having earlier blocked their vision, can now restore it. Experience proves the wisdom of the manipulation of contraries, as physicians have found by careful observation of nature and experimentation with animals, which enable them beneficially to counteract the deadly properties of one poison with those of another, to salutary effect, drawing good from evil even without understanding the process involved. In just this way did the astonished soul, still in a state of shock, withdraw her attention, with her reasoning power so impaired as to allow her only a muddled embryo of thought, an unstable chaos of species incessantly coming together and coming apart in complete disorder—the result of trying to cram such a vast array of objects into a tiny container, the mind, inadequate for even the most minute.

The overconfident ship of the soul, having run afoul of wind and waves, perforce washed ashore in a shattered state on the beach of the vast sea of knowledge. There, to refit herself, she fell into a wiser and more prudent line of thought: she would consider one thing at a time, either by itself, or by mounting step by step the ladder of those scholastic categories that make it possible to think abstractly in terms of the universals. Thus she would compensate for the mind's inability to encompass all the universe in one intuitive act.

Both the substance of such scholastic doctrine and the mental hygiene involved in its progressive acquisition give the mind energy to climb the arduous peak of learning to the summit, there to find self-assurance and honor. Thus, my mind proposed to take up first the lowest level of being—the inanimate or mineral realm, the one least favored by Nature—then advance to the nobler vegetal kingdom, moving up the scale of plants from the first forms to emerge in the sea and draw sustenance from water. Four operations characterize this second realm: attraction, selection, expulsion, and conversion. My mind would then survey the more beautiful animal kingdom—sentient and endowed with powers of mental perception—and thus superior to even the brightest or loftiest star. From this basis in knowing via sense, it would ascend to the creature who combines the three lower natures: the vegetal, the sensitive, and the rational; the link between the lowliest of the creatures and the purest (the angel). He is not only endowed by God with the five outer senses but with the three inner faculties which control them: will, understanding, and memory. He is thus supreme among all of God's creatures, His main concern and special delight, after creating whom He rested, on the seventh day. Capable of the loftiest aspiration heavenward, yet only mortal, he might be represented by Saint John's apocalyptic vision of a creature belonging to heaven and earth, or by the golden statue with feet of clay seen by Nebuchadnezzar in a dream.

This creature is man, the greatest wonder imaginable, who combines in himself the natures of angel, animal, and plant. Why such a blend? Perhaps that man might be uplifted through the loving union of the earthly and the divine in the Incarnation—a grace often given human lip service, yet still so unacknowledged and unappreciated.

Such was my ambition, yet there were times when it seemed much too bold in one who could not even understand the most commonplace phenomena. How did the brook hold to its course, now meandering, now, like Arethusa, disappearing underground, now flowing through countryside as beautiful as the Elysian Fields, once site of the nuptials of Pluto and Persephone. (From her underground wanderings the river Arethusa was at least able to bring back to the pining and tirelessly searching Demeter news of her missing daughter Persephone.) The mind could not even account for the delicate loveliness of pattern and color, the fragrance, the continual burgeoning, the subtle texture, of the tiniest flower which, when fully opened, displays the rosy hue of Venus or mixes the white of daybreak with the red of dawn in an iridescence which is the admiration of surrounding Nature. But perhaps the flower shows up the vanity, or flaunts the feminine duplicity, of that coating of poisonous material in women's makeup which adds further noxiousness to that of an already deceptive appearance.

Cowardly doubts kept assailing my mind, asking how, if it could not so much as grasp one object set aside for that very purpose, it could hope to take in the total system of the universe, so astounding and vast. If not sustained by God as its center, such a system would be judged far more of a burden by Atlas or Hercules than the heavens their shoulders upheld. The investigation of Nature would be a harder task than their feat of strength.

Fired at other times by the feat of Phaethon in driving the chariot of his father, Apollo, even though he came to grief, my mind would consider daring supreme, holding back cowardly. No fear of punishment will ever curb the lofty flight of spirit in its determination to achieve fame, even at a ruinous price. Let the penalty paid remain unknown lest broadcasting the feat influence others. Or let ignorance of it be feigned, or it be duly punished in secret, since publicizing it makes it the more contagious, hence the more dangerous.

But as the mind found itself thus frustrated, the heat engendered in the stomach had consumed the food that maintained it, converting it into itself. The noisy combining of moist and hot humors had ceased for lack of sustenance; there were thus fewer and fewer humors to cloud the brain and relax the limbs, and sleep was growing lighter, with the limbs beginning to stir spontaneously and the senses to resume their operation. The eyes were half-open and the brain rapidly clearing, with its phantasms departing in just the way the magic lantern projects at a duly determined distance on a white wall as fleeting two-dimensional shadows the silhouettes of three-dimensional colored figures.

Meanwhile the Sun, as the hour of his rising in our East approached, was simultaneously departing from our antipodes in their West. Venus, the morning star, preceded him in the beautiful, dewy Dawn, who boldly warded off the night with her brightness as morning lighted her brow. The Sun was busily marshaling his untried troops in the van, his veterans in the rear, for the assault against the usurping tyrant girt round with shadows awesome even to her. But as Dawn unfurled her pennant and the birds trumpeted their unschooled call to arms, Night, fearful and cowardly despite her brave front and her black cloak—vain protection against the light beams piercing it—summoned her dark squadrons to join her in an orderly retreat.

Just then the first sunbeam shot past her and caught the highest point on earth. The Sun now appeared, having completed the circle of the zodiac, and darted brilliance everywhere. Night kept falling all over herself in her rush to reach the West with her shadowy cohorts. Once there, she decided to conquer the half of the globe left defenseless by the Sun. He distributed his light impartially and abundantly, restoring full color to the world, setting the senses to functioning again, and waking me up.

First Dream

*So entitled and so composed by Mother Juana Inés de la Cruz, in
imitation of Góngora*

Pyramidal, lugubrious,
a shadow born of earth
pushed heavenward its towering tips
like vacuous obelisks bent on scaling stars,
although those splendid lights
forever free, aglow forever,
spurned the shadowy war
which the dreadful moving shade
was waging in gaseous blackness, so far below
that even its frowning gloom stopped short
before it reached the convex side
of that fair goddess' orb—
she, I mean, who shows herself
in threefold beauty,
the beauty of her three faces.
There was left it as sole domain
the air it kept defiling
with each dense breath exhaled,
within which soundless purview
of its silent realm,
it brooked none but the muted voices
of the birds of darkness,
sounds so deep and dim
as not to break the silence.

that fair goddess' orb: The sphere of the moon is the innermost of the ten
which revolve around Earth in the Ptolemaic system. The moon's three
faces (waxing, waning, dark) correspond to the three forms in which the
moon goddess is worshiped; see note to poem 8.

With sluggish flight and song,
jarring on ear and even more on spirit,
shamefaced Nyctimene keeps watch
by chinks in sacred portals
or at those gaping openings
of lofty, rounded windows
best suited to her purpose:
to desecrate the brightly shining
holy lamps perpetually lit,
extinguishing, even defiling them,
while drinking in clear liquid form
rich substance that Minerva's tree,
constrained by press, has sweated forth
out of her fruit, a tribute forced.

And those women who saw their house
become an out-of-doors; their weft, the grass;
defiant of Bacchus' godhead—
no longer telling various tales
but changed now ignominiously—
create an added fog,
fearing even in darkness to be seen,
featherless wingèd birds—
those three sisters I mean,
daringly laborious,
whose frightful punishment
gave them such ill-shaped wings
of drab and naked membranes
as to bring them jeers from other baleful birds.

They, with Pluto's telltale
one-time henchman, now an omen
to superstitious persons,
alone made up

Nyctimene: For tricking her father into incest with her, this girl of Lesbos
was changed into an owl, a bird believed to drink the oil of holy lamps in
order to extinguish them. The olive tree was a gift of Athena (Minerva) to
the Greeks.

those women: The daughters of Minyas of Thebes refused Bacchus'
summons to join his cult, clinging instead to their looms in defense of
Athena and telling stories to while away the time. As punishment, they
were changed into bats, their weft into greenery (Ovid, *Metamorphoses*,
4.1–30, 389–415).

one-time henchman: Ascalaphus, son of a nymph of the underworld and
the river Acheron, revealed that Persephone had eaten seven pomegranate
seeds while below; for this indiscretion he was changed into a screech owl,
a bird of ill omen (Ovid, *Metamorphoses* 5.533–550).

the fearsome jangling choir,
droning long and longer lengthened notes,
and pausing more than singing,
to hang on the torpid, lazy measure,
more dragged out still at times, kept by the wind
to a phlegmatic beat,
so slow in tempo, so sustained,
that sometimes the wind would doze between two notes.

   This dismal intermittent dirge
of the fearful shadowy band
insisted on attention less
than it coaxed a listener asleep.
Indeed, with all deliberation
its dull and drawn-out harmony
invited all to rest,
urging repose on weary limbs,
while Night, an index finger
sealing her two dark lips—
silent Harpocrates—enjoined
silence on all things living,
a summons, however peremptory,
complied with easily
and promptly obeyed by all.
The dog asleep, the wind at rest—
one prone, the other quiet—
stir not a single atom,
fearing lest sough or sigh should make
a sacrilegious noise, however slight,
to violate the reign of silence.
The sea, no longer roiled,
did not so much as rock the azure
unsteady cradle where the sun lay sleeping.
The fish, mute always, now asleep
in the oozy beds
of their cavernous dark coves
were doubly silent,
and Halcyon in their midst,

Harpocrates: Greek version of a name of the Egyptian sun god Horus,
represented as a boy with a finger on his mouth. This pose, misunderstood
by the Greeks, led to their worshiping him as god of silence.

Halcyon: This daughter of Aeolus, god of the winds, threw herself from
the shore onto the body of her drowned husband, Ceyx, King of Thrace,
and along with him was changed into a kingfisher (halcyon). Thus, her
earlier rejected suitors, metaphorically caught like fish in the nets of her
allurements, were avenged (Ovid, *Metamorphoses* 9.710–748).

enchantress and deceiver,
by her own transformation brought revenge
to guileless lovers once transformed by her.

   In remote mountain hideaways,
misshapen hollow crags
whose ruggedness is less defense
than their darkness is protection,
abodes of utter blackness
where night is safe from daylight's glare,
to which sure foot of practiced hunter
has never yet ascended,
the legions of wild animals lay resting—
some shedding all ferocity,
others, their timorousness—
each to Nature's power
paying the tribute
imposed by her on all alike.
The king of beasts, though open-eyed
pretending to keep watch, lay fast asleep.
That once-illustrious monarch
cornered by his own dogs,
now a timid hart,
pricks up an ear
to catch the slightest motion
of the peaceful surrounding night,
the merest shift of atom,
and twitching each ear in turn,
perceives the faint and muffled sound
uneasily through his sleep.
In the quietude of the nest
built out of twigs and mud—
hammock hung where foliage is thickest—
the light-pinioned tribe
slumbers away and gives the wind
a respite from the slashes of its wings.

   Jupiter's majestic bird,
the dutiful king of fowl, rejects

once-illustrious monarch: Actaeon, not himself a monarch but grandson of
the king of Thebes, having inadvertently surprised Diana at her bath, was
changed by her into a stag and torn to pieces by his own hounds (Ovid,
Metamorphoses 3.155–252).

Jupiter's majestic bird: Sor Juana attributes to the eagle a practice ascribed
since Pliny (*Natural History* 10.23) to the crane, a traditional symbol of
vigilance. The sound of the pebble falling once the bird's grasp is relaxed
in sleep supposedly would awaken it.

complete repose, holding it a vice,
too far indulged, and taking care
not to fall unwittingly asleep.
Entrusting all his weight to a single leg,
he keeps a pebble in the other foot—
an alarm for his light sleep—
so that, when slumber impends,
it may not be prolonged,
will rather be interrupted
by kingly pastoral concern.
Uneasy lies the head that wears a crown!
Not for one instant may he lay it down.
Mysterious explanation this may be
why crowns are circular,
the golden round betokening
the unending obligation of the king.

　　All was now bound in sleep,
all by silence occupied.
Even the thief was slumbering,
even the lover had closed his eyes.
　　The hour of silence is drawing to a close,
the dark time is half over
when, worn out by daily tasks—
oppressed not only
by the heavy burden
of bodily exertion, but fatigued
by pleasure as well (for any object
continually before the senses,
even if pleasurable, will cloy them:
hence Nature is always shifting weight
from one side of the balance to the other,
setting the unsettled needle to its task
of logging all activity—now leisurely,
now toilsome—as she directs
the universe's complicated clockwork);
the limbs, then, all were occupied
by deep and welcome sleep,
leaving the senses for a time
if not deprived, relieved
of their customary labor—
labor indeed but labor greatly loved,
if labor can be loved—
the senses, I say, had yielded
to the likeness of life's opponent,
who, slow to arm and cowardly in attack,

with sleepy weapons is a lazy victor
over lowly shepherd's crook and lofty scepter
and all that stands between,
purple and sackcloth being all one for him.
His level is all-powerful:
it never makes exceptions
for any man alive,
be he one who wears the sovereign tiara
made up of triple crowns, or one
who dwells in hut of straw,
a man whom the Danube gilds in mirrored glory
or a denizen of humble rushes:
with one unvarying measuring-rod
(Morpheus being, after all,
a powerful image of death)
he graduates brocade and sackcloth.

The soul now being released
from outward governance, activity
which keeps her materially employed
for better or for worse the whole day through,
at some remove although not quite cut off,
pays out their wages
of vegetal heat only
to listless limbs and resting bones
oppressed by temporary death.
The body in unbroken calm,
a corpse with soul,
is dead to living, living to the dead,
the human clock attesting
by faintest signs of life
its vital wound-up state,
wound not by hand but by arterial concert:
by throbbings which give tiny measured signs
of its well-regulated movement.

This sovereign member, very core of vital spirits,
with its allied breathing bellows—
the lung, a magnet drawing in the wind—
which, with movement always even,
now compressing, now expanding
the sinewy, soft aqueduct,
effects the inhalation
of the cool surrounding atmosphere,

triple crowns: The papal tiara is made up of three superimposed crowns.

warming it up;
but the latter, angered at being expelled,
continually carries off small traces
of native warmth one day to be lamented,
never to be recovered, although now
not even noticed by their possessor—
still no theft is small if it keeps recurring;
these two witnesses, then,
reliable, unimpeachable in fact,
as I was saying, kept life going
while the silent senses, vocal silently,
impugned their testimony,
citing their very silence,
and the torpid tongue by silence of its own
disputed them as well.

And that most marvelous and scientific
manufacturer of heat,
provident supplier of the limbs,
always at work and never stinting,
which neither favors the closest member
nor overlooks the farthest
but keeps exact account
on her natural dial
of the share she apportions to each one
in the chyle, which unceasing heat distills
from the food—well-meaning intercessor,
innocent interposer of its substance
between heat and humid radical,
who has to pay in full for good intentions
or foolish arrogance that leaves that food
exposed to its enemy's voracity,
punishment well deserved although unneeded
for one who intervenes when others quarrel—
so this, if not forge of Vulcan,
moderate bonfire of human warmth,
was sending to the brain
vapors from the four well-tempered humors,
humid but so clear
it not only failed to cloud with them

---

humid radical: In ancient physiology this was a "lymphatic humor, sweet, thin, and balmlike, which gave flexibility and elasticity to the body's tendons" (Espasa Dict. [Span.]). It was constantly contending with the body's "natural heat," which was unable to overcome it because the interposition of food kept restoring its destructiveness.

the images which the estimative sense
furnished to the imaginative
and the latter, for safer keeping,
passed on in purer form
to diligent memory
to incise retentively and store with care,
but also offered the fantasy
a chance to put together
further images. In just the way
that on the polished surface—
a glassy marvel and unique protection
of Pharos Island—could be seen
far, far away, despite the distance,
in the quicksilver moon,
almost the entire realm of Neptune
with the ships that plowed it so far off,
their number, size, and fortune
and the risk they ran
in the transparent
unsteady country of the deep
as their light sails cleaved the wind,
their heavy hulls the waters:
so the fantasy was calmly copying
the images of everything,
and the invisible brush was shaping
in the mind's colors, without light
yet beautiful still, the likenesses
not just of all created things
here in this sublunary world, but those as well
that are the intellect's bright stars,
and as far as in her power lay
the conception of things invisible,
was picturing them ingeniously in herself
and displaying them to the soul.

    Meanwhile the latter, all intent
on her immaterial being,
was contemplating that most lovely spark,
that portion of highest being
in whose likeness in herself she took delight.
She thought herself almost loosed
from that bodily chain,

estimative sense: Father Méndez Plancarte (*OC*, I, 590) believes Sor Juana
means the inner sense common to the five outer senses, which receives
their percepts and passes them on to the other senses located in the brain:
the image-making, the memory, and the fantasy.

that always blocks her path,
obstructing crudely and grossly interfering
with the flight of intellect through which she plumbs
the vast immensity of the firmament
or ponders the well-regulated orbits
in which the celestial bodies
variously run their courses—
a heavy sin with punishment inherent,
the relentless shattering of inner peace,
when it lapses into vain astrology—
placed, so she thought, on the towering crest
of a mountain next to which that very Atlas,
which like a giant dominates all others,
becomes a mere obedient dwarf,
and Olympus, whose tranquil brow
has never admitted violation
by buffeting winds,
is unworthy of foothill status.
For the clouds that form an opaque crown
for the topmost mass
of the loftiest volcano that from earth,
a rearing giant, goads high heaven to war,
scarcely form a heavy sash
around its soaring height
or a girdle round its huge waist,
a turbulent one, rough and poorly fashioned,
which winds undo
or the nearness of the sun evaporates.

    The first level of its elevation
(the bottommost, I mean, if you divide
its limitless awesome body into three)
no rapid surging flight could ever reach
of eagle soaring to the very heavens,
drinking in sunbeams and aspiring
to build her nest amidst the sun's own lights,
however hard she presses upward
with great flappings of her feathered sails
or combings of the air
with open talons, as she strives,
fashioning ladders out of atoms,
to pierce the inviolate precincts of the peak.

rearing giant: After their unsuccessful assault on Olympus, the Giants
were condemned by the gods to imprisonment under mountains.

drinking in sunbeams: The eagle was considered the only living creature
capable of gazing directly into the sun (Pliny, *Nat. Hist.* 29. 123–160)

The two Pyramids—proud boast
of vainglorious Memphis, ultimate refinement
of architecture, pennants, if not fixed,
no fluttering ones surely—whose great mass,
crowned with barbaric trophies,
was tomb and ensign to the Ptolemies,
broadcasting to the wind and clouds
(if not to heaven as well)
Egyptian glories, deeds of Memphian prowess—
of that great city, Cairo now, I mean,
forever undefeated—
deeds never sung by Fame, too dumbstruck
by their very abundance,
glories still written in the wind and sky;
these Pyramids, in lifting higher and higher
in smooth and level stages, their vast bulk,
shrank so in girth and with such art
that the closer the lynxlike gaze
of the observing eye approached the heavens,
the more it lost its way amid the winds,
unable to discern the minute tip
that feigns a juncture with the lowest heaven,
until, worn out by sheer astonishment,
it found itself below by the spacious base
after, not smooth descent, but downward plunge
in giddiness that only gradually
gave way to level-headedness—
no minor punishment
for the wingèd boldness of the eyes.
The two opaque bodies,
not contraries to the sun, instead
on best of terms with sunlight, indeed
confederate by contiguity,
were so completely bathed
in brilliance that, all aglow,
they never offered tired feet
or panting breath of sweltering traveler
so much as a carpet's breadth
of even the slightest shade.
These, be they glories of Egypt
or high points of idolatry,

two Pyramids: No doubt those of Cheops and Khafre, 140 meters high, at
Giza outside Memphis, identified here with modern Cairo. These pyramids
were in fact erected long before the Ptolemies by the pharoahs of the
Fourth Dynasty.

a carpet's breadth: Legend held that the pyramids cast no shade.

barbaric hieroglyphics
of purblind error, as that singer says,
that Greek, blind also, and a sweetest poet—
unless the history-writing clan
lays claim to him for his account
of Achillean deeds of valor,
or the wily warring of Ulysses,
or lists him in their catalogue
as adding in prestige
(though not in numbers) to their ranks—
from whose sweet rhythmic sequences
the theft of just a single
hemistich dictated by Apollo
would be a harder task
than robbing the fearsome Thunderer
of a flashing thunderbolt
or stealing from Alcides
his heavy iron-studded mace:

In Homer's opinion, then,
the pyramids were mere material versions,
outward manifestations only
of inner dimensions instancing
the human spirit's attitude:
for just as the ambitious fiery flame
assumes pyramidal shape when mounting
heavenward, so the human mind
assumes this very shape
in ever aspiring to the one First Cause,
the center toward which the straight line tends,
if not indeed the circumference
containing every essence ad infinitum.

These two artificial mountains, then
(be they miracles or marvels),
and that lofty blasphemous Tower
whose unhappy remnants to this day—
languages diversely shaped, not stones,

that Greek: This reference to Homer must allude to a hermetic
interpretation of his text since nowhere in his epics is there a reference to
the pyramids.

Thunderer: Zeus

Alcides: Hercules

the center: From Nicholas of Cusa, via Athanasius Kircher, comes this
definition of God, to which Sor Juana returns in her *Reply* to Sor Philothea
de la Cruz.

lest voracious time devour them—
are the divers tongues which still obstruct
the easy intercourse of humankind
(causing those Nature formed as one
to seem entirely different
simply because their tongues are unfamiliar),
if those three were compared
to the elevated pyramid of mind
on which, not knowing how, the soul
found herself now placed, they would see themselves
so far below that anyone
would assume her perch was in another sphere,
since her ambitious urge,
making of her very flight a summit,
lifted her to the highest point
of her own mentality,
mounted so high above herself, she thought
she had emerged in some new region.

   At this almost limitless elevation,
jubilant but perplexed,
perplexed yet full of pride,
and astonished although proud,
the sovereign queen of this sublunary world
let the probing gaze, by lenses unencumbered,
of her beautiful intellectual eyes
(unperturbed by distance
or worry lest some opaque obstacle
by intervening hide objects from her view)
range unrestricted over all creation.
Such an immense assemblage,
a mass so unencompassable,
though holding out to sight
some chance of being taken in,
held none to the understanding, which being dazed
by objects in such profusion, its powers
surpassed by their very magnitude,
turned coward and drew back.

   The eyes were far less quick
to reel, contrite, from their bold purpose.
Instead, they overreached and tried
in vain to prove themselves
against an object which in excellence exceeds
all visual lines—
against the sun, I mean, the shining body

whose rays impose a punishment of fire
which, scorning unmatched forces,
chastises beam by beam
the self-assured, originally bold,
now lachrymose attempt
(silly experiment which cost so dear
that Icarus was drowned
in his own self-pitying tears).
Far less quick, I say, than the mind, which, overcome
no less by the immense agglomeration
of a congeries so weighty
(a globe compounded
of multiple species densely packed)
than by the several qualities of each,
gave in, so overwhelmed
that, amid the copiousness,
impoverished by embarrassment of riches,
helpless to choose in so astounding a sea,
it foundered, bearings lost,
and, trying to look at everything, saw nothing,
unable to discern
(its intellective faculty gone blunt
in the face of so diffuse a quantity
of species beyond its grasp,
that stretched from the axis on which is poised
the revolving mechanism of the sphere
to the opposite pole)
those parts not simply
which it thinks of as perfecting
the universe and belonging
merely to its decorative detail,
but even those fully integrated parts,
limbs of its extensive body,
each with its function duly set.

But, as one who has been deprived
by lengthy darkness of all color
in visible objects,
if suddenly assaulted by bright light
is made the blinder by its very brilliance—
for excess produces opposite effects

Icarus: Wearing wings fashioned by his father, Daedalus, for their escape
from Crete, Icarus flew too close to the sun. The wax which held his wings
in place melted, and he plunged into the sea now called Icarian.

those parts: The ensuing distinction between integral and perfecting parts
is basic in scholastic philosophy.

in the dulled faculty, which cannot all at once
admit the brightness of the sun
for want of practice—
and appeals to that same shade which formerly
had been a shadowy obstacle to the sight,
against the light's offenses,
and over and over with the hand protects
the wavering beams
of the weak and dazzled eyes;
so the shadow, merciful mediator,
now serving as an instrument
to bring about the eyes' recovery,
their gradual restoration,
so that, unfalteringly,
reliably, they may discharge their task—
natural procedure, this inborn wisdom,
which, with confirmation by experience,
a silent teacher perhaps,
but exemplary persuader,
has led physicians more than once
to mete out scrupulously
in proportions carefully determined
the secret harmful qualities
of deadly poisons,
now via an excess
of properties hot or cold,
now through the unknown sympathies
or antipathies whereby
natural causes carry out their action
(providing our astonished admiration
with a sure effect born of an unknown cause,
by taking endless pains and with observant
empirical attention tested first
in experiments performed on animals,
where the danger is not so great)
so that they might concoct in a healthful brew—
final goal of Apollonian science—
a marvelous counterpoison,
for thus at times from evil good arises;
not otherwise, then, did the soul,
astounded by the sight of such a mass
of objects, pull the attention back,
which, scattered over such diversity,
as yet had found recovery impossible
from the portentous shock
that had blocked her reasoning power,

allowing her scarcely more
than a rudimentary embryo
of muddled discourse, one so shapeless,
that from the confusion of species it embraced
it formed a picture of disordered chaos—
associating species in no order,
dissociating them in none,
so that the more they mix and intermingle,
the more they come apart in disarray
from sheer diversity—
forcibly cramming the vast overflow
of objects into a tiny vessel
unfit to hold even the humblest, most minute.

   In fine, the ship of the soul, sails furled,
whose inexperience she entrusted
to the treacherous sea, the fanning wind,
thoughtlessly presuming
the sea to be loyal, constant the wind,
against her will was forced
to run ashore on the beach
of the vast sea of knowing,
with rudder broken, yardarms snapped,
kissing each grain of sand
with every splinter.
Recovering there,
for calking she resorted
to prudent rumination,
the temperate wisdom born of thoughtful judgment,
which, reining in its operation,
considered as more appropriate
restriction to a single subject
or taking separate account
of each thing, one by one,
contained in every one
of those artfully constructed
categories, ten in number:
a metaphysical reduction teaching
(by encompassing generic entities
in the purely mental constructs
of abstract thought, eschewing
embodiment in matter)
the art of forming universals,

categories: The categories of being of Aristotelian logic adopted by the
scholastics: substance, quantity, relation, qualification, doing,
being-affected, where, when, being-in-a-position, having.

sagely compensating by such art
for a deficiency:
the inability to know by one sole act
of intuition every created thing,
the need instead to move up, step by step,
as on a ladder, from one concept
to the next, adopting of necessity
the relative order of understanding
required by the restricted power of Mind,
which must entrust its progress
to a graduated form of reasoning.

The imparting of such doctrine fortifies
Mind's weaknesses with learnèd nourishment
and the lengthy, although smooth,
continuing course of discipline
endows it with lusty energies,
wherewith inspirited, its pride aspires
to the glorious banner that rewards
the most arduous undertaking:
to ascend the lofty stair,
by cultivation, first of one,
then of another form of knowledge
till honor's summit gradually comes in view,
the easeful goal of a most laborious climb
(from bitter seed a fruit delighting taste,
which even at such expense is inexpensive)
and treading valiantly, Mind implants
sure footsteps on the summit's lofty brow.

Of this series now my mind
desired to pursue the method:
namely, from the basest level
of being—the inanimate
(the one least favored
by the second productive cause,
yet still not wholly destitute)—
to move on to the nobler hierarchy,
which, in respect to vegetative vigor,
is the firstborn, however rude,
of Thetis—and the first to cling

second productive cause: The first productive cause being God, the second
is Nature, entrusted by God as His vice-gerent with overseeing the
functioning of the universe.

Thetis: Following Father Méndez Plancarte (*OC*, I, 596), I emend the
"Themis" of earlier texts to "Thetis." As the wife of Ocean, Thetis suits
the context far better than Themis, the goddess of justice.

to her fruitful maternal breasts
and draw by power of suction on the sweet
and gushing springs of that terrestrial humor
which for its natural sustenance
is a sweetest nutriment—
a hierarchy furnished with some four
operations diverging in their action,
now attracting, now excluding carefully
whatever it judges unsuited to itself,
now expelling superfluities and making
the most useful of countless substances its own;

    then, this form once examined,
to scrutinize another form, more beautiful—
one that possesses feeling
(and, what is more, equipped with powers
of apprehending through imagination):
grounds for legitimate complaint—
if not indeed for claiming insult—
on the part of the brightest star
that sparkles, yet lacks all feeling,
however magnificent its brilliant light—
for the lowest, tiniest creature
surpasses even the loftiest of stars,
arousing envy;
and making of this bodily way of knowing
a foundation, however meager,
to move on to the wondrous
composite, triplicate
(set up on three concordant lines)
mysterious compendium
of all the lower forms:
the hinge that makes the link
between the purest nature,
that which occupies the highest throne,
and the least noble of the creatures,
the most abject,
equipped not only with the five
faculties of sense,
but ennobled also by the inner ones,
the three that rule the rest;
for not for nothing was he fitted out
by the powerful and knowing hand
to be supreme over all the others:

hierarchy: This enumeration of the operations characteristic of vegetal
matter appears to derive from Galen.

the goal of all his works, the circle
clasping heaven and earth in one,
utmost perfection of creation,
utmost delight of its Eternal Author,
with whom well pleased, well satisfied,
His immense magnificence took His rest;
creature of portentous fashioning
who may stretch proud arms to heaven
yet suffers sealing of his mouth with dust;
whose mysterious image might be found
in the sacred vision seen in Patmos
by the evangelic eagle, that strange vision
which trod the stars and soil with equal step;
or else in that looming statue
with sumptuous lofty brow
made of the most prized metal,
who took his stance on flimsy feet
made of the material least regarded,
and subject to collapse at the slightest shudder.

   In short, I speak of man, the greatest wonder
the human mind can ponder,
complete compendium
resembling angel, plant, and beast alike;
whose haughty lowliness
partook of every nature. Why?
Perhaps that, being more fortunate
than any, he might be lifted high
by a grace of loving union.
Oh, grace repeated often,
yet never recognized sufficiently,
overlooked, so one might think,
so unappreciated is it,
so unacknowledged it remains.

   These then were the stages over which
I sometimes wished to range; yet other times
I changed my mind, considering much too daring
for one to try to take in everything,

evangelic eagle: The eagle is the iconographic emblem of Saint John the
Evangelist. Though the congruence is not perfect, the "strange vision"
appears to be that of Apocalypse 10:1–2: "And I saw another mighty angel
come down from heaven . . . and he set his right foot upon the sea and his
left foot upon the earth."
looming statue: The "great statue" of Nebuchadnezzar's dream in Daniel
2:32–35.

who failed to understand the very smallest,
the easiest part
of those effects of nature
that lie so close at hand;
who, seeing the laughing brook, could never grasp
the hidden means whereby
she steers her crystal course,
pausing at times for roundabout meanders,
conducting her bright search
through Pluto's grim recesses
and through the frightful caverns
of the deep and terrifying chasm,
through lovely countryside,
the pleasant Elysian Fields,
once bridal chamber for his triform wife
(useful inquisitiveness, however trivial,
that brought the goddess of the flaxen hair
sure word of her fair missing daughter
when, searching high and low through woods and hills,
investigating every field and grove,
she sought her very life and all the while
was losing her life from grief);
who, seeing a tiny flower, could not tell
why with an ivory pattern
its fragile beauty is girt about;
why a mixture of colors—
scarlet blending into white of dawn—
tints its fragrant costume,
why its scent is of amber,
why it unravels in the breeze
a wrapping so delicately beautiful
(renewed in its every newborn child)
and makes a bright show of flounces
fluted with golden streaks,
which, once the bud's white seal is broken,
boastfully display the tincture

Pluto's grim recesses: There is an implicit reference to Arethusa, a nymph
of Artemis, who, pursued by the river Alpheus, was changed into a stream
which went underground and under the sea to the island of Ortygia in the
harbor of Syracuse, where she surfaced as a spring (Ovid, *Metamorphoses*
5.504–508, 572–641).

bridal chamber: The reference is to Pluto's abduction of Persephone to be
his consort in the underworld. Her three forms: as maiden, the daughter
of Demeter and Zeus; then, for half of the year, queen of the underworld;
for the other half, goddess of agriculture.

goddess of the flaxen hair: Demeter (Ceres), goddess of grains and harvests.

born of the Cyprian goddess' sweet wound,
unless, indeed, the whiteness of the daybreak
or the redness of the dawn
has overwhelmed it, fusing
red snowflake with snow-whitened rose,
such opalescence soon eliciting
acclaim sought from the meadow;
perhaps a tutor in the vanity—
unless indeed an impious demonstration
of the feminine duplicity which makes
the deadliest poison twice as deadly
in the conspicuous overlay
of the woman who feigns a glowing countenance.

   Now if, from a single object—
my timid thought kept saying—
true knowledge shies away,
and reason ingloriously turns aside;
if on a species set apart
as independent of all others—
thought of as unrelated—
understanding turns her back;
if reason, overwhelmed, recoils
before so difficult a challenge,
refusing to take action resolutely,
doubting in her cowardice
that she can grasp even this single object,
how can she hope to function in the face
of so astounding and immense a system?
Its burden, terrible, unendurable—
were it not upheld at its very center—
would make the shoulders even of Atlas sag,
outdo the strength of Hercules,
and they, who proved sufficient counterweight
to the sphere of heaven,
would judge its fabric far less burdensome,
its framework less oppressive,
than the task of investigating Nature.

goddess' sweet wound: The red rose was said to have arisen from the
blood of Venus when a thorn pricked her foot as she rushed to the aid of
Adonis, wounded by a wild boar.

were it not upheld: The omniscience and omnipotence of God sustain the
universe.

Atlas: A Titan, King of Mauretania, Atlas was turned by Perseus into the
mountain that upholds the sky.

Hercules: Hercules for a time relieved Atlas of the burden of the heavens.

Bolder at other times,
my mind denounced as height of cowardice
yielding the laurels without one attempt
to meet the challenge of the lists.
Then it would seize upon the brave example
set by that famous youth, high-minded
charioteer of the chariot of flame;
then courage would be fired
by his grand and bold, if hapless, impulse,
in which the spirit finds
not, like timidity, a chastening lesson
but a pathway summoning it to dare;
once treading this, no punishment can deter
the spirit bent upon a fresh attempt
(I mean a thrust of new ambition).
Neither the nether pantheon—
cerulean tomb of his unhappy ashes—
nor the vengeful lightning bolt,
for all their warnings, ever will convince
the soaring spirit once resolved,
in lofty disregard of living,
to pluck from ruin an everlasting fame.
Rather, that youth is the very type, the model:
a most pernicious instance
(causing wings to sprout for further flights)
of that ambitious mettle,
which, finding in terror itself a spur
to prick up courage,
pieces together the name of glory
from letters spelling endless havoc.
Either the punishment should not be known
so that the crime would never become contagious,
a politic silence covering up instead,
with a statesman's circumspection,
all record of the proceedings;
or let a show of ignorance prevail,
or the insolent excess
meet its just deserts by secret sentence
without the noxious example
ever reaching public notice,
for broadcasting makes the wickedness
of the greatest crime all the greater
till it threatens a widespread epidemic,
while, left in unknown isolation,
repetition is far less likely
than if broadcast to all as a would-be lesson.

But as judgment foundered in confusion
amid the reefs and skirted whirlpools
of no return, no matter which direction
it sought to follow, heat, no longer finding
the sustenance it needed,
since its tempered flame (however temperate,
a flame still, which, actively engaging
in its function, uses up materials
or else inflames them),
unable to act otherwise
had gradually
transformed its nutriment,
converting foreign matter into own.
The noisy boiling that resulted
from uniting the burning humor with the moist
in that most wonderful
and natural of vessels now had ceased,
with nothing left to feed on. In consequence
the humid and sleep-inducing vapors
arising from it,
were affecting the seat of reason
(from which they carried to the limbs
a pleasant drowsiness);
and consumed by the gentle warming
resulting from the heat,
were loosening the chains of sleep.
The overtired limbs,
worn out by rest,
reacting to the lack of sustenance,
and neither wide-awake nor fast asleep,
were showing signs of wishing
to be stirring once again
by the languid, drawn-out stretching
the torpid sinews were engaging in.
Even without their owner's full assent,
the limbs were turning tired bones
from side to side;
the senses were beginning to resume
their functioning, despite mild interference
caused by the natural toxin,

sleep-inducing vapors: Sleep, according to Saint Thomas, following
Aristotle, occurs when vapors from digestion rise to the brain ("the seat of
reason") and numb the senses. With the ending of the digestive process,
one awakens.

natural toxin: The last lingering vapors arising from the digestive process.

half-opening the eyes;
and from the brain, now cleared,
phantasms had taken leave
and, being formed of lightest vapor,
converted easily to smoke or wind,
now let their shapes be dissipated.
Just so, the magic lantern
casts on white of wall
simulations of different painted figures,
made possible by shadow no less than light.
Maintaining amid shimmering reflections
the distances required
by the science of perspective
and confirmed in its true measurements
by a number of experiments,
the fleeting shadow
that fades into the brilliance of the light
simulates a body's form,
one possessing all dimensions, though it merits
no consideration even as surface.

 Meanwhile the father of flaming light
saw that the appointed hour was arriving
when he must climb the East.
He took his leave of our antipodes
with light departing down the West,
for through the flickers of his fading light
the same point serves to mark his going down
as ushers in the brightening of our East.
But not till Venus as the morning star,
beautiful and serene,
had pierced the first faint dawnlight,
and the fair wife of old Tithonus—
amazon arrayed in countless lights
(her armor against the night),
beautiful though bold,
valiant although tearful—
had let her lovely brow be seen
crowned with the lights of morning,

magic lantern: A recent invention whose functioning was explained and
illustrated in the *Ars Magna Lucis et Umbrae* (The Great Art of Light and
Shade) of Athanasius Kircher (Amsterdam, 1667), a work frequented by
Sor Juana.

wife of old Tithonus: Eos or Aurora, the Dawn, whose youth is renewed
every day, while her husband Tithonus, originally a mortal, grows older
and older.

a tender prelude though a spirited one,
to the fiery planet,
who was busy marshaling his troops
of glimmering novices—
reserving glowing veterans, more robust,
to fill the rearguard—
against the tyrannical usurper
of the empire of daylight,
who wore a laurel girdle with countless shadows
and with her dreadful nighttime scepter
ruled over shadows
of whom she stood in awe herself.
But scarcely had the lovely harbinger
and standard-bearer of the Sun, unfurled
her luminous pennant in the East,
as all the bugles of the birds,
soft yet bellicose, sounded the call to arms
(resonant trumpeters and skilled,
though uninstructed)
when—cowardly as tyrants always are,
and beset by timorous misgivings—
although trying to put up a valiant front
with her forces, although flaunting
her funereal cloak as shield,
that took short wounds
from the stabbing brightness
(even though her uneasy bravery
was merely a crude cover for her fear
since she knew how weak was her resistance)—
as if relying more on flight
than belligerence for her salvation,
Night was blowing her raucous horn
to gather her swarthy squadrons in
and make an orderly retreat—
when a burst of bouncing light
assaulted her from closer by
as it bathed the topmost tip
of the loftiest of turrets in the world.

    The Sun appeared, the circle now complete
which he carves in gold against the sapphire blue.
From his luminous circumference there sprang
a thousand times a thousand golden specks,
a thousand streams of gold—
lines, I mean, of brilliant light
ruled on heaven's cerulean page,

drawn up for orderly attack
upon the dismal despot of his realm
who, in hasty headlong flight,
stumbling over her native terrors,
was treading on her very shadow
as she sought to reach the West
with the routed, broken ranks
of her shadow army, harassed by light
in close pursuit upon her heels.
At last her fleeing footsteps reached the point
where the West came into view
and, though rushing, regaining her composure,
plucking courage up from her very ruin,
she resolved, rebelling once again,
to see herself made sovereign
in that half of the globe
left unprotected by the sun
when the beauty of his golden locks
brought luster to our hemisphere.
Dealing judiciously with his light,
by orderly distribution he dispensed
to all things visible their colors,
restoring to every outer sense
full functioning,
flooding with light whatever had been opaque
throughout the world, and summoning me awake.

Self-Justification
In Reply to an Admonishment

Admonishment:
The Letter of Sor Philothea de la Cruz

Madam:

I have seen the letter in which you take issue with the Reverend Father Antonio de Vieira regarding the signs of Christ's love treated by him in his Maundy Thursday sermon.[1] So subtle is his treatment that the most erudite persons have opined that, like a second Apocalyptic Eagle, his singular talent outsoared itself as it followed the scheme set forth earlier by the Most Illustrious César Meneses, a Portuguese talent of the first rank.[2] In my opinion, however, anyone following your exposition must admit that your quill was cut finer than either of theirs and that they might well have rejoiced at finding themselves confuted by a woman who does honor to her sex.

I at least have admired the keenness of your concepts, the skill of your proofs, and the vigorous clarity that lends conviction to the subject, a quality inseparably linked with wisdom. This is why the first word uttered by Divine Wisdom was light, *for without illumination there can be no word of wisdom. Even Christ's words, cloaked in parables when He spoke of the deepest mysteries, were not held to be marvelous in the world. Only when He spoke out clearly did He win acclaim for knowing everything. This is one of the many special favors you owe to God, for clarity is not acquired by toil and diligence; it is a gift infused with the soul.*

So that you may read yourself in clearer lettering in that document, I have had it printed; likewise, so that you may acknowledge

1. Antonio de Vieira (1608–1697) was a celebrated Portuguese Jesuit whose sermons had been translated into Spanish several times. The sermon in question had been preached in Lisbon at some time between 1642 and 1652.

2. Diogo César Meneses (1604–1661), another Portuguese preacher, was Vieira's mentor.

the treasures God has placed in your soul and, being made thus
more aware, may be more grateful, for gratitude and awareness
are always born twins. And if, as you say in your letter, the more
one has received from God, the more one is obligated to reciprocate,
I fear you may find yourself at a loss, for few of God's creatures
owe His Majesty greater natural talents, or incur such a debt of
gratitude to Him for them. So if heretofore you have made good
use of them (and I must think this the case with one who professes
religion as you do), henceforth you may make still better use.

My judgment is not so stern a censor as to disapprove of verse,
an endowment for which you have found yourself so highly
acclaimed; after all, Saint Teresa, Saint Gregory of Nazianzus,
and other saints have sanctified this skill by their example.[3] But I
could wish that, as you imitate them in meter, you might do so as
well in choice of subject.

I do not subscribe to the commonplace view of those who condemn the practice of letters in women, since so many have applied
themselves to literary study, not failing to win praise from Saint
Jerome. True, Saint Paul says women should not teach, but he does
not order women not to study so as to grow wiser. He wished only
to preclude any risk of presumptuousness in our sex, inclined as it
is to vanity.[4] Divine Wisdom took one letter away from Sarai and
added one to the name of Abram, not because man is meant to be
more lettered than woman, as many falsely claim, but because the i
appended to the name of Sara connoted being swollen up and dom-
ineering [Gen. 17:5, 15]. Sarai is interpreted as My lady, and it
was unfitting that one should be the lady of Abraham's house whose
position was a subordinate one.

Letters that breed arrogance God does not want in women. But
the Apostle does not reject them so long as they do not remove
women from a position of obedience. No one could say that study
and learning have caused you to exceed your subordinate status.
Indeed, they have served to perfect in you the finer forms of obedience. For if other nuns sacrifice their wills for the sake of obedience, you hold the mind captive, which is the most arduous and the
most welcome sacrifice one can offer on the altars of Religion.

3. Saint Teresa (1515–1582), the Spanish Carmelite mystic canonized in
1622, is known principally for her prose writings. She is the author of a
small body of devotional verse. Saint Gregory of Nazianzus (ca. 329 – ca.
389), one of the four great fathers of the Eastern Church, wrote epigrams
and elegies in his later years as a form of recreation.

4. Saint Jerome (ca. 340–420), founder of the Hieronymite order to
which Sor Juana belonged, was a prolific writer on religious subjects. Some
of his letters deal with the education of women. Saint Paul wrote: "But I
suffer not a woman to teach [nor to use authority over the man but to be
in silence]" (1 Tim. 2:12).

As this judgment shows, I do not mean you to modify your natural predisposition by giving up books; I do mean that you should improve it by sometimes reading the book of Jesus Christ. None of the Evangelists called the genealogy of Christ a book, except Saint Matthew [Matt. 1:1].This was because at his conversion our Lord's wish was not so much to change his natural bent, as to improve upon it, so that, if earlier as a publican his occupation was to keep books recording his transactions and interest, as an apostle he might better his nature, transforming the books of his ruin into the book of Jesus Christ. You have spent much time studying philosophers and poets. Surely it is only right for you now to better your occupation and upgrade your books.

Was there ever a nation more learned than Egypt? In it the world's first letters had their beginning and there were admirable hieroglyphics. In order to underscore Joseph's wisdom, Holy Scripture calls him a past master of Egyptian learning.[5] Notwithstanding this, the Holy Ghost openly calls the people of Egypt barbarians, because all their learning served at most for probing into the courses of the stars and the heavens; it was not applied to curbing the unruliness of the passions. Their entire learning had as its goal perfecting men for political life, not lighting their way to the eternal. And learning which does not enlighten men for their salvation is deemed folly by God, who knows everything.

This was how Justus Lipsius (that marvel of erudition) felt when close to death, a time, it would seem, when the mind is at its most lucid.[6] As his friends consoled him with the thought of the many scholarly books he had written, he said, pointing to a crucifix: Scholarship not devoted to Christ Crucified is folly and sheer vanity.

I do not on this account censure the reading of these authors, but I pass on to you some advice of Gerson's:[7] Lend yourself to these studies; do not sell yourself to them, nor yet allow yourself to be carried away by them. The humanities are slaves and as such they have their usefulness for sacred studies. But they must be rejected when they dislodge Divine Wisdom from possession of the human mind and, though destined to be menials, take over as masters. They are to be recommended when the curiosity that has motivated them, which is a vice, gives way to studiousness, a virtue.

5. This reference appears to be not to Joseph but to Moses, whom Stephen calls "instructed in all the wisdom of the Egyptians" (Acts 7:22).

6. Belgian classical scholar, teacher and editor (1547–1606) associated with Christian neo-stoicism and author of a famous edition of Seneca.

7. This was the name given to Jean Charlier (1363–1429), theologian and chancellor of the University of Paris to whom the *Imitation of Christ* of Thomas à Kempis was long attributed.

Saint Jerome was scourged by angels for reading Cicero and, like a wretch, not a free man, preferring the seductiveness of his eloquence to the solidity of Holy Scripture.[8] But this Holy Sage of the Church made good use of the learning and secular eloquence which he acquired from such authors.

You have devoted no little time to these intriguing subjects. Move on now, like the great Boethius, to edifying ones; complement the subtleties of natural philosophy with the usefulness of the moral kind.[9]

It is a pity that so great a mind should stoop to lowly earthbound knowledge and not desire to probe into what transpires in heaven. But since it does lower itself to ground level, may it not descend further still and ponder what goes on in hell! And, if sometimes it enjoys sweet and tender conceits, let it apply its powers of understanding to Calvary, where, seeing how considerate the Redeemer was and how ungrateful the redeemed, it will have ample scope for reflecting on the excesses of infinite love and, not without tears, will find words of atonement for the highest degree of ingratitude. Or, at other times, let the rich galleon of your mind sail usefully forth upon the high seas of the perfections of God. I have no doubt that it would happen with you as with Apelles, when painting the portrait of Campaspe, that for every line he applied to the canvas with his brush, Cupid's arrow made a wound in his heart, so that at one and the same time the portrait was finished to perfection and the painter's heart mortally wounded with love for the sitter.[10]

I am wholly convinced that if, with your keen mental powers, you formed and depicted an idea of divine perfections (insofar as the shadows of faith allow), you would at the same time find your soul bathed in light and your will afire and sweetly wounded by love of its God, so that this Lord who, in the order of Nature, has so copiously showered you with outright blessings, may not find Himself obliged to grant you only negative ones in the supernatural order. For, though your clever mind is forever calling them exquisite favors, I consider them punishments. That only is a blessing which God bestows on the human heart when He predisposes it by means of His grace to reciprocate with gratitude and to prepare itself, having received one acknowledged blessing, to receive from God's generosity, free of restraints, other greater ones.

8. This pious tale is found in *The Golden Legend* of Jacobus de Voragine.

9. Fernández de Santa Cruz evidently subscribes to the notion, now discredited, that Boethius (480–524), last of the Roman philosophers and author of the *Consolation of Philosophy*, was in fact a Christian.

10. Apelles was the favorite painter of Alexander the Great, whose mistress Campaspe he was commissioned to paint and subsequently allowed to marry.

This is desired for you by one who, since kissing your hand many years ago, has remained enamored of your soul, time or distance being powerless to cool this love, for spiritual love is not subject to the vicissitudes of change, nor does it know any except in the direction of increase. May His Divine Majesty hear my entreaties and make you most saintly and preserve you for me in all good fortune.

From this Convent of the Most Holy Trinity in Puebla de los Angeles, November 25, 1690,

Your devoted servant kisses your hands.

Philothea de la Cruz

The *Reply to Sor Philothea*

My most illustrious Lady:

It is no will of mine, but poor health and a legitimate timidity that have held up my reply these many days. It can hardly be a surprise that at the outset my bungling pen encountered two obstacles. The first (and for me the most obdurate) has been not knowing how to reply to your most learned, prudent, pious, and loving letter. When I recall how that Angel of the Schools, Saint Thomas, on being questioned about his silence toward Albertus Magnus, his mentor, replied that he was keeping silent because there was nothing he could say worthy of Albertus, how much more reason must there be for me to keep silent—not, like the Saint, out of humility, but because in reality I know nothing worthy of you. The second obstacle was finding an adequate way to thank you for a favor as undeserved as it was unexpected—committing my poor scribblings to print—a favor so huge as to surpass the wildest dreams or most ambitious hope, one that could never have entered my mind, as a creature of reason; one of such magnitude, in a word, that not only does it defy confinement within the bounds of language; it exceeds the very capacity for gratitude, in both scale and surprise. In Quintilian's words: *Minorem spei, maiorem benefacti gloriam pereunt.*[11] It is one of those that leave the beneficiary speechless.

When the felicitously barren (only to become miraculously fruitful) mother of the Baptist saw in her

11. Apparently Sor Juana is recalling *Institutio Oratoria* 3.7.13: *quo minores opes fuerunt, maiorem benefactis gloriam parit* ("The glory of good deeds may be enhanced by the smallness of their resources"). Her recollection is evidently faulty, for the Latin is defective. (English cited from the Loeb edition [Cambridge, Mass.: Harvard University Press; London: Heinemann, 1969]).

two women meeting ✓

house a visitor as extraordinary as the Mother of the Word,
her mind went blank and words failed her [Luke 1:43].
Whence she burst forth with questions and disbelief rather
than with thanksgiving: *Et unde hoc mihi?* [And whence is
this to me?] The same happened to Saul on seeing himself
selected and then anointed King of Israel: *Numquid non
filius Jemini ego sum de minima tribu Israel, et cognatio mea
novissima inter omnes de tribu Beniamin? Quare igitur locutus es
mihi sermonem istum?* ["Am I not a son of Jemini of the least
tribe of Israel . . . Why then hast thou spoken this word to
me?" (1 Kings [1 Sam.] 9:21)]. So shall I say: Whence,
revered Lady, whence such partiality to me? Am I,
perchance, anything but a poor nun, the least of all the
world's creatures, and the most unworthy of engaging your
attention? So, *quare locutus es mihi sermonem istum? Et unde
hoc mihi?*

Neither have I any reply to make to the first objection,
except that I am completely unworthy of your notice, nor
to the second, except wonderment—this rather than
gratitude, incapable as I am of thanking you for the tiniest
portion of what I owe you. It is no affectation of modesty
on my part, Madam, but the simple truth of my entire soul,
to say that when the letter that you chose to call
Athenagoric[12] came into my hands, I burst into tears of
embarrassment, something I do not very easily do. It
seemed to me that your attention was simply a reproof
from God for my poor reciprocation of His favors, and
that, just as He corrects others through punishment, He
wants to curb me by signs of benevolence. A special favor,
this, for which I recognize my indebtedness to Him, as I do
for many other favors I owe to His immense kindness; but
also a special way of making me ashamed and embarrassed,
for it is a most exquisite type of punishment to make me,
knowing myself as I do, be my own judge, deliver my own
sentence, and condemn my own ingratitude. And thus,
when I reflect on all this, here by myself, I am wont to say:
Blessed art Thou, Lord, who wert not only unwilling to
place my judgment in the hands of others, or even in my
own, but reserved it for Thine and delivered me from
myself and from the sentence I would have passed on
myself—which, in the light of my self-knowledge, could

12. Worthy of Athena, goddess of wisdom. The reference is to the *Carta
atenagórica*, Sor Juana's critique of Vieira's Maundy Thursday sermon,
which takes as its theme Christ's enjoining the disciples "as I have loved
you, that you also love one another" (John 13:34).

only have been one of damnation—reserving it for Thy mercy to pass sentence, because Thou lovest me more than I can ever love myself.

Forgive, my Lady, the digression wrung from me by the force of truth; and, to tell the whole truth, as a way of eluding the difficulty of answering; indeed I had almost made up my mind to let silence be my answer. Yet, since silence is something negative, although it explains a great deal by its insistence on not explaining, some brief label is needed to enable one to understand what it is intended to mean. Otherwise, silence will say nothing, since its function is precisely that: to say nothing. The vessel of election[13] was transported to the third Heaven and, having seen the arcane secrets of God, he says: *Audivit arcana Dei, quae non licet homini loqui* ["He heard secret words, which it is not granted to man to utter" (2 Cor. 12:4)]. He does not tell what he saw; he says that he cannot tell it. Thus, of those things that cannot be spoken, it must at least be said that they cannot be, to make clear that keeping silent does not mean having nothing to say, but rather that words cannot encompass all there is to say. Saint John says [21:25] that were he to write down all the miracles worked by our Redeemer, there would be insufficient room in the whole world for the resultant books. About this passage Vieira says that the Evangelist spoke more in this one sentence than in everything else he wrote. And this is very well said (and does the Lusitanian Phoenix ever fail to say things well, even when it would be as well not to say them?), because with these words Saint John says all that he had left unsaid, and expresses whatever he had left unexpressed. Thus, I, my Lady, will answer only that I do not know what to answer; my only thanks will be to say that I am incapable of thanking you; and I will say, as a brief indication of what I leave to silence, that only with the assurance of your favor and on the strength of your honoring me, can I dare to talk with Your Greatness. If I speak nonsense, forgive me, since it is a warrant of well-being. I will thereby provide Your Benevolence with more grounds, and you will give me further cause, for gratitude.

Moses, as a stammerer, did not consider himself worthy of talking to Pharaoh. Later, the knowledge that he was favored by God instilled such powers in him that he not only spoke to God Himself but dared to ask of Him a thing impossible: *Ostende mihi faciem tuam* ["And he said, shew me

13. Paul, so called by the Lord (Acts 9:15).

like moses, she is emboldened by the favors shown her

Thy glory ... And again He said, Thou canst not see my
face: for man shall not see me and live" (Exod. 33:18, 20)].
So it is with me, dear Madam: when I reflect upon the
extent of your favors to me, I no longer consider
insuperable those obstacles I mentioned at the outset. One
who had the Letter printed so completely without my
knowledge, gave it a title, underwrote the expense, and
honored it so greatly (though it was so totally unworthy
both in itself and in its author)—what will she not do, what
not forgive, what leave undone, what unpardoned?
Therefore, on the assumption that I am speaking under
the safe conduct of your favor and with the assurance of
your good will, and that, like another Ahasuerus, you have
given me the tip of the golden sceptre of your affection to
kiss as a sign that you benevolently grant me permission to
speak and declare my thoughts in your venerable presence,
I shall say that I receive in my soul your most holy
admonition to apply my study to the Sacred Books.[14]
Though this comes in the guise of counsel, it will for me be
equivalent to a precept, since I take no little comfort in the
thought that my obedience seems to have anticipated your
pastoral suggestion, as if at your direction, as may be
inferred from the subject and the proofs of the Letter
itself. I well recognize that your very sage advice does not
apply to *it*, but to all those writings of mine which you will
have seen on human subjects. And thus, everything I have
said is simply to make amends through the Letter, for the
failure to apply myself which you will have presumed (quite
correctly) from other writings of mine.

her letter was on the subject of the scripture / (for Philotea must be referring to other subjects)

Coming down to particulars, I confess to you, with the
ingenuousness owed to you and the truth and clarity
natural and habitual with me, that my not having written
much on sacred subjects is not from disinclination or lack
of application, but from an excess of the awe and reverence
due those Sacred Letters, for the understanding of which I
acknowledge myself so ill-equipped and which I am so
unworthy to treat. There ever resounds in my ears, with no
little dread, our Lord's threat and interdiction to sinners
like me: *Quare tu enarras iustitias meas, et assumis testamentum
meum per os tuum?* ["Why dost thou declare my justices, and
take my covenant in thy mouth?" (Ps. 49:16)]. This
question and the awareness that even to learned men the

14. "And when he saw Esther the queen standing, she pleased his eyes,
and he held out toward her the golden sceptre, which he held in his hand;
and she drew near, and kissed the top of his sceptre" (Esth. 5:2).

reading of the Canticle of Canticles [Song of Songs] was forbidden until they were over thirty, and that of Genesis as well, the latter on account of its obscurity, the former lest the appeal of those epithalamiums give imprudent youth cause to apply their sense to carnal affections. My great father Saint Jerome confirms this, requiring that the former be the last thing studied, for the same reason: *At ultimum sine periculo discat Canticum Canticorum, ne si in exordio legerit, sub carnalibus verbis spiritualium Nuptiarum Epithalamium non intelligens, vulneretur* ["But last of all, let her, without risk, study the Canticle of Canticles; lest she suffer harm by reading it at the outset without grasping the epithalamium of spiritual marriage beneath the carnal words" (*Epistle to Laeta*)]. And Seneca says: *Teneris in annis haut clara est fides* [Faith is not clearly defined in youth (*On public honors*)]. Then how should I dare to take this into my unworthy hands, when my sex, age, and especially my way of life all oppose it? And so I confess that many times this fear has taken the pen from my hand and caused the subject to sink back into the very mind from which it sought to emerge.

I encountered no such problem in secular subjects, since heresy against art is punished, not by the Holy Office, but by the laughter of the intelligent and the censure of the critical. The censure, *iusta vel iniusta, timenda non est* [whether deserved or not, is not to be feared], for it does not interfere with communion and attending mass, whence it concerns me little or not at all. For, in the opinion of the very people who slander me for writing, I am under no obligation to be learned nor do I possess the capacity never to err. Therefore my failure involves neither fault nor discredit: no fault since there is no chance of my not erring and *ad impossibilia nemo tenetur* [no one is obliged to attempt the impossible]. And in truth I have never written except when pressured and forced to and then only to please others and even then not only without enjoyment but with actual repugnance because I have never thought of myself as possessing the intelligence and educational background required of a writer. Hence my usual reply to those who urge me on, especially where sacred matters are involved: what aptitude have I, what preparation, what subjects, what familiarity do I possess for such a task, beyond a handful of superficial sophistries? Let such things be left to those who understand them; I want no trouble with the Holy Office. I am ignorant and I shudder to think that I might utter some disreputable proposition or distort the proper understanding of some passage or other. My purpose in studying is not to write, much less to teach (this would be overbearing pride in my case), but simply to see whether studying makes me less ignorant. This is my reply and these are my feelings.

I have never written of my own accord, but only when pressured by others. I could truthfully say to them: *Vos me coegistis* ["You have compelled me" (2 Cor. 12:11)]. What is true and I will not deny (first because it is public knowledge and then—even if this counts against me—because God, in His goodness, has favored me with a great love of the truth) is that from my first glimmers of reason, my inclination to letters was of such power and vehemence, that neither the reprimands of others—and I have received many—nor my own considerations—and there have been not a few of these—have succeeded in making me abandon this natural impulse which God has implanted in me—only His Majesty knows why and wherefore and His Majesty also knows that I have prayed to Him to extinguish the light of my mind, only leaving sufficient to keep His Law, since any more is overmuch, so some say, in a woman, and there are even those who say it is harmful. His Majesty also knows that, not succeeding in this, I have tried to inter my name along with my mind and sacrifice it to Him alone who gave it to me; and that this was precisely my motivation in taking the veil, even though the exercises and shared life which a community entails were repellent to the independence and tranquillity which my inclination to study needed. And once in the community, the Lord God knows and, in the world, he knows who alone had the right to know it, how hard I tried to conceal my name, and that he did not allow this, saying that it was temptation, which no doubt it was.[15] If I could repay you some part of what I owe you, my Lady, I think I would be paying you simply by relating this, for it has never escaped my lips before, except when addressed to one who had the right to know it. But I want you to know that, in throwing wide open to you the gates of my heart, exposing to your gaze its most tightly guarded secrets, my justification for the liberty I am taking is the great debt I owe to your venerable person and overly generous favors.

To go on with the account of this strong bent of mine, about which I want you to be fully informed, let me say that when I was not yet three, my mother sent a sister of

15. A probable allusion to her confessor, Antonio Núñez de Miranda, S.J.

mine, older than I, to learn to read in one of those establishments called Amigas [girls' elementary schools], at which point affection and mischievousness on my part led me to follow her. Seeing that she was being given lessons, I became so inflamed with the desire to learn to read, that I tricked the mistress—or so I thought—by telling her that my mother had directed her to give me lessons. This was not believable and she did not believe me, but falling in with my little trick, she did give me lessons. I continued attending and she went on teaching me, no longer as a joke, since the event opened her eyes. I learned to read in so short a time that I already knew how when my mother found out, for the mistress kept it from her in order to give her a pleasant surprise and receive her recompense all at one time. I kept still, since I thought I would be whipped for having acted on my own initiative. The person who taught me is still alive (may God preserve her) and can attest to this.

I remember that at this period, though I loved to eat, as children do at that age, I refrained from eating cheese, because someone had told me it made you stupid, and my urge to learn was stronger than my wish to eat, powerful as this is in children. Afterward, when I was six or seven and already knew how to read and write, along with all the sewing skills and needlework that women learn, I discovered that in the City of Mexico there was a university with schools where the different branches of learning could be studied, and as soon as I learned this I began to deluge my mother with urgent and insistent pleas to change my manner of dress and send me to stay with relatives in the City of Mexico so that I might study and take courses at the university. She refused, and rightly so; nevertheless, I found a way to read many different books my grandfather owned, notwithstanding the punishments and reproofs this entailed, so that when I went to the City of Mexico people were astonished, not so much at my intelligence as at the memory and store of knowledge I had at an age at which it would seem I had scarcely had time to learn to speak.

I began to study Latin, in which I do not believe I had twenty lessons in all, and I was so intensely studious that despite the natural concern of women—especially in the flower of their youth—with dressing their hair, I used to cut four or five fingers' width from mine, keeping track of how far it had formerly reached, and making it my rule that if by the time it grew back to that point, I did not know such-and-such a thing which I had set out to learn as

cutting hair to measure learning time

it grew, I would cut it again as a penalty for my dullness. Thus it would happen that it would grow back and I still would not know what I had set myself to learn, because my hair grew rapidly, whereas I was a slow learner, and I did indeed cut it as a punishment for my slowness, for I did not consider it right that a head so bare of knowledge should be dressed with hair, knowledge being the more desirable ornament. I became a nun because, although I knew that that way of life involved much that was repellent to my nature—I refer to its incidental, not its central aspects—nevertheless, given my total disinclination to marriage, it was the least unreasonable and most becoming choice I could make to assure my ardently desired salvation. To which first consideration, as most important, all the other small frivolities of my nature yielded and gave way, such as my wish to live alone, to have no fixed occupation which might curtail my freedom to study, nor the noise of a community to interfere with the tranquil stillness of my books. This made me hesitate a little before making up my mind, until, enlightened by learned persons that hesitation was temptation, I overcame it by the grace of God and entered upon the life I now pursue so unworthily. I thought I was escaping from myself, but, alas for me, I had brought myself along. In this propensity I brought my greatest enemy, given me by Heaven whether as a boon or a punishment I cannot decide, for, far from dying out or being hindered by all the exercises religion entails, it exploded like gunpowder. *Privatio est causa appetitus* [Privation arouses the appetite] had its confirmation in me.

I went back (I misspeak: I had never stopped); I went on with the studious pursuit (in which I found relaxation during all the free time remaining from my obligations) of reading and more reading, study and more study, with no other teacher than books themselves. One can readily imagine how hard it is to study from those lifeless letters, lacking a teacher's live voice and explanations. Still I happily put up with all those drawbacks, for the sheer love of learning. Oh, if it had only been for the love of God, which would have been the sound way, what merit would have been mine! I *will* say that I tried to uplift my study as much as I could and direct it to serving Him, since the goal I aspired to was the study of theology, it seeming to me a mean sort of ineptitude for a Catholic not to know all that can be found out in this life through natural means concerning divine mysteries. I also felt that being a nun and not a lay person, I should, because of my ecclesiastical status, make a profession of letters—and furthermore that, as a daughter of Saint Jerome and Saint Paula, it would be a great disservice for the daughter of such learned parents to be a fool.[16] This is what I took upon myself, and it seemed right to do so, unless of course—and this is probably the case—it was simply a way of flattering and applauding my own natural tendency, proposing its own pleasure to it as an obligation.

In this way I went on, continually directing the course of my study, as I have said, toward the eminence of sacred theology. To reach this goal, I considered it necessary to ascend the steps of human arts and sciences, for how can one who has not mastered the style of the ancillary branches of learning hope to understand that of the queen of them all? How, lacking logic, was I to understand the general and specific methodologies of which Holy Scripture is composed? How, without rhetoric, could I understand its figures, tropes, and locutions? How, without physics, all the natural questions concerning the nature of sacrificial animals, which symbolize so many things already explicated, and so many others? How, whether Saul's being cured by the sound of David's harp [1 Kings (1 Sam.) 16:23] came about by virtue of the natural power of music, or through supernatural powers which God was pleased to bestow on David? How, lacking arithmetic, could one understand such mysterious computations of years, days, months, hours, weeks, as those of Daniel and others, for the intelligence of which one needs to know the natures, concordances, and properties of numbers? How, without geometry, could one measure the sacred ark of the covenant and the holy city of Jerusalem, whose mysterious measurements form a cube in all its dimensions, and the marvelous proportional distribution of all its parts? How, without a knowledge of architecture, is one to understand Solomon's great temple, of which God Himself was the artificer who provided the arrangement and layout, the wise king being only the overseer who carried it out? In it, no column's base was without its mystery, no column without its symbolic sense, no cornice without allusiveness, no architrave without meaning, and so on with all its parts, not even the most

value of other branches of knowledge

16. Paula (d. 414) was a Roman matron who, with her two daughters, Blesilla and Eustochium, followed Jerome to Bethlehem, where she built and presided over the first nunneries of the Hieronymite order. She was a patron saint of Sor Juana's convent.

miniscule fillet serving solely as support or complement to the design of the whole, but rather itself symbolizing greater things. How will one understand the historical books without a full knowledge of the principles and divisions of which history consists? Those recapitulations in the narrative which postpone what actually occurred first? How will one understand the legal books without a complete acquaintance with both codes of law? How, without a great deal of erudition, all the matters of secular history mentioned in Holy Writ, all the customs of the Gentiles, the rites, the ways of speaking? How, without many rules and much reading of the Church Fathers, will one be able to understand the prophets' obscure forms of expression? And how, unless one is thoroughly versed in music, will one understand those musical proportions, with all their fine points, found in so many passages, especially in Abraham's petitions to God for the cities, asking whether He would forgive them, providing there were fifty righteous men, from which number he went down to forty-five, which is the sesquinone and is as from mi to re: thence to forty, which is the sesquioctave and as from re to mi; thence to thirty, which is the sesquitierce, or the proportion of the diatessaron; thence to twenty, which is the sesqualter, or that of the diapente; thence to ten, which is the duple, or diapason—and went no further, there being no other harmonic proportions.[17] Now, how is this to be understood without music?

In the book of Job, God says to him: *Numquid coniungere valebis micantes stellas Pleiadas, aut gyrum Arcturi poteris dissipare? Numquid producis Luciferum in tempore suo, et Vesperum super filios terrae consurgere facis?* ["Shalt thou be able to join together the shining stars the Pleiades, or canst thou stop the turning about of Arcturus? Canst thou bring forth the day star in its time and make the evening star to rise upon the children of the earth?" (Job 38:31–32)]. Such terms will be incomprehensible without a knowledge of astrology. And it is not only these noble disciplines; no mechanical art goes unmentioned. In sum, how to understand the book which takes in all books, and the knowledge which embraces all types of knowledge, to the

17. Petitions of Abraham for the just men in Sodom and Gomorrah (Gen. 18:23–32). To the descending fives of Abraham's petitions to God, Sor Juana has applied intervals of the Pythagorean musical theory of her day, as taken from the work of Pietro Cerone whose translated title reads: *The Musicmaker and Master: A Treatise on Theoretical and Practical Music* (Naples, 1613).

understanding of which they all contribute? After one has mastered them all (which is evidently not easy nor, in fact, possible), a further circumstance going beyond all those mentioned is required: a continuing prayer and purity of life, so as to be visited by God with that cleansing of the spirit and illumination of the mind which the understanding of such lofty matters demands, in the absence of which none of the rest is any use.

Of the Angelic Doctor Saint Thomas, the Church says these words: *In difficultatibus locorum Sacrae Scripturae ad orationem ieiunium adhibebat. Quin etiam sodali Fratri Reginaldo dicere solebat, quidquid sciret, non tam studio, aut labore suo peperisse, quam divinitus traditum accepisse* [When in difficulty over passages in Holy Scripture, he added fasting to prayer. Indeed he used to say to his companion Friar Reginald that whatever he knew he had not so much achieved by study and hard work as received as a gift from God (Roman Breviary, Office of the Feast of Saint Thomas Aquinas, March 7, Fifth Lesson)]. How then, could I, remote as I was from virtue and learning, find the strength to write? Thus, for the acquisition of certain fundamentals, I would constantly study divers things, without inclining in particular to any given one, inclined rather to all generally. So it happened that my having concentrated on some more than others was not a matter of choice but came about through the chance of having found books dealing with the former subjects closer to hand, which gave them preference without any decision of mine. As I had no material goal in mind, nor any limitation of time constraining me to the study of any one thing to meet degree requirements, almost at once I was studying different things or dropping some to take up others, although this was not wholly unsystematic since some I called study and others diversion. The latter brought me relaxation from the former. It follows from this that I have studied many things, yet know nothing because each one always interfered with some other. True, I am referring to the operative aspect of those which have one, for, obviously, while the pen is in motion, the compass is at rest, and while the harp is being played, the organ is still, *et sic de caeteris*. For, because much bodily practice is required to develop a skill, one who spreads herself out over a number of exercises willl never acquire any one skill perfectly. In the formal and speculative realms, however, the opposite is true, and I should like to convince everyone by my own experience not only that different subjects do not interfere with one another, but that they actually

all cohesive

support one another, since certain ones shed light on others, opening a way into them by means of variations and occult connections. It was to form this universal chain that the wisdom of their Author so put them in place that they appear correlated and bound together with marvelous concert and bonding. This is the chain that the ancients pretended emerged from Jupiter's mouth, on which all things were strung and linked together. So much is demonstrated by the Reverend Father Athanasius Kircher in his curious book *De Magnete* [On the Magnet]. All things proceed from God, who is at once the center and the circumference from which all existing lines proceed and at which all end up.[18]

For my own part I can attest that what I do not understand in an author writing on one subject, I can usually understand in one writing on another seemingly far removed from it, and that authors, in developing their thought, will come up with metaphorical examples from other fields, as when the logicians say that the middle term is to the two other terms as a measuring rod is to two distant bodies, with respect to determining whether they are equidistant, and that the logician's sentence proceeds in a straight line, taking the shortest way, while the rhetorician's moves in a curve, taking the longest, but that the two end up at the same point; and when it is said that expositors are like an open hand and scholastics like a closed fist. Thus I am not excusing myself, nor do I mean to, for having studied different things, since they are in fact mutually supportive. I am simply stating that my failure to progress in them has been due to my ineptitude and poor mind and has not been caused by such diversity.

What I might point out in self-justification is how severe a hardship it is to work not only without a teacher but also

18. As Sor Juana says, she takes the image, with its syncretic and hermetic overtones, from a work by the German Jesuit Athanasius Kircher (1601–1680). (Her title is inexact.) The image figures in and adorns the frontispieces of three of Kircher's works: *Magnes, sive de arte magnetica* (Magnet, or On the Art of the Magnet [Rome, 1641]); *Mundus Subterraneus* (The Subterranean World [Amsterdam, 1665]); *Magneticum Naturae Regnum* (Nature's Magnetic Realm [Rome, 1667]). It stems from a passage in the *Iliad* (8.14–18) and reappears in Macrobius' *Commentary* on the *Dream of Scipio*, ch. 14. The matter is treated in full in Octavio Paz, *Sor Juana*, ch. 24. Though drawn from Kircher, the image originates in the *De Docta Ignorantia* (On Learned Ignorance) of Nicholas of Cusa (1440). He sees God as both center and circumference of the cosmos. See Paz, *Sor Juana*, ch. 21.

without fellow students with whom to compare notes and try out what has been studied. Instead I have had nothing but a mute book as teacher, an unfeeling inkwell as fellow student, and, in place of explanation and exercises, many hindrances, arising not only from my religious duties (it goes without saying that these occupy one's time most profitably and beneficially) but also from things implicit in the life of a religious community—such as when I am reading, those in a neighboring cell take it upon themselves to play music and sing. Or when I am studying and two maids quarrel and come to me to settle their dispute. Or when I am writing and a friend comes to visit, doing me a great disservice with the best of intentions, whereupon I not only must put up with the bother but act grateful for the injury. This goes on all the time, because, since the times I devote to my studies are those remaining when the regular duties of the community are over, the others are also free then to come and bother me. Only those who have experienced communal religious life can know how true this is. Only the strength of my vocation allows my nature to take pleasure in it—this and the great bond of love between me and my beloved sisters, for since love is union, there are no poles too distant for it.

I do confess that in this respect my hardship has been beyond description; hence I cannot say what I have with envy heard from others: that learning has not been hard work for them. Lucky they! For me, not learning (for I am not yet learned), merely wanting to learn has been so hard that I might say, with my Father Saint Jerome (although not so edifyingly): *Quid ibi laboris insumpserim, quid sustinuerim difficultatis, quoties desperavim, quotiesque cessaverim et contentione discendi rursus inceperim; testis est conscientia, tam mea, qui passus sum, quam eorum qui mecum duxerunt vitam* ·[My conscience is witness to the effort I expended, all the difficulties I suffered, the many times I gave up and stopped, then started in again from the sheer urge to learn—and not only my own conscience, which was a party to this suffering, but the consciences of those who shared my life (Letter of Saint Jerome to the monk Rusticus)]. Except for the companions and witnesses (for I have lacked even this alleviation), I can most truthfully vouch for the rest. And to think that this unlucky bent of mine has been strong enough to overcome all these things!

As I owe to God, among other good things, so gentle and accommodating a nature, and the nuns are so fond of me on account of it (and kindly overlook my faults) and thus greatly enjoy my company, it would often happen that, aware of this and spurred on by my great love for them (more understandable than theirs for me), during the free time we both had, I would go and comfort them and relax in their company. I realized that at such times I was neglecting my study and so made a vow not to enter a single cell unless obedience or charity required it of me. For, in the absence of a curb as harsh as this, love would have broken through a control arising from mere resolve. Knowing my frailty, I would make this vow for a month or a fortnight and then, allowing myself a recess of a day or two, I would renew it. The free day was intended not so much to give me a rest as to prevent their considering me unbending, withdrawn, and unappreciative of the undeserved affection of those dearest sisters.

This shows only too clearly the strength of my inclination. Blessed be God for his will to direct it toward learning and not toward some vice or other that would have proved all but irresistible to me. And one can easily deduce how very much against the stream my poor studies have had to row—or rather to founder. Well, the most arduous part of the difficulties still remains to be told, for those related up to now have been simply necessary or incidental annoyances which are such only indirectly. Still to come are the outright ones which have worked directly to hinder and to prohibit my pursuit of learning. Who could fail to believe, in view of such widespread plaudits, that I have sailed with a following wind on a glassy sea to the encomiums of general acclaim? Well, the Lord knows that it has hardly been so, for amidst the bouquets of that very acclaim, asps of such invidiousness and relentlessness as I could never describe have stirred and reared up. Those most harmful and painful to me are not the persons who have pursued me with open hatred and ill will, but those who, while loving me and wishing me well (and being possibly very meritorious in God's eyes for their good intentions), have mortified and tortured me much more than the others, with their: "This study is incompatible with the blessed ignorance to which you are bound. You will lose your way, at such heights your head will be turned by your very perspicacity and sharpness of mind." What have I not gone through to hold out against this? Strange sort of martyrdom, in which I was both the martyr and my own executioner!

Why, for the ability (doubly infelicitous in my case) to compose verse, even when it was sacred verse, what nastiness have I not been subjected to, what unpleasantness has not come my way! I must say, Madam, that sometimes I stop and reflect that anyone who stands out—or whom God singles out, for He alone can do so—is viewed as everyone's enemy, because it seems to some that he is usurping the applause due them or deflecting the admiration which they have coveted, for which reason they pursue him.

That politically barbarous law of the Athenians, whereby anyone eminent in natural endowments and virtues was to be exiled from their republic so that he might not tyrannize public liberty, still holds, and is still observed in our day, although the reasoning of the Athenians no longer applies.[19] There is a different consideration, however, no less efficacious though less well grounded, for it might be a maxim of that godless Machiavelli: hate anyone who stands out because he tarnishes the luster of others. So it goes, so it has always gone.

What, if not this, was the cause of that furious hatred the Pharisees conceived for Christ, when they had so many reasons to feel just the opposite? For if we consider His person, what trait could be more worthy of love than His divine beauty? Which more capable of stealing men's hearts? If human beauty of any sort holds sway over men's minds and is able to enthrall them with mild and welcome violence, what must have been the power of Christ's, with all its prerogatives and supreme gifts? How efficacious, how moving that unfathomable beauty must have been, with the radiance of Godhead showing through the beautiful face as through smooth, polished glass! How could that countenance fail to be moving when over and above perfections of a human order it displayed glimmers of the divine?

If the face of Moses, merely from conversing with God, became unbearable to weak human sight, what must that of God Himself made flesh have been?[20] As for the other traits, could any invite more love than His heavenly modesty, or the gentleness and mildness that spread loving-kindness with His every movement, or His deep humbleness and meekness, His words of eternal life and

19. Ostracism, instituted probably by Cleisthenes in 508 B.C., was not exile, as Sor Juana states, but a ten-year banishment involving no loss of status or property.

20. "When Moses came down from the mount Sinai . . . Aaron and the children of Israel, seeing the face of Moses horned, were afraid to come near" (Ex. 34:29–30).

eternal wisdom? So, how can it be that these traits did not captivate men's souls, that men did not follow in His train, uplifted and loving?

The Holy Mother, my mother Teresa, tells how, once she had beheld the beauty of Christ, she was cured of any inclination toward human beings, because nothing she could see was not ugly, in comparison with that beauty. Then how could it have had such opposite effects on men? Or, granting they were too base and uncouth to recognize or appreciate His perfections, why did not their own self-interest at least motivate them to see how much they stood to gain and profit from the benefits He brought them by healing the sick, raising the dead, curing those possessed by devils? Then how could they not love Him? Ah Lord, for that very reason they did not love Him, for that reason they hated Him. So they themselves attest.

They sit in council and say: *Quid facimus, quia hic homo multa signa facit?* ["What do we, for this man doth many miracles" (John 11:47)]. What reasoning! If they had said This man is a ne'er-do-well, a transgressor of the law, a rabble-rouser who stirs up the people by deceit, in so saying they would have been lying, but at least those would have been reasons more in keeping with what they were seeking, which was to put Him to death. But to cite as a reason His doing extraordinary things is hardly worthy of learned men, such as the Pharisees undoubtedly were. Yet so it goes: when learned men become aroused, they burst into such inconsistencies. In truth this was the only reason it was determined that Christ should die. Men—if indeed this name suits you, when you are such beasts—why so cruel a judgment? You answer only: *signa facit*. Heaven help me, then doing extraordinary things is sufficient reason for putting someone to death! This *multa signa facit* goes back to that *radix Iesse, qui stat in signum populorum* ["root of Jesse, who standeth for an ensign of the people" (Isaias 11:10)], and additionally, to that *in signum cui contradicetur* ["for a sign which shall be contradicted" (Luke 2:34: Simeon speaking of Jesus at the Presentation in the Temple)]. On account of a miracle? Then let Him die! Outstanding? Then let Him suffer, that being the reward of anyone who excels.

At the topmost point of temples, figures of the Winds and of Fame are commonly placed as ornaments; to protect them from the birds, they cover them all over with barbs. This sounds like a defense; in fact it is an obligatory adjunct. No one in a superior position will be able to avoid barbs that cut into him: the resentment of the wind, the harshness of the elements, lightning bolts venting their rage, stones and arrows finding their mark. Oh unlucky summit, exposed to so many risks! Oh singularity, set up as a target for envy and an object for contradiction! Any eminence, be it in dignity, nobility, wealth, beauty, learning, is subject to this penalty, but most implacably subject to it is eminence of mind. First of all, because it is the most defenseless, since wealth and power punish anyone daring to challenge them; but not mind, for the greater it is, the more modest and long-suffering, and the less prone to defend itself. Secondly, because, as Gracián so learnedly put it, superiority of mind goes with superiority of the whole being.[21] The angel is superior to man for no other reason than superiority of mind; man surpasses animals in mind alone. Thus, as no one wishes to be inferior to anyone else, no one will admit that another is superior in mind, since this proceeds from natural superiority. Anyone will allow and admit that another is nobler than he, richer, handsomer, and even more knowledgeable, but that someone else has a better mind scarcely anyone will grant. *Rarus est, qui velit cedere ingenio* [Rare is the man willing to acknowledge another's superiority of mind (Martial, *Epigrams* 8.8)]. That is why assaults on this gift are so successful.

When the soldiers made Our Lord Jesus Christ their amusement, entertainment, and laughingstock, they brought a worn scarlet robe and a hollow reed and a crown of thorns to crown Him king in jest. Now then, the reed and the purple robe, though an affront, were not hurtful; why is the crown alone so? Is it not enough for it, like the other insignia, to be a sneering gibe, that being the object? No, because the sacred head of Christ and His divine brain were a storehouse of wisdom, and in the world it is not enough for a wise mind to be scorned; it must also be bruised and hurt. Let the head that is a treasure-house of wisdom expect no crowning other than the thorns! What wreath can human intelligence expect when it sees what is bestowed on the divine? Roman arrogance crowned the various feats of arms of its captains with different crowns: the civic was for one who defended the citizenry; the military, for one who penetrated an opposing army; the

21. The Aragonese Jesuit Baltasar Gracián (1601–1658) in "Genio y ingenio" (Character and Wit), the first essay of his treatise *El discreto* (The Worldly Wit).

mural, for one who scaled a city wall; the obsidional, for one who raised the siege of a city or an encircled army, encampment, or headquarters; the naval, the oval, the triumphal, for other feats, of which Pliny and Aulus Gellius tell. Seeing so many varieties of crown, I was uncertain what kind Christ's was. I think it must have been obsidional, which (as you, my Lady, know) was the most honored and was so called from *obsidio,* which means siege. This was not made of gold or silver but of the actual grass or plants of the field in which the operation was carried out. The feat of Christ was to make the Prince of Darkness lift his siege, which had the whole world encircled, as is said in the Book of Job: *Circuivi terram et ambulavi per eam* ["(And the Lord said to him, Whence comest thou? And he answered:) I have gone round about the earth, and walked through it" (Job 1:7)]; and told in Saint Peter: *Circuit, quaerens quem devoret* ["(The devil) . . . goeth about seeking whom he may devour" (1 Peter 5:8)]. Our Chieftain then came and made him lift the siege: *nunc princeps huius mundi eicietur foras* ["Now shall the prince of this world be cast out" (John 12:31)]. Thus the soldiers crowned Him, not with gold or silver, but with the natural product of the world, which was the seat of the struggle, and which, after the curse—*spinas et tribulos germinabit tibi* ["Thorns and thistles shall it bring forth to thee" (Gen. 3:18)]—produced nothing but thorns. Thus the crown with which His mother, the Synagogue, crowned the valiant wise . Conqueror was most fitting. The daughters of Zion came forth in tears to behold the sorrowful triumph, as they had come rejoicing to that of the other Solomon, for the triumph of the wise is obtained in sorrow and celebrated with weeping; that is how wisdom triumphs. It was Christ, as prince of the wise, who first tried out the crown, in order that, having been sanctified on His temples, it should lose its horror for other men of wisdom, and make them realize that they may aspire to no other honor.

The very Life was willing to go and give life to the deceased Lazarus. The disciples, not knowing His purpose, objected: *Rabbi, nunc quaerebant te Judaei lapidare, et iterum vadis illuc?* ["Rabbi, the Jews but now sought to stone thee: and goest thou thither again?" (John 11:8)]. The Redeemer quieted their fears: *Nonne duodecim sunt horae diei?* ["Are there not twelve hours of the day?" (John 11:9)]. Up to this point they seem to have been afraid because they had in mind the precedent of the Jews' wanting to stone Him for having reproved them by calling them thieves and not shepherds of their flocks. And thus, they feared that, if He went forth with the same end in view (reproofs, however well deserved, being usually taken ill), His life would be in danger. But once set right and made aware that His going is to restore life to Lazarus, what could have caused Thomas, showing as much bravery as Peter in the garden, to say: *Eamus et nos, ut moriamur cum eo* ["Let us also go, that we may die with Him" (John 11:16)]. Blessed apostle, what are you saying? The Lord is not going forth to die—why such misgivings? For Christ's aim is not to reprimand, but to perform an act of mercy, and they therefore can do Him no harm. The Jews themselves might have been your reassurance, for when He reproved them for wishing to stone Him, saying: *Multa bona opera ostendi vobis ex Patre meo, propter quod eorum opus me lapidatis?* ["Many good works I have shewed you from my Father; for which of those works do you stone me?" (John 10:32)], they answered Him: *De bono opere non lapidamus te, sed de blasphemia* ["For a good work we stone thee not, but for blasphemy" (John 10:33)]. So, if they do not want to stone Him on account of His good works, and He is now going to do them such a good one in giving life to Lazarus, of what are they afraid and why? Would it not be better to say: Let us go and enjoy the fruit of gratitude for the good deed that our Master is about to perform? To see Him applauded and given thanks for the benefaction? To see their own astonishment at the miracle? And not to say to them something so evidently beside the point as: *Eamus et nos, ut moriamur cum eo.* But, alas, the Saint was well-advised to be afraid and spoke like an apostle. Is Christ not going to perform a miracle? What greater danger can there be? Pride finds it less intolerable to hear a reproof, than envy to see a miracle. In all I am saying, venerable Lady, I do not mean that I have been persecuted for being learned, only for my love of learning and letters, not because I have been successful in either.

The Prince of the Apostles found himself, at one point, as remote from wisdom as is emphatically brought out by those words: *Petrus vero sequebatur eum a longe* ["But Peter followed afar off" (Luke 22:54)], so far from being applauded for learning that he was called ignorant: *Nesciens quid diceret* ["not knowing what he said" (Luke 9:33)]. And even when questioned about his acquaintance with wisdom, he himself said that he had not attained the slightest notion thereof: *Mulier [sic], nescio quid dicis* ["Man, I know not what thou sayest" (Luke 22:60)]. *Mulier, non novi illum* ["Woman, I know Him not" (Luke 22:57)]. And what happens to him next? Simply that, with all these credentials for ignorance, he did not have the prestige but did have the afflictions of a man of wisdom. Why? No other reason was given except: *Et hic cum illo erat.* ["This man also was with Him" (Luke 22:56)]. He was partial to wisdom, it had won his heart, he followed its trail, prided himself on his pursuit of and love for it, and though this was at such a distance that he neither understood nor attained it, it sufficed to make him incur its tortures. There was not a single alien soldier who did not give him trouble nor any maidservant who did not bother him. I confess that I am far removed from wisdom's confines and that I have wished to pursue it, though *a longe*. But the sole result has been to draw me closer to the flames of persecution, the crucible of torture, and this has even gone so far as a formal request that study be forbidden me.

This was successful in one instance involving a very holy and very ingenuous prelate who thought studying was something for the Inquisition and ordered me to cease. I obeyed her (for the three months her right to so order me lasted) as regarded not taking a book in hand, but as to ceasing study altogether, it not being in my power, I could not carry it out. For, although I did not study from books, I did from everything God has created, all of it being my letters, and all this universal chain of being my book. I saw nothing without reflecting on it; I heard nothing without wondering at it—not even the tiniest, most material thing. For, as there is no created thing, no matter how lowly, in which one cannot recognize the *me fecit Deus* [God made me], there is none that does not confound the mind once it stops to consider it. Thus, I repeat, I looked and marveled at all of them, so much so that simply from the person with whom I spoke, and from what that person said to me, countless reflections arose in my mind. What could be the origin of so great a variety of characters and minds, when all belonged to one species? Which humors and hidden qualities could bring this about? If I saw a figure, I at once fell to working out the relationship of its lines, measuring it with my mind and recasting it along different ones. Sometimes I would walk back and forth across the front of a sleeping-room of ours—a very large one—and observe how, though the lines of its two sides were parallel and its ceiling horizontal, one's vision made it appear as if the lines inclined toward each other and the ceiling were lower at the far end, from which I inferred that visual lines run straight but not parallel, tending rather toward a pyramidal figure. And I asked myself whether this could be the reason the ancients questioned whether the world was spherical or not. Because, although it appears to be, this could be an optical illusion, and show concavities where there might in fact be none.

This type of observation would occur to me about everything and still does, without my having any say in the matter; indeed, it continually irritates me because it tires my mind. I thought the same thing occurred in everyone's case, and with writing verse as well, until experience proved me wrong. This turn, or habit, of mind is so strong that I can look upon nothing without reflecting on it. Two little girls were playing with a top in my presence. The moment I saw its movement and form, I began, in my crazy way, to consider the easy motion of the spherical form, and how, the impulse once given, it continued independently of its cause, since at a distance from the girl's hand, which originated the motion, the top went on dancing. Nor was this enough for me. I had flour brought and sifted, so as to tell, when the top danced over it, whether the circles its motion described were perfect or not. I discovered that they were simply spirals which moved farther and farther from the circular in proportion as the impulse wore down. Other girls were playing with pins—childhood's most frivolous game. I would approach and observe the shapes the pins took, and on noticing that three chanced to form a triangle, I would set about actually connecting them, recalling that this was the shape the mysterious ring of Solomon was said to have taken—that ring on which there were distant glimmerings and depictions of the Most Holy Trinity, by virtue of which it worked such prodigious and marvelous things.[22] This was also said to be the shape of David's harp, for which reason Saul was said to have been cured by its sound. The harps of our day have retained the same shape.

What could I not tell you, my Lady, of the secrets of Nature which I have discovered in cooking! That an egg hangs together and fries in fat or oil, and that, on the contrary, it disintegrates in syrup. That, to keep sugar liquid, it suffices to add the tiniest part of water in which a quince or some other tart fruit has been. That the yolk and white of the same egg are so different in nature, that when eggs are used with sugar, the yolks must be used separately

22. No such ring is mentioned in the Bible. An occult tradition is perhaps being drawn on.

from the whites, never together with them. I do not wish to tire you with such trivia, which I relate only to give you a full picture of my native turn of mind, which will, no doubt, make you laugh. But, Madam, what is there for us women to know, if not bits of kitchen philosophy? As Lupercio Leonardo said: One can perfectly well philosophize while cooking supper.[23] And I am always saying, when I observe these small details: If Aristotle had been a cook, he would have written much more.

But to continue with the workings of my mind, let me say that this line of thought is so constant with me that I have no need of books. On one occasion, when, owing to some serious stomach trouble, the doctor forbade my studying, I obeyed for several days, but then I pointed out that allowing me books would be much less harmful, since my mental activity was so vigorous, so vehement, that it used up more spirits in a quarter of an hour than studying from books did in four days. So they agreed reluctantly to allow me to read. And not only that, my Lady: even my sleep was not free from this constant activity of my brain. In fact, it seems to go on during sleep with all the more freedom and lack of restraint, putting together the separate images it has carried over from waking hours with greater clarity and tranquillity, debating with itself, composing verses, of which I could draw up a whole catalogue for you, including certain thoughts and subtleties I have arrived at more easily while asleep than while awake, which I won't go into, not wishing to bore you. What has been said suffices for your own acumen and high-mindedness to grasp with clarity and full understanding my native disposition of mind and the origin, methods, and present state of my studies.

Even if these studies were to be viewed, my Lady, as to one's credit (as I see they are indeed celebrated in men), none would be due me, since I pursue them involuntarily. If they are seen as reprehensible, for the same reason I do not think I should be blamed. Still, though, I am so unsure of myself, that neither in this nor in anything do I trust my own judgment. Hence I leave the decision up to your supreme talent, and will abide by whatever it decrees, with no antagonism and no reluctance, for this has been nothing more than a simple account of my inclination to letters.

23. The Aragonese poet Bartolomé Leonardo de Argensola (1562–1631), not his brother Lupercio, is the source of the saying ("First Satire," lines 143–144).

I must admit, likewise, that although, as I have said, a truth such as this requires no exemplification; nevertheless the many precedents I have read about in both divine and humane letters have greatly assisted me. For I see a Debbora [Judges 4 and 5] setting up laws in both military and political spheres, and governing a nation that could boast so many learned men. I see a most wise Queen of Sheba [3 (1) Kings 10; 2 Paralipomenon (Chronicles) 9], so learned that she dared to challenge with enigmas the wisdom of the wisest of the wise, without suffering on that account any reproof. Rather, thanks to that, she becomes judge of the unbelieving. I see so many and such outstanding women, like Abigail [1 Kings (1 Sam.) 25], endowed with the gift of prophecy; others, like Esther, with that of persuasiveness; others, like Rahab [Josue 2], with piety; others, like Anna, mother of Samuel [1 Kings (1 Sam.) 1 and 2], with perseverance; and an infinite number of others, all possessing other gifts and virtues.

If I look among the Gentiles, the first I come upon are the Sybils, chosen by God to prophesy the principal mysteries of our faith—and to do so in such learned and refined verse that it holds wonderment itself in suspense. I see worshiped as goddess of learning a woman like Minerva, daughter of the first Jupiter and giver of all the learning of Athens. I see a Polla Argentaria helping her husband Lucan write the Pharsalian Battle.[24] I see divine Tiresias' daughter, more learned than her father.[25] I see a Zenobia, queen of the Palmyrans, as wise as she is brave.[26] An Arete, daughter of Aristippus, learned in the extreme.[27] A Nicostrata, inventor of Latin letters and extremely erudite in the Greek.[28] An Aspasia of Miletus, teacher of philosophy and rhetoric and instructress of the philosopher Pericles.[29] A Hypatia, who taught astrology

24. Statius asserts that Polla Argentaria assisted her husband, Lucan (A.D. 39–65), in correcting the first three books of his epic, *Pharsalia.*

25. Manto, a seer like her father, is mentioned by Ovid, *Metamorphoses* 6.7

26. Zenobia, an ambitious ruler of Palmyra, A.D. 266–272, embarked on military campaigns in Asia Minor and Egypt.

27. Arete was tutor to her son, the philosopher Aristippus the Younger (fourth century B.C.).

28. Nicostrata, also called Carmenta, was an oracle credited by Saint Isidore with the invention of Latin letters (*Etymologies* 1.4.1).

29. This highly accomplished woman and renowned teacher of eloquence in Athens became the mistress of Pericles.

and lectured for a long time in Alexandria.[30] A Leoncia, the Greek woman who wrote in opposition to Theophrastus, the philosopher, and won him over.[31] A Jucia, a Corinna, a Cornelia[32]—in sum, the whole throng of those who earned a name for themselves—Grecians, muses, oracles, who all were simply women of learning, considered such, celebrated as such, and venerated as such by the ancients. Not to mention innumerable others, of whom the books are full, for I see that Egyptian Catherine, lecturing and winning over to her view all the wisdom of the sages of Egypt. I see a Gertrude reading, writing, and teaching.[33] And, to stay with examples close to home, I see a most holy mother of mine, Paula, learned in the Hebrew, Greek, and Latin languages and most skilled at interpreting the Scriptures. And how could she fail to be, when the supreme Jerome, her chronicler, considered himself scarcely worthy of being such, for with that striking emphasis and power of expression, of which he has the secret, he says: If all the limbs in my body were tongues, they would still not suffice to publish abroad the wisdom and virtue of Paula. He was moved to similar praise of the widow Blesilla and the illustrious virgin Eustochium, daughters both of the same Saint, the latter so noteworthy that, by reason of her learning, she was called the Wonder of the World. Fabiola, the Roman woman, was also most versed in Holy Scripture.[34] Proba Falconia, a Roman woman, wrote an elegant book on the mysteries of our

30. A leader of the Alexandrian Neoplatonic School, Hypatia (d. A.D. 415) taught astronomy and commented on Plato and Aristotle. Sor Juana must have found a similarity between her own situation and the persecution (and death) of Hypatia at the hands of fanatic monks; see Paz, *Sor Juana*, ch. 26, toward end.

31. Leontium, a renowned courtesan, pupil of Epicurus, wrote in support of his doctrines against those of Theophrastus (fourth/third centuries B.C.).

32. Jucia is in all likelihood an erratum for Julia, also known as Domna, a Syrian woman of great intelligence and learning who became the second wife of the emperor Septimus Severus (A.D. 194–211) and a patroness of the arts. Corinna was a celebrated lyric poet of the sixth century B.C., traditionally considered the teacher of Pindar. Daughter of Scipio Africanus and mother of the Gracchi, Cornelia was a woman of great accomplishments, some of whose epistles are preserved (second century B.C.).

33. Saint Gertrude the Great, a German Benedictine (1256–1302/3), abandoned her early literary study after Christ in a vision reproved her. She became famous for her writings on the Fathers and Holy Scripture.

34. A disciple of Saint Jerome praised by him in an epistle.

Women may study, but not preach

Holy Faith, by putting together quotations from Virgil.[35] Our Queen Isabella, the wife of Alfonso X, is known to have written on astrology.[36] Not to mention others whom I shall pass over to avoid relaying what others have said (a vice I've always detested) and because in our day there flourishes the great Christina Alexandra, Queen of Sweden, as learned as she is courageous and great-hearted, and their Excellencies the Duchess of Aveiro and the Countess of Villaumbrosa.[37]

The venerable Dr. Arce (in virtue and cultivation a worthy professor of Scripture) in his *Studioso Bibliorum,* raises this question: *An liceat foeminis sacrorum Bibliorum studio incumbere? eaque interpretari?* [Is it legitimate for women to apply themselves to study of the Holy Bible and to interpret it?][38] He brings in many opinions of saints in support of the opposing view, especially that of the Apostle: *Mulieres in Ecclesiis taceant, non enim permittitur eis loqui* etc. ["Let women keep silence in the churches, for it is not permitted them to speak" (1 Cor. 14:34)]. He then brings in other opinions and especially that of the same Apostle addressing Titus: *Anus similiter in habitu sancto, bene docentes* ["The aged women, in like manner, in holy attire . . . teaching well" (Tit. 2:3)], with interpretations of the Church Fathers. He finally decides, in his judicious way, that to lecture publicly in the classroom and to preach in the pulpit are not legitimate activities for women, but that studying, writing, and teaching privately are not only allowable but most edifying and useful. Of course this does not apply to all women—only to those whom God has endowed with particular virtue and discernment and who have become highly accomplished and erudite, and possess

35. Falconia Proba, a fourth-century Roman poet, composed a history of the Old and New Testaments made up entirely of lines from Virgil.

36. A probable reference to a supposed collaboration in the *Books of Astronomical Knowledge* of her husband, Alfonso the Wise (1221–1284).

37. The Swedish queen (1626–1689), shortly after abdicating the throne in 1654, converted to Catholicism, was baptized Alexandra, and was received with great ceremony at Rome. She had a lively lifelong interest in the arts and sciences. Maria Guadalupe Alencastre, Duchess of Aveiro, a Portuguese contemporary of Sor Juana, was called "Mother of the Missions" because of her benefactions to the Jesuit missions of Mexico. The unidentified Countess of Villaumbrosa may be included out of courtesy.

38. Juan Díaz de Arce (d. 1653) was a Mexican cleric, theologian, and university professor. The full title of his work is *Fourth Book of Expository Questions for the Fuller Understanding of the Holy Bible* or *For the Bible Student* (1648).

the talents and other qualities needed for such holy pursuits. So true is this that the interpretation of Holy Scripture should be forbidden not only to women, considered so very inept, but to men, who merely by virtue of being men consider themselves sages, unless they are very learned and virtuous, with receptive and properly trained minds. Failure to do so, in my view, has given rise precisely to all those sectarians and been the root cause of all the heresies. For there are many who study in order to become ignorant, especially those of an arrogant, restless, and overbearing turn of mind, who are partial to new interpretations of the Law (where precisely they are to be rejected). Hence, until they have uttered something heretical merely in order to say what no one else has, they will not rest. Of these the Holy Spirit says: *In malevolam animam no introibit sapientia* ["For wisdom will not enter into a malicious soul" (Wisdom 1:4)]. Learning does more harm to such than remaining ignorant would. A clever man once said that a person who does not know Latin is not a complete fool, but that one who does is well qualified to be one. And I add he is even better (if stupidity is a qualification) who has studied his bit of philosophy and theology and has a smattering of languages, for therewith he becomes a fool in many branches of learning and language, his mother tongue not offering room enough for a great fool.

These, I repeat, are harmed by study, for it is like placing a sword in the hands of a madman.[39] While a sword is a most noble instrument for self-defense, in the hands of a fool it is the death of himself and many others. Such the Divine Writ became in the possession of wicked Pelagius, perverse Arius, wicked Luther, and the other heresiarchs, such as our Dr. (he was never ours nor a doctor of anything) Cazalla.[40] Their learning did them

39. Sor Juana is thinking of a much-reproduced emblem of Andrea Alciato (1492–1550), the pioneer of Renaissance emblem literature: "Insani gladius" (The Sword in the Hands of a Madman).

40. Pelagius (ca. 360–ca. 420), British-born theologian, held that the will is free at any moment to choose between good and evil. He thus severely limited the role of God's grace and denied the efficacy of original sin. His doctrine was strongly combatted by both Jerome and Augustine. The heresy of Arius (280?–336) considered the Son a subordinate being created by the Father, rather than his uncreated coequal. This position was defeated at the Council of Nicaea (325). Agustín Cazalla (1510–1559), a Spanish Lutheran, onetime canon of Salamanca Cathedral and chaplain to the King, was burned to death by the Inquisition.

harm, even though it is the best sustenance and the very life of the soul. Just as the better the nourishment a distempered and morbidly hot stomach receives, the more arid, rotten, and putrid the humors it produces, so the more these evilly inclined persons study, the worse the opinions they bring forth. Their understanding becomes obstructed by the very substance that should have nourished it; this is because they study a great deal and digest very little, in a way wholly disproportionate to the limited capacity of their understanding. On this the Apostle writes: *Dico enim per gratiam quae data est mihi, omnibus qui sunt inter vos: Non plus sapere quam oportet sapere, sed sapere ad sobrietatem: et unicuique sicut Deus divisit mensuram fidei* ["For I say, by the grace that is given me, to all that are among you, not to be more wise than it behoveth to be wise, but to be wise unto sobriety and according as God hath divided to everyone the measure of faith" (Rom. 12:3)]. And truthfully the Apostle said this not to women but to men, so the *taceant* applies not only to women but to everyone not properly endowed. I will never succeed in knowing as much or more than Aristotle or Saint Augustine if I lack the aptitude of Saint Augustine or Aristotle, even though I study more than the two of them. Not only that, but I will diminish and dull the workings of my weak mind by its lack of proportion to the objective.

Oh, if all of us—and myself first of all, weak woman that I am—would size up our talents before undertaking study and, even more, before writing out of a driving ambition to equal and even excel others, how little heart we would have left for it, how many errors we would spare ourselves, and how many wrong interpretations now making the rounds would not be circulating! My own errors I will put before all the rest, for if I recognized them as I ought to, I would not write this at all. I protest that I do so only to obey you, with such misgivings as to place you more in my debt for my taking pen in hand when feeling so timid, than you would be if the works I sent you were perfect. It is just as well that everything is subject to your correction: rub it out, tear it up and reprove me, and I will be more appreciative of that than of all the vain applause others may give me: *corripiet me iustus in misericordia, et increpabit: oleum autem peccatoris non impinguet caput meum*[41] ["The just man shall correct me in mercy and shall reprove me: but let not the oil of the sinner fatten my head" (Ps. 140.5)].

41. *Corripiet* is evidently an erratum for *corriget*.

Going back to our Arce, let me say that he cites in confirmation of his views those words of my Father Saint Jerome (*Ad Laetam, de institutione filiae*) [To Laeta, on the education of her daughter]) where he says: *Adhuc tenera lingua psalmis dulcibus imbuatur. Ipsa nomina per quae consuescit paulatim verba contexere; non sint fortuita, sed certa et coacervata de industria. Prophetarum videlicet, atque Apostolorum, et omnis ab Adam Patriarchum series, de Matthaeo, Lucaque descendat, ut dum aliud agit, futurae memoriae praeparetur. Reddat tibi pensum quotidie, de Scripturarum floribus carptum* [Let her tongue, however, be initiated into the sweetness of the psalms. Let the very names out of which she is beginning to form phrases be not random ones but chosen on purpose. For example, those of the Prophets and the Apostles, and let the whole succession of Patriarchs beginning with Adam be taken from Matthew and Luke, so that, while otherwise engaged, she may be made ready for future tasks of memorization. Have her bring you a daily quota culled from the flowers of Scripture]. Now if the Saint wished a girl just beginning to talk to be educated in this way, what would he not wish for his nuns and his spiritual daughters? That is quite clear from the example of the above-mentioned Eustochium and Fabiola and from Marcela, her sister, Pacatula, and others whom the Saint honors in his epistles, exhorting them to follow this holy exercise, as one can tell from the epistle just cited where I quoted that *reddat tibi pensum,* which harks back to and harmonizes with the *bene docentes* of Saint Paul. For the *reddat tibi* of my great Father implies that the girl's teacher is to be none other than her mother, Laeta.

Oh, how much harm would be avoided in our country if older women were as learned as Laeta and knew how to teach in the way Saint Paul and my Father Saint Jerome direct! Instead of which, if fathers wish to educate their daughters beyond what is customary, for want of trained older women and on account of the extreme negligence which has become women's sad lot, since well-educated older women are unavailable, they are obliged to bring in men teachers to give instruction in reading, writing, and arithmetic, playing musical instruments, and other skills. No little harm is done by this, as we witness every day in the pitiful examples of ill-assorted unions; from the ease of contact and the close company kept over a period of time, there easily comes about something not thought possible. As a result of this, many fathers prefer leaving their daughters in a barbaric, uncultivated state to exposing them to an evident danger such as familiarity with men breeds. All of which would be eliminated if there were older women of learning, as Saint Paul desires, and instruction were passed down from one group to another, as is the case with needlework and other traditional activities.

For what drawback could there be to having an old woman, well-versed in letters and pious in conversation and way of life, in charge of the education of maidens? And what harm in preventing the latter from going to waste either for lack of instruction or from having it imparted to them through the dangerous medium of male masters? For even if there were no greater risk than the impropriety of having a strange man sit beside a bashful woman (who blushes even when her father looks directly at her) and treat her with offhand familiarity and with the informality of the classroom, her discomfiture at being in men's company and conversing with them suffices to forbid it. And I don't see how this method of having women taught by men can be free of danger, unless it is carried out in the severe judgment seat of the confessional or through distant instruction from the pulpit or by remote acquaintanceship with books, and not via the close contact that comes of proximity. Everyone recognizes the truth of this, yet it is permitted simply because well-educated older women are not to be found. It follows that their not being is very damaging. This should be taken into account by those who, being wedded to that *Mulieres in Ecclesia taceant*, rail against women's being educated and becoming teachers, as if the Apostle himself had never said: *bene docentes*. Besides which, that injunction referred to a historical circumstance related by Eusebius, namely, that in the early Church women had begun to indoctrinate one another in places of worship and the noise interfered with the apostles' preaching, for which reason they were told to keep still—exactly as now it is the case that while the preacher is preaching one does not pray out loud.[42]

The understanding of many passages doubtless requires much study of history, customs, ceremonies, proverbs, and even the ways of speaking of the times in which they were written, so as to learn to what certain locutions of Holy Writ are referring and alluding. Does not *Scindite corda vestra, et non vestimenta vestra* ["Rend your heart and not

42. Eusebius, Bishop of Caesarea (ca. 260–ca. 340), was a voluminous writer whose best-known work is his *History of the Christian Church*.

your garments" (Joel 2:13)] allude to the Hebrew ceremony of tearing the clothes as a sign of grief, as the evil priest did when he said that Christ had blasphemed! Do not many passages of the Apostle concerning the succoring of widows also reflect the customs of those times? And does not that saying regarding the strong woman: *Nobilis in portis vir eius* ["Her husband is honorable in the gates" (Prov. 31:23)] allude to the locating of judges' tribunals at the city gates? Does not the term *dare terram Deo* ["give the earth to God"] signify the taking of a vow? Were not public sinners called *hiemantes* because they did penance in the open, as against the others who did so beneath a portico? Was not that complaint of Christ to the Pharisee about his failure to kiss and wash His feet [Luke 7:44–45] based on the Jewish custom of doing precisely these things? And countless other places, not only in sacred writings but in secular, that one is continually coming across, such as the *adorate purpuram*, which meant obey the king; the *manumettere eum*, which meant to set free, an allusion to the custom and ceremony of giving a slave a pat on the cheek when giving him his freedom. The *intonuit caelum* of Virgil, an allusion to the omen of thunder in the west, which was considered favorable.[43] The *tu nunquam leporem edisti* of Martial [the words may mean either "You never ate hare" or "You never uttered a witticism"], which not only offers the delight of a pun in the *leporem*, but also an allusion to a supposed property of the hare.[44] That proverb: *Maleam legens, quae sunt domi obliviscere* ["Rounding Malea, forget domestic matters"], which alludes to the great danger of the Laconian promontory.[45] That reply of the virtuous matron to the irksome suitor: Hinges won't be greased nor will torches burn for me, a way of saying that she had no desire to marry, with an allusion to the ceremony of greasing doors with fat and lighting nuptial torches at marriages—as if we were now to say: there will be no outlay for dowry nor will the priest give his blessings on my account. And along these lines there are countless other observations of Virgil and Homer and all the poets and prose writers.

---

43. "Heaven thundered" appears to be an erratum for *intonuit laevum* (it thundered on the left), twice used in the *Aeneid* (2.693, 9.631) of favorable omens.

44. The hare was supposed to make one who ate it handsome for a week (Martial, *Epigrams* 5.30).

45. That is, concentrate on matters at hand, an allusion to the difficulty of sailing around this promontory in the southeastern Peloponnese.

Aside from these, how many difficulties cannot be found in Biblical passages, even in matters of grammar—the plural used for the singular, the second person giving way to the third, in those words of the *Canticle of Canticles: osculetur me osculo oris sui: quia meliora sunt ubera tua vino* ["Let him kiss me with the kiss of his mouth: for thy breasts are better than wine" (1:1)]? The adjective in the genitive instead of the accusative, as in *Calicem salutaris accipiam* ["I will take the chalice of salvation" (Ps. 115:13)]? The use of the feminine for the masculine and, on the contrary, calling any sin adultery?

All of this requires more study than is thought by some who, not having gone beyond the level of grammar or knowing at most a few terms of formal logic, undertake to interpret the Scriptures and fasten onto *Mulieres in Ecclesiis taceant*, with no idea of how it should be interpreted. And, from elsewhere in the Bible, onto: *Mulier in silentio discat* ["Let the woman learn in silence" (1 Tim. 2:11)], even though these words speak more in women's favor than against them, since they direct them to learn, and it is obvious that while women are learning they must keep silent.[46] And it is also written: *Audi, Israel, et tace* ["Hear, Israel, and hold thy peace"],[47] words which address the whole conglomeration of men and women telling them all to maintain silence, since anyone listening and learning must naturally be attentive and keep silent. If all those interpreters and expositors of Saint Paul think otherwise, I should like them to explain to me how they understand the passage *Mulieres in Ecclesia taceant.* Because they must understand it either as referring concretely to pulpits and clerics' chairs, or immaterially to the whole multitude of the faithful, which is the Church. If they take it in the first sense (which, in my view, is the true one, since we see that women are not in fact allowed to lecture or preach publicly in the Church), why do they reprimand those who study in

46. Nina M. Scott, who has thoroughly explored Sor Juana's handling of her sources in the *Reply*, points out that she tailored her quotations from Paul's epistles to Timothy and Titus, and from Jerome as well, to support her argument. She asks: "Was she aware of the liberties she was taking with her Scriptural authority? It seems difficult to believe otherwise, but she was so concerned with the lack of suitable women teachers that she would go to any length to prove her point." ("Sor Juana Inés de la Cruz: 'Let Your Women Keep Silence in the Churches . . .'," *Women's Studies International Forum*, 8 [1985], 516f.)

47. This is an inexact reminiscence of Job 33:31; "Attend, Job, and hearken to me: hold thy peace."

private? If they understand it in the second sense and take
the Apostle's prohibition so sweepingly as not even in secret
to allow women women to write or study, how is it that we
see the Church allowing a Gertrude, a Teresa, a Bridget,
the nun of Agreda, and many more to study?[48] And if it is
answered that these women were saints, I agree, but this
does not invalidate my argument: first, because Saint Paul's
affirmation is absolute and refers to all women, not
excluding saints—for in his day, in the fervor of the early
Church, Martha and Mary, Marcella, Mary mother of
Jacob, Salomé, and many other women were saints, and he
does not except them. And nowadays we see the Church
allowing women, both saints and not, to write, for the nun
of Agreda and Maria de la Antigua[49] are not canonized, yet
their writings circulate, nor were Saint Teresa and the
others when they wrote. Thus Saint Paul's prohibition
referred only to speaking in public from pulpits; if the
Apostle had prohibited writing, the Church would not
allow it. So today I am not so bold as to teach—it would be
the height of presumption in my case. Writing requires
greater talent than I possess and a great deal of thought.
So Saint Cyprian says: *Gravi consideratione indigent, quae
scribimus* [The things we write need to be very carefully
considered]. My whole wish has been to study so as to be
less ignorant, for, as Saint Augustine has it, some things are
learned with a view to action, others only for the sake of
knowing: *Discimus quaedam, ut sciamus; quaedam, ut
faciamus.*[50] So what is there so criminal, considering that I
refrain even from what is legitimate for women, which is to
teach through writing, knowing that I do not have the
background for it, and following the advice of Quintilian:
*Noscat quisque, et non tantum ex alieniis praeceptis, sed ex natura
sua capiat consilium* [Let everyone learn, and not so much
through the precepts of others as by consulting his own
nature]?

If the crime is in the Athenagoric Letter, was there
anything more to that than simply setting forth my views

48. Probably Saint Bridget of Sweden (ca. 1302–1373), greatly venerated
for her good works and founder of the order of Saint Savior. The nun of
Agreda was María de Jesús (1602–1665), who corresponded with and
advised Philip IV and wrote *La mystica ciudad de Dios* (The Mystical City of
God), a visionary work with which Sor Juana had some acquaintance. See
Marie-Cécile Bénassy-Berling, *Humanisme et religion chez Sor Juana* (Paris:
Editions de la Sorbonne, 1982), pp. 269–270, 464).

49. A Spanish nun (1544–1617), author of several spiritual works.

50. No loci in Cyprian or Augustine have been found.

without exceeding the limits our Holy Mother Church allows? If she with her most holy authority does not forbid my doing so, why should others forbit it? Was holding an opinion contrary to Vieira an act of boldness on my part, and not His Paternity's holding one opposing the three holy Church Fathers? Is not my mind, such as it is, as free as his, considering their common origin? Is his opinion one of the revealed precepts of Holy Faith, that we should have to believe it blindly? Besides which, I was not lacking in the respect owed to so great a man, as his local defender was, ignoring the affirmation of Titus Lucius: *Artes comitatur decor* [Decorousness befits the arts].[51] Nor did I touch the Sacred Company[52] with so much as the tip of my little finger. Nor did I write for the judgment of anyone beside the person who suggested my doing so. And according to Pliny, *non similis est conditio publicantis, et nominatim dicentis* [one who publishes is in a different position from one who speaks in his own name]. For had I thought my letter would be published, I would have polished its rough style. If it is heretical, as the censor says, why does he not denounce it? That way he will have his revenge and I will be satisfied, for I value more, as I should, being called a Catholic and an obedient daughter of the Holy Mother Church, than all the plaudits my learning may bring. If the letter sounds uncouth—in this he is right—let him laugh, even if the laugh is actually a snicker. I am not asking him to applaud me, since, just as I was free to dissent from Vieira, so anyone else is to dissent from my opinions.

But, what am I saying, Madam? This does not belong here, nor is it what you should be hearing. The simple fact is that, in talking of my detractors, I recalled the points made against me by one who has just appeared, and without realizing it, my pen slipped into attempting to answer him in particular, when my intention is actually to speak in general terms. So, going back to our Arce, he says he knew two nuns in this city: one in the Regina convent, who learned the Breviary by heart so well that in conversations she could bring in its verses and psalms, and dictums from the homilies of the saints, with remarkable rapidity and pertinence. The other, in the convent of the

51. Titus Lucius has not been identified. The preceding quotation from Quintilian refers, inexactly, to *Inst. Or.* 9.4.7. (I have corrected the spelling.)
52. The Jesuit order, to which Sor Juana's misogynist superior, the Archbishop of Mexico, a devotee of Vieira, belonged.

Conception, was so much in the habit of reading the Epistles of my father, Saint Jerome, and the sayings of the Saint, that Arce says: *Hieronymum ipsum hispane loquentem audire me existimarem* [I thought I was hearing Jerome himself speaking Spanish]. And he says of her that after her death he learned that she had translated the Epistles into the vernacular, and he laments the fact that so much talent was not devoted to higher studies on an orderly basis. He does not mention the name of either nun, but he does cite them in support of his contention that it is not only proper but most useful and necessary for women, and especially for nuns, to study sacred texts—the very thing that you, in your wisdom, have been exhorting me to do, one which so many good reasons recommend.

If I turn to the facility in writing verse which has been so censured in me, it is so innate that I am even doing violence to myself to keep this missive in prose and could cite that line *Quidquid conabar dicere, versus erat* [Anything I set out to say turned into verse (Ovid, *Tristia* 4.10.26, inexactly quoted)]. Seeing it so condemned and so impugned on all sides, I have expressly tried to determine what is so wrong about it and have not been able to. What I find instead is that verses are applauded on the lips of Sybils, sanctified in the pens of the Prophets, and especially of King David, of whom that great expounder and beloved father of mine, in explaining their metrical patterns, says: *In morem Flacci et Pindari nunc iambo currit, nunc alcaico personat, nunc sapphico tumet, nunc semipede ingreditur* [In the manner of Horace and Pindar, now it runs along in iambics, now it is resonant with alcaics, now it swells with sapphics, now it moves in half-feet].[53] Most of the sacred books are in meter—the Canticle of Moses, for example. As for the Book of Job, Saint Isidore in his *Etymologies* says it is in heroic verse. Solomon wrote verse in Epithalamiums, Jeremiah in Lamentations. Whence Cassiodorus: *Omnis poetica locutio a Divinis scripturis sumpsit exordium* [Every poetic expression originated in Holy Scripture].[54] Our Catholic Church not only does not frown upon them, but makes use of them in its Hymns and recites those of Saint Ambrose, Saint Thomas, Saint Isidore, and others. Saint

---

53. Jerome, preface to the second book of the *Chronicle* of Eusebius Pamphilus.

54. Cassidorus (ca. 490–ca. 585) founded a monastery for the purpose of preserving and transmitting knowledge, sacred and profane. The statement quoted has not been located in his works.

Bonaventure was so fond of them that one scarcely finds a single page of his which lacks them. One can see that Saint Paul has studied verse, since he cites some and translates that line of Aratus: *In ipso enim vivimus, et movemur, et sumus* ["For in him we live, and move, and are" (Acts 17:28)] and adduces a line of Parmenides: *Cretenses semper mendaces, malae bestiae, pigri* ["Cretans are always liars, evil beasts, slothful bellies" (Titus 1:12)]. Saint Gregory of Nazianzus debates the questions of matrimony and virginity in elegant verse. Why go on? The Queen of Wisdom, Our Lady, intoned on her sacred lips the Canticle of the Magnificat [Luke 1:46–55] and having once cited her as an exemplar, it would demean her to cite secular examples as proof, even those of the most solemn and learned men, since hers more than suffices. That and the knowledge that the Psalms still retain the name and divisions of verse, even though, Hebrew elegance not being compressible into Latin meters, the sacred translator [Jerome], attributing greater importance to the meaning, eschewed versification. What harm can verse possibly do in and of itself? After all, wrong usage is not the fault of art, but of the bad practitioner who vitiates verse, converting it into a snare of the devil, something that happens in every faculty and branch of learning.

Now if the wrong consists in the practice of verse by a woman, since so many have practiced it in a fashion so evidently praiseworthy, what can be so wrong about my being a poet? Though I readily confess that I am base and vile, I am not aware that anyone has seen an unseemly ditty by me. Furthermore, I have never written anything of my own volition, but always at the request, and to the specifications, of others. So much so that the only thing I can remember writing for my own pleasure is a trifle called *The Dream.* I wrote that Letter which you, Madam, have so greatly honored, with more reluctance than otherwise and that both because it dealt with sacred matters, of which (as I have said) I stand in reverent awe, and because it seemed to tend toward controversy, something to which I feel a natural aversion. And I do believe that if I had had any inkling of the happy lot awaiting it from birth—for I cast the foundling, like another Moses, into the waters of the Nile of silence, where you, a princess, found and fondled it—I do believe, I repeat, that I would have preferred to strangle it in the very hands into which it was born, for fear that the clumsy blemishes of my ignorance would find their way into the light of your knowledge. This plainly shows the vast extent of your kindness, for your will applauds that precisely from which your brilliant mind recoils.

However, since its fate has cast the letter up at your door, so completely a foundling and orphan that you even had to give it a name, it grieves me that, amidst its other deformities, it should also display the defects that come of hastiness. For I was in a hurry to finish for many reasons: continuing poor health; the excessive number of responsibilies to which obedience binds me; the lack of anyone to help me to write it out, so that everything had to be in my own hand; and because the matter went against my natural bent, and all I wanted was to keep my word to someone I could not disobey. Thus it was that I left out whole lines of thought and numerous proofs that came to mind; I dropped them so as not to extend myself further. Had I known the letter would be printed, I would not have omitted them, if for no other reason than to meet certain objections which it provoked and of which I could have taken account. But I will not be so disobliging as to place such unsuitable objects before your pure eyes, for it is enough for me to offend them with my own ignorance, without directing them to the audacious objections of others. If these should come flying your way on their own (they are of so little weight that they surely will), you will tell me what I must do. Unless your instructions intervene, as far as my natural defense is concerned, I will never put pen to paper because one who by the very fact of concealing himself acknowledges his wrongdoing, does not, in my view, need an answer from anyone else. For, as my father, Saint Jerome, says, *bonus sermo secreta non quaerit* [good words require no secrecy] and to quote Saint Ambrose: *latere criminosae est conscientiae* [concealing oneself is an admission of guilt]. Nor do I consider myself impugned, since a rule of law says: *Accusatio non tenetur si non curat de persona, quae produxerit illam* [A charge will not stand up if it does not take account of the person bringing it]. What cannot help striking one is the trouble he went to in making copies. What strange madness: to take more pains to destroy one's own reputation than one might have taken to gain one.

I, Madam, have preferred not to answer, although others have done so without my knowledge. It suffices for me to have seen some of these writings. One of them I am sending on to you for its erudition and so that the reading of it may recompense you for that part of your time I have wasted with what I am writing. If it should be your pleasure, my Lady, that I do the opposite of what I had proposed to your judgment and view, my decision will yield, as is right, to the least indication of your wishes. As I said, it had been to remain silent because, although Saint John Chrysostom says: *calumniatores convincere oportet, interrogatores docere* [slanderers should be won over, questioners enlightened], I see that Saint Gregory also says: *Victoria non minor est hostes tolerare, quam hostes vincere* [It is no less a victory to tolerate an enemy than to overcome him], and that patience conquers by tolerance and triumphs by sufferance. And it was the custom of the pagan Romans, at the highest peak of their captains' glory, when they returned home in triumph from the conquest of nations, dressed in purple and crowned with laurel; with, instead of animals, crowned heads of conquered kings pulling the chariot; with the rich spoils of the whole world in their train; with the victorious militia decorated with the insignia of their prowess; while they enjoyed the popular acclaim of such honorable and greatly reputed titles as Fathers of their Country, Mainstays of Empire, Bulwarks of Rome, Protectors of the Republic, and other titles to glory: it was, I say, the Romans' custom, in the full flush of human glory and felicity, to have a soldier go alongside the conquerer, saying to him in a loud voice, as if expressing his own sentiments and acting on the Senate's order: Don't forget you are mortal, that you have such and such a flaw, without sparing them the most shameful, as happened at Caesar's triumphs, when the lowliest soldiers shouted into his ears: *Cavete romani, adducimus vobis adulterum calvum* [Beware, Romans, we bring you one who is bald and adulterous!][55] This was done so that such great honors should not go to the conqueror's head, and so that the ballast of these affronts should counterbalance the sails of such acclaim, in order that the ship of judgment should not be endangered by the winds of so much cheering.

If this, I say, was done by pagans having solely the light of natural law, is it so much for us Catholics, who are required to love our enemies, to tolerate them? For my part, I can assure you that calumnies have sometimes mystified me but have never harmed me, since I consider very stupid the person who, having the opportunity to win merit, takes no less trouble to lose it, like those people who resist the thought of dying, yet die in the end, their resistance being of no avail in avoiding death and serving

55. Suetonius, *The Twelve Caesars*, "Julius Caesar," 51.

only to deprive them of the merit of acceptance and turning what could have been a fine death into a poor one. Thus, Madam, I consider these things more beneficial than harmful and hold the risk of applause the greater one for human weakness, which has a way of appropriating what does not belong to it. One must be very wary and keep those words of the Apostle written in one's heart: *Quid autem habes quod non accepisti? Si autem accepisti, quid gloriaris quasi no acceperis?* ["Or what hast thou that thou hast not received? And if thou hast received, why dost thou glory, as if thou hadst not received it?" (1 Cor. 4:7)], that they may serve as a shield to resist the sharp spikes of praise, a lance which, when not attributed to God, to whom it belongs, takes our lives and turns us into robbers of God's honor and usurpers of the talents He has entrusted to us and the gifts He has lent us, of which we must give a most exact reckoning. I therefore fear praise more than censure, my Lady, for the latter, by only the simplest act of patience, may be turned to advantage, while the former, if it is not to do one harm, requires many reciprocal acts of humility and self-knowledge. So in my case I recognize and realize that it is by God's special grace that I have understood this, that I may be able in either case to comport myself in accordance with that saying of Saint Augustine: *Amico laudanti credendum non est sicut nec inimico detrahenti* [One should no more believe a friend's praise than an enemy's detraction]. Though I am the sort of person who will usually spoil everything, or infuse such defects and imperfections into it that I corrupt a thing that, in itself, would have been good. Thus, as regards what little of mine has been printed, not merely my name but the very decision to publish has been out of my hands, a liberty taken by others, for which I am not responsible. Such was the case with the Athenagoric Letter. Only certain *Exercises on the Incarnation* and *Offerings of the Sorrows* were printed with my blessing, though without my name, as being useful for public worship. I am sending along some copies for you to distribute, if you wish, among our sisters, the nuns of your sacred community, and the other nuns of your city. Only one of the *Sorrows* is included because they are all used up and I could find no more. I wrote them years ago solely for use in my sisters' worship, but subsequently they circulated abroad. Their subjects are as far beyond the scope of my tepid ability as they are beyond my ignorance, and only their connection with our great Queen enabled me to compose them. There is something about treating the Most

Blessed Virgin that sets the frostiest heart ablaze. I would ask nothing better, my venerable Lady, than to offer you works worthy of your virtue and learning, but, as the Poet said: *Ut desint vires, tamen est laudanda voluntas: / hac ego contentos, auguror esse deos* [Though my strength fails, my good intention still deserves praise. / I predict that the gods will be satisfied with it (Ovid, *Ex Ponto* [From the Black Sea] 3.4.79–80)].

Should I compose any other trifles, they will ever seek sanctuary at your feet and safety through your correction, for they are the only currency in which I can repay you, and in Seneca's view anyone who has begun to repay favors has incurred an obligation to continue doing so. Thus, your own generosity will be your payment, for only in this way can I properly discharge my obligation and avoid having those words of the same Seneca apply to me: *Turpe est beneficiis vinci* [It is shameful to be second-best in doing favors (Seneca, *On Public Honors*, 5.2.1)]. The generous creditor shows his mettle in giving an impoverished debtor the wherewithal to satisfy his debt. So God did with a world unable to pay; He gave the world His very own Son so that He might be offered up as a suitable payment.

If the style of this letter, my venerable Lady, should not have been such as is owed to you, I ask you to pardon my homespun familiarity or inadequate respect, in treating you as a veiled nun, sister to me, and forgetting the distance that separates me from your most illustrious person. Had I seen you with no veil, this would have not have happened. But with your good and benign judgment, you will fill in or emend the forms of address, and if you find incongruous my addressing you with no title, because I felt that considering the reverence I owe you, the title of Your Reverence would actually show very little reverence, replace my familiarity with any form of address you deem worthy of your merits, for I have not had the daring to exceed the limits of your style nor to infringe the margins of your modesty.

And keep me in your grace in order to obtain God's for me, and may He grant you great increase thereof and keep you, as I beg and need Him to do. From this convent of Our Father Saint Jerome of the City of Mexico, the first day of the month of March of the year sixteen hundred ninety-one. Your most favored servant kisses your hands,

Juana Inés de la Cruz

Key to Poem Numbers

Spanish	English	Spanish	English
2	26	147	31
6	17	149	29
8	41	150	30
19	3	151	32
48	1	152	33
50	2	157	34
51	36	160	38
56	25	164	22
61	8	165	23
70	19	169	15
71	39	170	16
72	40	189	35
77	6	195	14
78	20	211	18
79	7	221	42
82	4	224	43
84	21	258	44
89	11	279	46
91	5	281	47
92	37	283	48
102	13	287	49
103	12	312	50
126	9	316	51
127	10	322	52
145	27	384	24
146	28	xxxvii	45

Index of First Lines

English